79

The Catalans

also by Jan Read

THE WINES OF SPAIN AND PORTUGAL

THE MOORS IN SPAIN AND PORTUGAL

WAR IN THE PENINSULA

THE CATALANS

Jan Read

FABER AND FABER
London & Boston

First published in 1978
by Faber and Faber Limited
3 Queen Square London WC1
Printed in Great Britain by
The Bowering Press Ltd
Plymouth and London
All rights reserved

946.7
Rea

British Library Cataloguing in Publication Data

Read, Jan
  The Catalans.
  1. Catalonia—History
  I. Title
  946'.7   DP302.C62
  ISBN 0–571–10969–1

Contents

Illustrations

FIGURES

Acknowledgements

I am grateful to the following authors and publishers for the use of short extracts: Mr. W. S. Merwin and J. M. Dent & Sons for the verse translation from the *Poem of the Cid* on p. 46; Sr. Ferran Soldevila and Editorial Alpha for the quotation on p. 73; Mr. Alfonso Lowe and Routledge & Kegan Paul Ltd. for the translation from Nikephoros Gregoras on p. 80; the late Professor J. Trueta and the Oxford University Press for the translations from Ramon Llull and Joan Lluís Vives on pp. 97 and 100; the late Professor J. Vicens Vives, Editorial Vicens Vives and the University of California Press for the quotations on pp. 121 and 180; and Professor J. H. Elliott and the Cambridge University Press for the translations on pp. 107 and 126. I am also obliged to Jonathan Cape Ltd. for permission to reproduce the verses from A. E. Housman's *Epitaph on an Army of Mercenaries* on p. 88. Other short quotations are acknowledged in the text.

Parts of Chapter IV, 'The "Catholic" and the "Believers"' have previously appeared in *History Today*.

The Picasso drawing of 'Els Quatre Gats' is reproduced by kind permission of Ediciones 62, S.A., Barcelona.

Catalan Spelling

It is a point of pride for Catalan writers to spell the names of people and places in Catalan rather than Castilian—understandably so, because recurrent bans on the use of the language, the last during the period following the Civil War, have been a major grievance.

The general reader is, however, a great deal more familiar with Castilian forms, especially of place names, such as Lérida (Lleida) or Gerona (Girona); and it would seem pedantic to use names which cannot be found on a map. I have therefore used Castilian where the use of Catalan might lead to confusion. Similarly, I have preferred French for an area such as Roussillon, rather than Rosselló.

As regards kings and other well-known personages, the names have been anglicized; but on first mention and in the index the original Catalan has been placed in brackets, e.g. Peter (Pere) the Ceremonious or James (Jaume) of Urgell. The names of lesser-known people and places are in the form current in Catalonia.

It is almost impossible to be entirely consistent; and the choice of one form or the other has been made simply on the grounds of intelligibility.

Foreword

Separatist movements are a recurrent theme in modern Spanish history. At various times during the last half century, Catalonia, the Basque provinces, Valencia, Murcia, Galicia and parts of Andalusia have all demanded more say in the ordering of their affairs. Calls for local autonomy are, in the last place, a protest against rigid central government from Madrid that will not admit of social change; but to interpret them solely in terms of economics is very far from the whole truth. As in Scotland and Wales nearer home, nationalism is nourished by pride in the historic past and a belief in cultural individuality, which awake few echoes in the capital. Hence the strident cry of the Andalusian poet, Antonio Machado:

> *Castilla miserable, ayer dominadora*
> *envuelta in sus andrajos, desprecia cuanto ignora.*

> Wretched Castile, the ruler of yesterday,
> Wrapped in rags, despises what she does not know.

It is significant that such claims for a degree of independence have been most persistent in Catalonia and the Basque country, both of which possess living languages of their own and were the last of the independent kingdoms of Spain to be integrated with Castile— Catalonia in 1479 and Navarre in 1512 (although Alava and Guipúzcoa, once part of Navarre, had been annexed by Castile in 1200)—and then with a large measure of regional autonomy. In recent history and until the royal decree of 29 September 1977, Catalonia was officially no more than its parts, the provinces of Barcelona, Gerona (Girona), Tarragona and Lérida (Lleida), administered no differently from the other forty-six provinces of the country; but the inhabitants of these four provinces have always considered that Catalonia is not merely a region apart, but a nation in its own right. From the standpoint of Madrid, others of the ancient kingdoms of Hispania—the word 'Spain' only became current during the twelfth century, and then as a Provençal invention—like León or the Asturias, which coalesced with Castile during the expulsion of the Moors, might also claim autonomy with equally disruptive results. But this is to overlook the facts that as long ago as 1068 Catalonia, in its *usatges*, established an embryo form of democracy quite different from the political customs of the rest of the Peninsula; that it was ahead of Castile in developing an outward-looking mercantile economy and in winning an empire overseas; and that its full incorporation into Spain by the Bourbons was accomplished only in the face of bitter opposition. Portugal was markedly less differentiated when it broke away in 1179 at a time when the great era of Catalan expansion was yet to come; and it is an irony of history that, when both countries revolted against Castilian domination in 1640, Portugal should have succeeded in achieving final independence while Catalonia did not. If Portugal is now free, why not Catalonia, which, despite its small area, has a larger population than half a dozen European countries?

Few Catalans today would argue for outright separation; but implemention of the demand for regional autonomy is in the forefront of Spanish politics. The 'Catalan Problem' can only be understood in the light of history, and it is the purpose of this book to sketch that history from a period when Catalonia first began to assume a distinctive role of its own in the troubled annals of the Iberian Peninsula. It would, however, be a bold man who set out to write a formal history of Catalonia, and for various reasons I have preferred the title of *The Catalans*.

In the first place, Catalonia means much more to a Catalan than its present four provinces and loosely comprises all the areas where variations of the Catalan language are still spoken. These include the larger part of the provinces of Valencia, Castellón and Alicante, the Balearic Islands, parts of Aragon and Andorra, and the Roussillon in France. In the name of the Crown of Aragon, it was the Catalans and their ruling dynasty for five hundred years, the Counts of Barcelona, who were the driving force behind the Aragonese expansion into these areas—and further afield in Sicily, Sardinia, Corsica, the Kingdom of Naples, and even a region in Greece.

Furthermore, *The Catalans* is a better expression of the form in which I have shaped this account of a people's rise to power and influence; of their language, laws and culture; of the soldiers, writers and politicians who helped to mould their destiny; and of their aspirations for the future.

As an example of extremes in the treatment of an historical

theme one might instance two books: A *History of Aragon and Catalonia*, written by H. J. Chaytor in 1933, and Pierre Vilar's *La Catalogne dans l'Espagne moderne*, published in 1962. Chaytor's book is typical of the now outmoded 'narrative' history, which hinges on the description of kings and battles, of dynastic entanglements and, in short, of the exceptional individual. Vilar, on the other hand, is of the socio-economic school of Lucien Febvre and the Paris *Annales*, which as a much-needed corrective, maintains that history is made by common men in their multiplicity and their behaviour in response to the geographic milieu and the demographic and economic background of the times. The shortcomings of the first approach are only too obvious; the second attempts to unearth 'the short and simple annals of the poor' by systematic research into state and local archives and the compilation of statistics relating to population, trade, monetary values and technical resources.

For the professional historian such statistics provide a powerful new tool and a touchstone for testing the validity of opinionated views on politics and the wisdom, or otherwise, of rulers and statesmen; but for the layman the marshalling of facts and figures often reads not so much as intelligible history, but the raw material of history. One of the most pungent critics of the method has been Américo Castro, who, in *The Spaniards, An Approach to their History*, writes with some justification of Fernand Braudel's great study of *The Mediterranean*:

> Seduced by the actions of mountains, plains, and bodies of water, Braudel confers the function of actors in human history on natural elements and population statistics. We can glimpse a desire to reduce to spatial coordinates and numerical calculations, for those of us who are interested in what is itself relevant, in what is unique, singular, problematical, in what has value in itself, what is simply irreducible to arithmetic, geometry, or even topology . . . For Braudel, the Mediterranean is a living entity which creates problems and resolves them by itself. For me it is like an empty wall on which we can hang either a Goya or a dirty rag.

To take a specific example, during the reign of Philip IV Castile suffered from chronic inflation and debasement of the currency. This has been charted with precision and was undoubtedly the cause of widespread hardship among the working population. But it was not, as one might almost suppose from studying the work of the historico-materialistic school, an entirely natural and inevitable disaster. It also arose as a direct consequence of the deliberate decision of the Count Duke of Olivares to continue a fruitless war in Flanders and so to broadcast South American silver and squander human resources which might otherwise have been put to productive use. It is naturally important to establish a precise level of inflation rather than to talk in terms of generalities; but at least of equal interest to the reader who wishes to understand the period is a study of the Count Duke and his motives for pursuing the will-o'-the-wisp of Spanish hegemony in Europe. The study of mankind is man, and in the last resort economic crises spring from individual human decisions—and this was especially true when power was concentrated in the hands of small ruling minority. This, of course, is not to deny that there are natural disasters, such as plague and failure of crops, which have played their part in shaping the destinies of nations.

In his interesting introduction to a book which throws a great deal of light on the evolution of Catalonia, *Moments crucials de la història de Catalunya*, a collection of essays by various distinguished Catalan historians, Ramon d'Abadal makes a point which also seems relevant: 'To understand the past and to judge it by the norms and from the standpoint of the present day is to falsify history', and again, 'To believe that history is totally conditioned by physical and socio-economic laws, as dialectical materialism would have it, is, in my estimation, an error.'

It is particularly in relation to the deeply-held religious beliefs of mediaeval times that the materialistic approach seems anachronistic and misleading. While the enumerations of *focs* (or 'hearths'— literally 'fires') affords a rough guide to population, or the counting of tombstones to the death-roll of an epidemic, how is one to understand the intensity of conflicting interpretations of Christianity which led to the massacre of the Albigenses and indirectly to the loss of the greater part of the Catalan territories in France? Certainly not by a tabulated analysis of ecclesiastical tithes or Papal revenues.

Again, Américo Castro writes (of Braudel) that 'Anyone who does not belong to one of the Utopian or Messianic sects which base their beliefs mainly on economics and geopolitics . . . reads with stupefaction that "the proof of the overpopulation of Mediterranean Europe is the fact of the repeated expulsion of Jews, who were forced to leave Castile and Portugal in 1492 . . ."' In regard to Portugal this is a plain mis-statement of fact; the Jews were *not* expelled in 1492. And, as Castro has convincingly demonstrated, the whole passage is an attempt to apply 'an extra-human "law of numbers"' and takes no account of the Cluniac-led Christian revival in northern Spain, which supplied the spiritual impetus for the fight against the Moors, or of the further complex racial and economic rivalries which militated against the Jews.

A much happier example of the application of socio-economic methods is J. Vicens Vives's reassessment of the policies of Ferdinand the Catholic, who has been passionately denounced by nationalistic historians for denying Catalonia a share in the new trade with South America, quoted on page 121.

Enough has perhaps been said to justify the view that the history of the Catalans and their present problems cannot profitably be discussed solely in terms of economics and statistical fact. And it would be a dull narrative indeed which did not seek to illumine the character of a people without some account of the personal achievements of a James the Conqueror, Roger de Flor or Ramon Llull. For the benefit of the general reader, who cannot be expected to be versed in such matters, there are digressions on topics such as the Catalan language, the Knights Templars, the Provençal troubadours, the Great Schism of the Church, the Thirty Years War, the war of the Spanish Succession and the Spanish Civil War, all relevant to events in the Principality.

It remains to set the stage with some preliminary remarks about the land and its inhabitants.

The four provinces of the Principality (or Catalonia proper) form a rough triangle with its apex at Tortosa in the south, on the delta of the Ebro. To the north, the frontier with France (now, but not in the past) lies along the Pyrenees; on the west is the ancient Kingdom of Aragon, and to the east the Mediterranean. The total land mass is about the size of Holland or Belgium. Two mountain spurs extend southwards from the Pyrenees, one towards Barcelona and the other further and deeper inland, so that apart from a narrow coastal plain the landscape is rugged and broken and has been described as a flight of stairs rising from the coast towards the 11,350-ft peak of Mount Aneto in the Pyrenees. The existence of passes through the eastern Pyrenees has from the earliest times made Catalonia a corridor between the Iberian Peninsula and the rest of Europe and laid it open to successive incursions, usually short-lived as the invaders passed on, from Carthaginians, Romans, Visigoths, Moors and, of course, the Franks to their descendants, the French.

Catalonia has sometimes been described as rich in natural resources, but this is not so. It possesses few minerals and only two
sizeable tracts of arable land: the plains of Empordá at the foot of
the Pyrenees and of Urgell on the borders of Andorra—hence the
recurrent need to import wheat from Sicily in mediaeval times. An
abundance of fish from the Mediterranean, and the cultivation of
vines, fruit and olives and of rice in the sub-tropical Ebro delta
have nevertheless made Catalonia self-sufficient in food in all but
exceptional years of dearth.

The traditional wealth of Catalonia—which was a legend by
the time of the Count Duke of Olivares, sadly misinformed as he
was—has therefore resulted from the industry of its people in pro-
cessing raw materials imported from abroad. An exception has
been its wine and spirit trade, with native-produced cork as a valuable
ancillary; but the most important manufacture has always been
textiles.

By the fourteenth century Catalonia was the largest mercantile
country in the Mediterranean, with her fleet bringing back gold and
slaves from North Africa, and spices from as far afield as Syria and
Egypt. Barcelona became the market place and point of supply for
such commodities for an extensive hinterland reaching far beyond
the Principality, and, like her rivals, Genoa and Venice, was one
of the great banking places of mediaeval Europe. After plumbing the
depths of economic depression during the sixteenth and seventeenth centuries, the city regained her position as one of the most
important Mediterranean ports and commercial centres during the
nineteenth; but her supremacy as the banking centre of Spain was
lost to the Basques and has never been regained.

It is a heady, but dangerous exercise to generalize about national
character; and the task is complicated by successive and massive
immigrations of peasants from the poorer parts of Spain, notably
Murcia and the south, which have swelled the present population
to about six million. None the less, the Spaniards themselves would
be the first to admit that the Catalans do possess very marked
characteristics of their own.

Writing in his *Handbook for Travellers in Spain* in 1847, Richard
Ford declared with his usual verve:

No province of the unamalgamated bundle which forms the con-
ventional monarchy of Spain hangs more loosely to the crown
than Catalonia, this classical country of revolt, which is ever

ready to fly off: rebellious and republicans, well may the natives
wear the blood-coloured cap of the much prostituted name of
liberty.

There is still much truth in this, but Ford touches on another and
fundamental aspect of the Catalans, when he further describes them
as 'frugal, industrious, honest and rough diamonds.' According to
the Castilian proverb, 'The Catalans get bread out of stones'; and
it has been a capacity for hard work, often in the face of defeat and
disaster, which has enabled them to make a country with few
natural resources one of the richest regions of Spain. Theirs is a
tradition very different from that of Castile and the south, where,
in the period following the fall of Granada in 1492, the Old Christians tended to leave manual jobs to the Mudejars (or Moors living
in the reconquered territories) and the professions and trade to the
Jews, in the belief that such employment was unworthy of a Christian, who was held to be specially fitted for soldiering, priesthood
or government. To the Catalan, on the other hand, manual work
or trading activity was a source of pride; and this resulted in the
emergence of a *bourgeoisie* with no counterpart in Castile; in less
differentiation between social classes; and in possibilities for an
individual to move from one class to another by dint of his own
efforts.

An innate respect for the rights of the individual took tangible
shape much earlier in 1068, when the *usatges* (a code of usage) was
drawn up, defining the mutual rights and responsibilities of the ruler
on the one side and of his subjects on the other; and the *usatges*
were reinforced by the formation in the thirteenth century of the
Corts (or Parliament) with much greater powers than the Castilian
Cortes.

A facet of the Catalan's individuality is that he has always remained intensely conscious of his ancient rights and privileges. There
is a Catalan expression *no hi ha dret*, meaning that it is not right, or
against the agreed law of the land. If Ford was implying that when
the Catalan dons the 'blood-coloured cap of the much prostituted
name of liberty' he wears it *well*, it is perhaps a justified comment,
in that, for all their violence, revolutions in Catalonia have been
an outraged reaction to the infringement of traditional or natural
liberties. Contradictory as it may sound, the Catalan has often
been a conservative revolutionary; and, whether or not a long-
standing custom was still sensible or applicable in changed circum-

stances, he has fought to retain it. This was basically the cause of the revolution of 1640, when the Count Duke of Olivares, convinced that Spain must unite to survive, insisted on billeting troops in Catalonia and drafting Catalans for military service abroad—both practices expressly forbidden by the long-hallowed *Constitucions* of Catalonia. Rather than yield, the Catalans appealed to France for aid and in the upshot lost the last of their territory beyond the Pyrenees to their erstwhile ally.

This stubborn conservatism, which manifests itself in other ways, as in the tradition that the eldest son of the *masia* (or farm) inherits the whole property and the younger fends for himself, or the reluctance of small manufactories to modernize or combine, is still to be reckoned with in a world where multinational business organizations and foreign-inspired labour movements are undermining the traditional concepts of nationalism.

I

Beginnings

Prior to the arrival of the Romans the indigenous tribes which inhabited the north-eastern corner of the Iberian Peninsula could in no sense be called a nation. Apart from the French immigrants of the sixteenth and seventeenth centuries and the more recent arrivals from Andalusia, the great bulk of Catalans are descendants of the people who lived in the area in pre-Roman times and have left traces of a primitive culture; but, as Miquel Tarradell has shrewdly observed, 'If we are a Latin people it is because for seven centuries we lived under the great civilizing influence of the Romans—and not because the role of nationhood had been assigned to us from the time of Adam and Eve.' There had been earlier foreign visitations from the Phoenicians and the Greeks, who are said to have introduced the vine and the olive and who formed trading posts at Ampurias and Rosas, but without attempting to move further from the coast. The Carthaginians made more determined inroads, especially in the south, and Hamilcar Barca gave his own name of Barcino to Barcelona, where he founded a base. It was as a result of the counter-offensive against Hannibal during the Second Punic War, when, after capturing Saguntum, in 219 B.C., he crossed into Italy via the passes of the eastern Pyrenees and the Alps, that the Romans landed at Ampurias to cut him off from his bases in Hispania. Thereafter the Romans moved into the region swiftly and in strength, no doubt because it was the gateway to the Peninsula and it was essential to secure it. It proved necessary to send a strong army under Cato in 197 B.C. before resistance was finally brought to an end; but in general the local tribes were too small and disorganized to offer effective resistance. Catalonia was therefore one of the first parts of the Peninsula to be pacified and colonized, and was indeed incorporated into the Roman Empire almost a century before Julius Caesar's conquest of Gaul.

The process of Romanization was gradual, but gathered pace during the reign of Augustus and the first two and a half centuries A.D. Peace and a settled regime were among the greatest benefits

that the Romans brought to the country; and as a result the indigenous population began to move from defensive positions in the
hills to the plains and to the Ebro delta, where a more developed
and intensive form of cultivation was possible.

With this shift in population came the development of cities,
each a miniature Rome, and perhaps the most potent of the Empire's
means of civilization. The largest of these in the region were
Valencia, Barcelona and Tarragona (Tarraco), which was the capital
of the province of Tarraconensis, embracing the whole of the north
and centre of Hispania. It is not often realized that the excavation
of Roman sites, with their accretion of modern buildings, poses more
of a problem than the systematic archaeological investigation of
prehistoric remains in open country; but comparison, for example,
of the ruined forum and great aqueduct at Tarragona with earlier
indigenous remains provides a measure of the advances made under
the Romans. The creation of cities, with their numerous function-
aries, merchants and artisans, resulted in the emergence of social
classes and in particular of a vigorous *bourgeoisie*, of which, as time
went on and intermarriage became common, the indigenous inhabitants formed the larger part.

The innovations in agriculture were not so much in the introduction of new crops, but in the more fruitful use of the land and
improvement in the yield of existing staples, such as cereals, olives
and vines. The rapid progress of agriculture in Catalonia has been
demonstrated by the discovery of enormous quantities of amphorae
belonging to the *early* period of Roman occupation and used for
bringing wine from Italy; but by the middle of the first century A.D.
it was found necessary to protect the Italian growers by enforcing
strict limitations on the planting of new vines in the Hispanic
provinces.

Aerial photography in North Africa has revealed that the custom
was to divide the land into 710-metre squares, each cultivated by an
individual family; and it seems that a similar system prevailed in
Catalonia. The exploitation of large estates or *latifundias*, which
was to have such far-reaching social consequences in the south, was
not typical of Catalonia. Although the wealthy *bourgeoisie* often
owned *villae* with extensive orchards and gardens on the outskirts
of the towns, they did not employ slave labour on a large scale.
The Roman *villa* was in fact the forerunner of the *mas* or *masia*, so
characteristic of Catalonia from the mediaeval period onwards.

As it exists today, a typical *masia* is a stoutly-built house, well adapted for defence in earlier days, on two floors with a sloping roof. The usual arrangement, emphasizing the close connection of the *masia* with the land on which it stood, was for much of the ground floor to accommodate animals and farm implements and also the kitchen, the centre of family life. The stairs at the back of the entrance hall, which ran from front to back of the house, led to a second floor, consisting of bedrooms and a large *sala*, used for formal occasions.

So important was the *masia* that it often gave its name to the family; and the paramount importance of keeping it within the family was enshrined in the tradition that the eldest son should inherit the whole estate or that, at best, in accordance with Roman law, any younger children should share the *legítima* or third part of the property. Although a younger son was thus compelled to leave home and seek his fortune elsewhere, he would acknowledge the authority of the *hereu* or heir. Even the famous Don Pedro Franqueza, favourite of the Duke of Lerma in the seventeenth century, could write to his humbler, but elder brother: 'His Majesty has honoured me with the title of Count of Villalonga, on which I send you my congratulations, since everything redounds to your authority and that of your house, of which you are the head and I the feet.' There was a reverse side to this coin: such close ties could lead to fierce inter-family feuds.

Until the period of decadence, which set in about the middle of the third century A.D., there was no fixed boundary between the city proper and the outlying *villae* and gardens. With the coming of the first 'barbarians' between 407 and 409 and during the centuries of Visigothic dominance that followed, all this changed. The cities began to take on their mediaeval appearance and were enclosed within walls, magnificent examples of which are those of Barcelona. Physical changes were matched by an impoverishment of life within the cities, a turning inwards on themselves, accompanied at the same time by the increased importance of the rural areas outside; but all was not lost, culturally or in concrete terms.

The Romans had for the first time established a network of properly engineered roads, which remained the only arteries of communication during the Middle Ages and survive in modified form today. The backbone of the system was the Via Augusta, crossing the Pyrenees at La Junquera and continuing through Gerona, Barcelona, Tarragona, Tortosa, Castellón and Valencia to Alicante. For much of its length it is followed by the murderous modern race-track taken by tourists heading for the Costa del Sol. The Triumphal Arch, islanded in the middle of the present road at Bará, just north of Tarragona, and constructed during the first years of the second century by one of Trajan's generals, Lucius Sergius Sura, indicates that at points the routes coincide. Further south, in the province of Castellón de la Plana, another such arch in a field near Cabanes is some ten kilometers to the west of the modern road.

There were two consequences of the Roman occupation of even more lasting significance than physical remains or technical advances in agriculture: the spread of Christianity and the birth of the Catalan language.

As happened elsewhere in the Roman world, Christianity first took root in the cities connected with Rome either by sea or by great internal routes such as the Via Augusta. It is difficult to say whether there is any truth in the legend that St. Paul visited Tarragona and was the country's first evangelist. Certain it is that clandestine groups of Christians were well established by the middle of the third century, when a bishop and two deacons of Tarragona, Fructuós, Auguri and Eulogi, suffered martyrdom. Somewhat later two missionaries from North Africa were executed: San Feliú at Gerona, and San Cugat at Barcelona.

The popular belief that the Romans habitually persecuted the Christians is nevertheless untrue. Sporadic repression, as at the time of Nero, has been luridly portrayed in many a Technicolor epic and is the stock-in-trade of sentimentalists; but for the Romans religion was always more of a matter of politics and accepted behaviour rather than of metaphysics, and it was only at times of national peril that men were bidden to choose between God and Caesar. For this reason, persecution reached its height during the crisis of the third century when Diocletian was trying to re-establish the Empire on new and more secure bases. By the fourth century, when the first 'barbarians' entered the Iberian Peninsula, the new faith was openly tolerated, and by the early years of the fifth century, coinciding with the first invasion of the Visigoths, and as in other parts of the tottering Empire, it had become the official religion of the country. So, there was a Bishop of Barcelona, Sant Pacià, active during the first half of the century; and churches and objects of worship dating from this period testify to a widespread belief in Christ.

In the first place Christianity was an urban religion and spread gradually to the country districts, where the peasants were slower to abandon their traditional beliefs. It seems, in fact, that in the more remote mountain districts it was the influence of the Church which induced the country people to abandon their native tongue in favour of Vulgar Latin, the forerunner of Catalan.

The acceptance of Latin as the *lingua franca* began first, of course, in the cities founded by the Romans. The processes by which conversational Latin was transformed into Catalan took place over many centuries and parallel those which led to the emergence of other Romance languages, such as Castilian, Provençal, Italian and Rumanian.

Even in Italy itself there had for long been a marked difference between the Latin of the classical Roman authors and the vernacular. In very general terms, the tendency was to abandon the declension of nouns and their separate cases and to use only one case, usually the accusative, in combination with a preposition. Hand in hand with this, conjugations and tenses were simplified. These changes naturally affected the word order and construction of sentences. And the words themselves changed, because in speaking rather than writing them, people often found it easier to elide vowels, slur consonants, and alter the stress.

One of the issues most fiercely debated by philologists is the influence of pre-Roman speech habits on the pronunciation and modification of Latin words. To what extent, for example, did the sound patterns of 'Iberian' contribute to the emergence of Castilian as a language in its own right? Whole treatises have been written on perhaps the best-known of Spanish sound changes—that of *f* to *h*. Thus, for example, *facere* (to do or make) became *hacer*; *filium* (son), *hijo*; *farina* (flour), *harina*. The Spanish scholar Ramón Menéndez Pidal maintained that the change sprang from habits of speech in the Basque country, the birthplace of the original Castilian; but his conclusions have been hotly challenged, for one reason because the change did not occur in the regions to the south and east, subsequently to be known as Aragon and Catalonia. The corresponding words in Catalan are *fer*, *fill* and *farina*. Although the issue is complicated, one reason for the difference was Catalonia's close ties with Carolingians during a period when the larger part of the Peninsula was dominated by the Moors; and Catalan is much closer to the *langue d'oc* of southern France—and therefore to Vulgar Latin— than Castilian, which was much influenced by a massive transfusion of Arabic words. Links with the Languedoc and Provence remained close during the whole mediaeval period; and indeed for a time most of southern France was feudatory to the Crown of Aragon and its ruling dynasty, the Counts of Barcelona, until the defeat of Peter (Pere) the Catholic at the Battle of Murat in 1213. Catalan poets, including Alfonso II of Aragon (1162–96), composed in Provençal in the style of the troubadours; and the standardization of Catalan and its subsequent use as a vehicle for chroniclers such as Muntaner and Desclot (see pages 70 and 98) or philosophers such as Llull in the late thirteenth and fourteenth centuries owed much to the example of James (Jaume) I.

A feature which distinguishes Catalan from the other better-known Romance languages is the occurrence of the curious diph-thongs, *au, eu* and *iu*, which together with the strong syllabic stress and the absence of nasal and silent terminations, gives the spoken language a somewhat harsh and rugged character. Nevertheless, literary Catalan has a clarity and elegance reminiscent of Elizabethan English; and its quality can be judged by a quotation from the *Llibre dels Feits* or *Chronicle* of James I (describing his embarkation for Majorca to campaign against the Moors):

> E *veus lo comencament que nós faem de passar a Mallorques. E empresem dia que a mitjant maig fóssem tuit a Salou. E ab aitant parti's la cort, e cada un pensà's d'aparellar-s'hi. E fo pres sagrament de tots los nobles `que el primer dia de maig, fossen a Salou, tots ab tot llur aparellament, per passar a Mallorques, e que no hi fallissen. E aquell dia fom-hi nós; e estiguem aquí entrò a entrada de setembre en aguiar lo pasatge, e esperant naus e llenys e galees que ens venien; e per çò esperavem tant, que l'estol fos complit. E hac una partida de l'estol de Cambrils, e la major partida, on nós érem fo en Tarragona, car eren d'aquell lloc. E la quantidad de l'estol fo aital que hi hac vint-e-cinc naus complides, e divuit tarides, e dotze galees, e entre buces e galiots cent.*

To anyone with a working knowledge of French and Castilian and the rudiments of his school Latin the meaning will perhaps be fairly clear; but a literal translation is given as a matter of interest:

See the beginning which we made for the crossing to Majorca. We settled a day in the middle of May when we should all be at Salou. And having left the court, each one of us thought of equipping himself. And it was the pledge of all the nobles that on the first day of May they would be at Salou, all completely equipped, to make passage to Majorca, and that they would not fail. And that very day we were there at the beginning of September prepared for the passage, waiting for the arrival of vessels and ships and galleys; and thus we waited until the fleet was complete. And the fleet left from Cambrils, and the main contingent from where we were in Tarragona, for they were from that place. And the number of the fleet was such that there were twenty five ships of war, and eighteen transports, and twelve galleys, and between barques and galliots, a hundred.

'Language is the perfect instrument of empire', remarked the Bishop of Avila to Isabel the Catholic, when presenting her with a copy of Nebrija's Spanish grammar in 1492. After the union of Catalonia with Castile this was an axiom taken to heart by successive rulers and statesmen in Madrid; and determined efforts were thereafter made to replace Catalan by Castilian. During the first decades of the seventeenth century a major point at issue between the Catalan clergy and the Count Duke of Olivares was their refusal to allow preaching in Catalan. When Catalonia had been deserted by her allies at the end of the War of the Spanish Succession, the first of the Spanish Bourbons, Philip V, absolutely forbade the official use of Catalan and closed down all the Faculties of Barcelona University except that of Medicine. The creation of a new university in the small provincial town of Cervera was presumably to limit Catalan studies and render them innocuous. Again, during the years following the Civil War, the Franco regime imposed a total ban on the employment of the language for official purposes and on the publication of books and periodicals in Catalan. None of these measures prevented the continued and general use of Catalan by the peasants and the working classes in the cities. And even today the children of immigrant labourers from other parts of Spain speak Catalan as their first language.

Since the literary renaissance or *Renaixença* of the nineteenth century it has been a point of pride for the intellectuals and better-to-do to maintain Catalan as a living and vital means of communication. Thus Professor W. D. Elcock writes in *The Romance Languages* that 'During the present century the local philologists have elaborated the language, pruning, polishing, and enriching, to a degree of flexible standardization reminiscent of French.' Most Catalan historians and novelists, though of course equally fluent in Castilian, and difficult as it may be for those who read their books to learn a different idiom, prefer to write in their native tongue.

What, under the Romans, started as a unifying influence and one of the means of forging the bonds of empire, has by a full turn of the wheel become an emblem of national independence.

The legacy of the Romans, who brought Catalonia her cities, her religion and her language and early established a social structure so different from that of Castile, cannot be over-estimated. During the dark and troubled centuries which followed, the Roman tradition was never entirely lost and provided a base on which a truly individual Catalonia was to take shape and flourish.

II

The Legacy of Charlemagne

That three centuries of Gothic rule did relatively little to efface the profound civilizing influence of the Romans was largely because of the role of the Church. The Visigoths, who supplanted the original Germanic invaders—the Vandals, Alans and Suevians—and who were to dominate the Peninsula during the seventh and eighth centuries, subscribed to the Arian heresy; but in 587 King Reccared was converted to Catholicism, which became the official religion after the Third Council of Toledo in 589. Thereafter, the Church took a leading part in mediating between the great mass of the Hispano-Roman population and their Visigothic overlords and in preserving Roman forms of legislation. The Visigoths met the most stubborn opposition from the three or four million inhabitants of the Mediterranean coast and established their capital inland at Toledo; and in this may be seen the beginnings of the divide between Castile and the territories later to be embraced by the Crown of Aragon. Nevertheless, the main achievement of the Visigoths was to impose unity of a sort on the Peninsula, fragile though it proved in face of the Moorish invasion of 711.

The rapid occupation of most of the Peninsula by the Moors and their predominance for a period of some five hundred years was more than an interruption in the country's evolution and has differentiated Spain from any of the other Western European countries born of the dissolution of the Roman Empire. Al-Andalus itself, because of feuds between Arab and Berber, and Arab and Arab, was always prone to disintegrate—a tendency combated by successive emirs and caliphs—and the small Christian kingdoms of the north displayed an even greater disarray. No part of Hispania was less firmly attached to the body general than the north-eastern corner; and it was as a direct result of the confrontation with the Moors that its inhabitants allied themselves with the Franks across the Pyrenees, so setting in train a course of events which was to culminate in the emergence of an independent Catalonia.

From the outset the territory enjoyed a rather different relationship with the Moors from that of any other part of the Visigothic kingdom. King Roderic, whose overthrow at the Battle of the Río Barbate at the hands of Tariq ibn-Ziyad left the country at the mercy of the Moors, had supplanted Akhila, the son of his predecessor, Witiza, and the heir designate. At this time Akhila was governing a sizeable part of the north, extending from Tarragona to Narbonne, and according to the Arab chroniclers not only suggested the Moorish invasion to the governor of Ifriqya, but through the defection of his sons and their followers from Roderic's army at a critical juncture in the battle, contributed to the Moorish victory.

To begin with, the Moors were therefore received as allies; and it was only after Akhila's replacement by King Ardon that they met with much resistance. Barcelona fell to the governor of al-Andalus, al-Hurr, in 717–19, but certain regions in the Pyrenees were never occupied.

The Moors did not stop short at the Pyrenees and during the next two decades made determined thrusts into Gaul, occupying Narbonne and the trans-Pyrenean province of Septimania and pillaging as far afield as the Rhône valley and Burgundy. They were finally checked in 732, when a Muslim army, which had crossed the Pyrenees at their western end and advanced towards Tours, was decisively beaten by Charles Martel, the energetic and forceful leader of the Franks. The Moorish general, al-Samh ibn-Malik al-Khawlani was killed, and his troops fled in disorder to Narbonne, which was later besieged by Charles Martel in 737. However, another twenty years were to elapse before his son, Pépin le Bref, recaptured the city and drove back the Moors beyond the Pyrenees.

Not content with expelling the Moors from Septimania, the Franks now set about securing their frontier against invasion from the west. It was thus that Charlemagne undertook his ambitious expedition against Saragossa in 778. In the absence of support from its renegade Moorish governor, Charlemagne was compelled to retreat, and the rearguard of his army was engulfed in the disaster of Roncesvalles, immortalized by the Chanson de Roland. He made no immediate attempt to avenge the defeat, limiting himself to the creation of the powerful buffer state of Aquitaine, comprising the dioceses of Bourges, Bordeaux, Auch and Narbonne, which he put in charge of his son Louis, later to succeed him under the name of 'the Pious'.

On the other side of the Pyrenees, many of the inhabitants of the Moorish-occupied territories were taking action on their own behalf in a manner that was to play an important part in the eventual liberation of their motherland. The important Frankish source, the *Chronicle* of the Abbey of Moissac, contains a vivid description of the so-called *Hispani*:

> Certain men, moved by the iniquitous oppression and the cruel yoke which those enemies of Christianity, the Saracens, had imposed on them, abandoned their houses and properties belonging to them by hereditary right. From Spain they came to us and settled in Septimania, and, escaping the domination of the Saracens, accepted our authority freely and spontaneously of their own volition.

And again:

> The Goths or Spaniards, inhabitants of the famous city of Barcelona or of the Castle of Terrassa, fleeing the cruel yoke of the Saracens, the enemies of Christ, approached us and freely gave or ceded their city to our authority; and, removing themselves from the power of the Saracens, they submitted to our rule by free and prompt decision.

In this voluntary submission to the Carolingians was founded the *Marca hispanica* (or Spanish Mark). Charlemagne on his side promised help in freeing Barcelona and the surrounding Moorish-occupied region, without at the same time exacting the same strict conditions as for territories conquered by force of arms. It was in fact with the active help of the *Hispani* that the Franks were able to make slow progress against the Moors, and the process was one of liberation rather than of conquest.

The first major success was the recapture of Gerona in 785, credited by local tradition to Charlemagne himself. In 793 the Moors, under 'Abd al-Malik ibn-Mughith, counter-attacked and, without regaining Gerona, struck at Narbonne, inflicted a disastrous defeat on Count Guillen of Toulouse at Carcassonne and, according to the *Analects* of al-Maqqari, carried back with them to Córdoba some 45,000 slaves—a figure which is obviously grossly inflated.

The key to the region beyond the Pyrenees was the rich town of Barcelona, and Louis of Aquitaine made a first and unsuccessful attempt to recapture the city in 798. If the Carolingian poet Ermolde el Negre is to be believed, its citizens were by now better disposed towards the Moors than the Franks. Frankish and Moorish sources

B

differ as to subsequent events. According to the Christian chronicles, the Moorish governor, Zado (Sa'dun al-Ru 'aini), travelled to Aix-en-Chapelle to see Charlemagne with an offer of surrender. Arabic chroniclers were not given to dwelling on Moorish defeats, and Ibn-Hayyan simply states that Zado, having sought help in vain from the Muslim chiefs in the region and held out for two years, capitulated in 801, whereupon Barcelona took the place of Gerona as the advance bastion of the Franks. It remained anything but secure, so that in 813 it was sacked by 'Ubayd Allah, a cousin of the Córdoban emir, al-Hakam I. In describing this Frankish disaster, Ibn-Hayyan recounts that the severed heads of the defenders were piled into a bloody pyramid, exceeding the height of a lance stuck into the ground, from the top of which a muezzin exhorted the victorious troops.

It would be an over-simplification to say that all the Gothic nobility supported the Franks in the liberation of the area. As in later times, there were those who inclined either to their powerful neighbours of the east or of the west according to the fortunes of war; and when 'Ubayd Allah struck at Barcelona again in 828 it was with the support of a Gothic nobleman, Aizón, who had fallen out with Louis the Pious.

The Carolingian occupation reached its limits with the offensive of Louis the Pious against Tortosa in the Ebro delta. Here again there is a discrepancy between Moorish and Christian chroniclers. According to Moorish sources, Louis was twice repulsed and completely routed in a final attempt on the town in 809. The Christian account is that Tortosa capitulated to him in 811, becoming tributary to the Franks, but nevertheless remaining in Moorish hands. In either case, it was not captured until 1148; and what is of more significance is that, after succeeding Charlemagne in 814, Louis, who as King of Aquitaine had fought so assiduously against the Moors, lost interest in the further expansion of the Spanish Mark and devoted his main energies to the pacification of other parts of his empire.

The Spanish Mark came into being as the result of a cooperation against the Moors by its inhabitants and the Franks; and the Carolingians honoured their pledge to respect the rights of those inhabitants. These included the individual right to property, the maintenance of Visigothic law, limitation of taxes and the restriction of military service to the immediate locality. In all of this may be seen the genesis of the *usatges* (see pages 41–5) and the Catalan's abiding attachment to his ancient rights and freedoms. Government was similarly left in the hands of local potentates: the first governor of Barcelona, Count Bera, although from the Roussillon, was a Goth and not a Frank.

There were, of course, centralizing influences: it was the king who was the fountain-head of authority and who could appoint or dismiss the counts of the various regions at will; and just as the counts were vassals of the king, so ordinary individuals held their lands and were given protection in return for services to their feudal overlords. Feudalism, as in other parts of the Holy Roman Empire, but not in the rest of the Peninsula, was therefore established in the eighth and ninth centuries. The king exercised his ultimate authority, both by regularly sending his legates to Catalonia and by summoning its counts to the General Assemblies of the realm.

Side by side with the civil administration, the Church played almost as important a part in ordering the country, both because of the influence of the ecclesiastical hierarchy in affairs of state and because it reached out to every section of the community through its parish priests. As the Moorish tide receded, the newly-established monasteries also exerted an important influence on social and economic life. Centuries were to pass before Tarragona was recaptured from the Moors, and its old ecclesiastical province was absorbed within that of Narbonne, so reinforcing the commanding position of the Franks.

The Spanish Mark remained a distant province of the Carolingian Empire; and even under Charlemagne and his immediate successors, Louis the Pious and Charles the Bald, there were internal revolts. Nevertheless, its detachment from the Empire came about not as the result of violent rebellion or the upsurge of nationalistic feeling, but more by default. On the one hand, the short-lived kings who followed Charles lacked the force and authority of their predecessors; and eleven years after his death in 877, the dynasty was supplanted by Odo the Robert. Catalonia, as the province became known from the time of Louis the Pious (the origins of the name are not clear), explicitly owed allegiance to its Carolingian sovereigns, but not to a ruler of different lineage, and had increasingly come to rely on its own efforts to maintain and expand its territories in face of the ever-present threat from the Moors.

While the power of the sovereign had decreased, that of the counts had steadily grown, so that in the final resort it was no longer the king who chose the counts, but the counts who chose the king. Not only Catalonia, but the Empire at large saw the formation of independent principalities, such as those of Burgundy and Flanders; and when, in 872, Bernat Plantipilosa obtained the country of Toulouse from Charles the Bald, a Count Ramon seized the opportunity to establish the independent county of Pallars-Ribagorça in Catalonia.

It was not a question of the counts, who accepted their feudal status of vassals, deliberately rebelling against the king, but of seeking to consolidate their authority over the regions which they controlled, particularly by making the office hereditary. In the course of time the right of a count to leave his lands to his sons went unchallenged. In Catalonia there was also a tendency for the Count of Barcelona to take precedence over his fellows. As early as 817—but without it implying formal authority over the other counties—Count Bera had been granted the title of Marquess of the Goths, which passed to the ambitious and forceful Bernat of Septimania, nominated in 826. As a son of Guillem of Toulouse, who had played a large part in the capture of Barcelona, he had already acceded to the Roussillon and so forged a solid link between Catalonia and the region beyond the Pyrenees.

The founder of the House of Barcelona, which was to shape the country's destinies for the next five centuries, was Wilfred the Hairy (Guifré el Pilós), whose great contribution to the emergence of an independent Catalonia is symbolized by legend. It is said that while fighting against the Moors with Charles the Bald, he was wounded, and that by dipping four fingers into the blood and drawing them across Wilfred's gilded shield, the king made a grant of arms, which was the origin of the Catalan flag with its red bars on a yellow ground. It would be naïve to read into this story the recognition by the Franks of an independent Catalonia, although by his death in 897 Wilfred had achieved the *de facto* separation of the Principality from the Empire. Prudent and well-balanced as he was, Wilfred could hardly afford to antagonize the Franks when he was involved in incessant skirmishing with the Moors on his other frontier.

As important as his successes against the Moors was his resettlement of the regions in the west, which had remained devastated and depopulated since 'Ubayd Allah's foray of 828 in support of the dissident Aizón. Wilfred was thus able to restore the county of Ausona (Vich) and add it to those already under his rule: Urgell, Cerdanya (Cerdagne), Barcelona, Gerona and Conflent. Only the counties of Empuriés-Roussillon and Pallars-Ribagorça, within the tra-

ditional orbit of Toulouse, remained outside his control. For the
first time, therefore, a Count of Barcelona had succeeded in uniting
the greater part of Catalonia; and although the process of unification was to suffer a setback on his death, when he divided his
possessions among his sons, the central nucleus of Barcelona-Ausona-
Gerona was henceforth to survive intact. It was the custom for a
ruler to divide his possession; but the fight against the Moors could
have been conducted more effectively had they remained intact, and
the loss of the county of Urgell proved to be particularly damaging,
since even at the time of Alfonso el Cast two centuries later the
Count of Urgell sided with the Castilians.

1. The red and yellow
shield of Catalonia,
from a 1504 edition
of the
Constitucions.

Wilfred the Hairy died as the result of a mortal wound received
at the hands of the Moorish governor of Lérida, Lope ibn-Muham-
mad. He was laid to rest at the Abbey of Ripoll, which he had re-
founded after its destruction by the Moors and which was to
become a cradle of the arts and sciences in Catalonia.

With the restoration of the Carolingian dynasty in the person
of Charles the Simple, efforts were made to bring back Catalonia
within the Frankish fold. Charles styled himself both 'Rex Fran-
chorum' and 'Rex Gothorum'; and in 899 the Count of Barcelona,
Guifred-Borrell, led a deputation of Catalan nobles to Tours-sur-
Marne and paid lip-service to a series of edicts confirming the earlier
rights and privileges of the Carolingians—no mention being made

of Odo. But the Count of Barcelona was in no mind to conform to an authority which in practice no longer existed apart from a tenuous jurisdiction over the monasteries.

By entering into negotiations with the Caliph al-Hakam II, Count Ramon Borrell of Barcelona (948–92) initiated a policy openly hostile to the Franks. Thus Ramon d'Abadal writes that 'If the first two legations of Borrell to Córdoba in 950 and 966 represented no more than pacts of peace and friendship, it is clear that the two last, in 971 and 974, had a much more precise purpose, and it is to be supposed that Count Borrell became the vassal of al-Hakam, consequently pledging his obedience and fidelity—a vassalage incompatible with fidelity to the Frank king. We can therefore affirm that the attraction of the Córdoban court, now so powerful and resplendent, contributed in large measure to the disappearance of the Frankish domination of our territory.'

After the death of al-Hakam II, the Caliphate was ruled by the masterful dictator al-Mansur (Ibn-Abi-'Amir), who launched a long series of attacks on the kingdoms of the Christian north. The thirty-second (or thirtieth according to Ibn-al-Khatib) of these was directed against Barcelona. Why he should have attacked a principality with which he was on friendly terms is not clear—but al-Mansur's ambitions were insatiable. There is perhaps a clue in Ibn-Khaldun's remark that, before invading the county of Barcelona, al-Mansur made sure that it was completely detached from the king of the Franks and said that the first Umayyads maintained relations with the 'kings of Barcelona', because if they fought them they would also have to fight the 'king of Rome' and also of Constantinople.

Al-Mansur struck north along the Mediterranean coast, sweeping aside opposition from Ramon Borrell, and on 7 July 985, entered Barcelona, which was ruthlessly sacked and then burnt to the ground. Most of the inhabitants were either killed or enslaved, and Borrell took refuge in the mountains until the Moorish garrison retired some six months later.

Pocketing his pride, Borrell now made a smart turn-about and applied to Lothaire, king of the Franks, for aid against a renewed attack. Lothaire died in 986, and his son Louis, the last of the Carolingians, in 987; and the new king, Hugh Capet, bode his time before sending Borrell a cool reply early in 988 :

In the name of King Hugh to Count Borrell. Since God in his mercy has blessed the Kingdom of the Franks with complete tranquility, we have decided with the advice of our counsellors to make prompt reply to your unease. If, then, you wish to keep the troth so often pledged by your legates to us and our fore-bears—so that we are not disappointed in your help on arriving in your country—at the time when our army encamps in Aqui-taine, you must present yourself to us with a few followers to swear fidelity and to guide the army on its way. If you wish to proceed in this fashion and in future to obey us rather than the Ishmaelites, send us legates before Easter to pledge your fidelity and to inform us precisely of your route.

By the time Borrell received this letter, al-Mansur was otherwise occupied in León and Castile, and the danger had passed. No legates were sent, nor did Borrell make the journey; and with this last ex-change the Counts of Barcelona broke off all political relations with Hugh and his successors. The Counts of Barcelona were now sover-eigns in their own land, although not formally recognized as such by a French monarch until the Treaty of Corbeil in 1258.

Catalonia remained a small state struggling for her existence. Al-Mansur died in 1002—'*mortuus est Almanzor, et sepultus est in inferno*' notes the *Chronicon Burgense* with evident relief—but the continuing threat from the Moors was underlined when his short-lived son 'Abd al-Malik mounted a damaging raid on the territories of the north-east in the summer of 1003. Left without a European ally, Catalonia turned to the Papacy in Rome, which was able to supply moral, if not material support. As has been well said by Ferran Soldevila,

> During the first period of their relations there was a certain similarity between the role played by Rome in Catalonia and the last of the Carolingians. We were looking for a moral guarantee from a power hierarchically and historically superior. The Counts of Barcelona, although enjoying a certain supremacy over the other counties, did not as yet exercise the required authority. It was a matter of necessity to form links with an established power outside the country.

Having severed their connection with the Franks, the Counts of Barcelona saw no reason why the powerful ecclesiastical establish-ment should still be controlled from Narbonne. As early as 971 Count Borrell had sought to revive the ecclesiastical province of Tarragona. Although Tarragona itself was still firmly in Moorish hands, the Pope issued bulls authorizing Ató, Bishop of Vich, to become metropolitan; but the initiative came to nothing because of his premature death. The issue came to the forefront again after the recovery from the Moors in 1085 of Toledo, the ancient Visigothic capital of Hispania, by Alfonso VI of Castile. In 1088 Pope Urban II promulgated a bull re-establishing the Archbishopric of Toledo and declaring it 'in totius Hispaniarum regnis.' This bull was officially communicated to 'Tarraconensibus et ceteris Hispaniarum archiepiscopis et episcopis.' Taking this to mean the revival of the province of Tarragona, Bishop Berenguer of Vich went to Rome to seek implementation of the papal concession of 971. It was confirmed in the summer of 1089; and despite opposition from Narbonne, the two dioceses were formally separated in 1091. A further decree of 1097 ended all the jurisdiction of Narbonne in the region beyond the Pyrenees; but it was not until 1154, after the union of Catalonia and Aragon during the reign of Ramon Berenguer IV, that the work was completed and the dioceses of Tarragona named as: Barcelona, Gerona, Urgell, Ausona, Tortosa, Lérida, Saragossa, Osca, Pamplona, Tarassona and Calahorra.

By cutting loose from the Archbishopric of Narbonne, the Counts of Barcelona completed the work of liberation from the Franks, which, on the political plane, had been accomplished a century earlier. Nevertheless the long and close association with the Carolingians was to stamp Catalonia as a region apart from the other kingdoms formed from the rump of Visigothic Hispania. By the end of the tenth century Catalonia was left with little of the feeling of historic continuity which inspired the kingdoms of León and Asturias, and differed from Castile both in language and in a feudally organized society.

There remained one all-important cohesive influence: if it was the Moors who had thrown Catalonia into the arms of the Franks, by their continuing presence they ensured that she should not entirely disattach herself from the rest of the country, but join in the task of Reconquest.

III

Counts of Barcelona

The death of al-Mansur in 1002 marks a turning point in the history of the Iberian Peninsula. It was very shortly followed by the disintegration of the Córdoban caliphate and the fragmentation of al-Andalus into some thirty small principalities governed by the so-called *reyes de taifas* or 'party kings'. Disunited as they were, they proved no match for the Christians of the north, who had found a new dynamic in their religion, a revival that gained impetus through the large-scale settlement of Cluniac monks from Burgundy. In the words of Ferdinand Lot in his *L'Espagne chrétienne de 711 à 1073*:

> If, instead of dwelling on details, one considers the period as a whole, the failures of the Christians disappear, the contradictions are of no account. There remains the spectacle of a resistance at first limited to a tiny corner of a great country, but invincible, since it survived all defeats. From the defensive the little Christian state passes to the offensive, and repopulation goes hand in hand with the excitement of Reconquest.

But if, in martial terms, the eleventh century belonged to the newly-born kingdom of Castile and to Ferdinand I, Alfonso VI and El Cid, there were to be significant developments in Catalonia. By a sudden reversal of roles it was now the Muslims, who, in return for protection or, at least, freedom from attack, became tributaries of the Christians. The moneys which began to flow into the coffers of the Counts of Barcelona from the time of Ramon Borrell were to swell during the reign of Ramon Berenguer I (1035–1076) and, together with the repopulation of the devastated areas, were to pave the way for economic expansion. Ramon Berenguer ('The Old') extended his territories both to the north and south, but made his most significant contribution in the promulgation of the *usatges*, a written code defining the reciprocal rights and responsibilities of the sovereign and his subjects, which preceded *Magna Carta* by some century and a half.

B*

The researches of José Balari Jovany into the *Archivo de la Corona de Aragón* have thrown a great deal of light on the circumstances in which this historic declaration of rights was made. In their original form of 1068 the laws were approved by a council of eighteen persons of high rank under the presidency of the Count and his wife Almodis. Of the eighteen, only one, Ponç Bofill March, was a cleric; and it seems likely that it was he who drafted the *usatges*.

Ponç Bofill March was appointed *juez de palacio* ('judge of the palace') in 1030, when Ramon Berenguer was only six, and in all probability acted as tutor and mentor to the young prince until, in 1035, at the age of fifteen or sixteen, Ramon Berenguer married his first wife, Isabel, and took the government into his own hands. In this same year Ponç ceased signing documents of state and retired from the office of *juez*. It was at this point, according to Balari, that he began the long work of drafting the code.

In support of this Balari instances the *usatge* '*Quoniam per iniquum principem*', which defines the responsibilities of the prince: 'It is easy to see that whoever drafted it was not a warrior equipped with a sword and encased in armour. Its author, who expected much of a prince and accorded him semi-divine status, must necessarily have been an ecclesiastic well-versed in the scriptures. This emerges from the first words of the *usatge*: "Without truth and justice the iniquitous prince destroys himself together with his lands and their inhabitants." These words are a paraphrase of Verse 3, Chapter X of Ecclesiasticus, which runs: "An unwise king destroyeth his people; but through the prudence of them which are in authority the city shall be inhabited." '

Immediate comparison of the two texts is even more striking:

Ecclesiasticus	Usatge
Rex insipiens perdet populum suum et civitates inhabituntur per sensum potentium	*Quoniam per iniquum principem, et sine veritate, et sine justitia perdit omni tempore terra et habitatores eius, etc.*

The derivation of the word *usatge* is from the Latin *us-us*, with the addition of the suffix *aticus*. This emerged in Catalan as *usatge* and in the Castilian as *usaje*; it therefore means a 'usage' or custom hallowed by long practice. The *usatges* did not, however, become law simply because they embodied established custom; they are rather the expression of sovereign will, freely exercised. The original *Código ó Compilación de los Usatges* was promulgated in 1068, but many

North-eastern Spain in 1086.

of the laws were subsequently emended or are of later date. The original *usatges* can be identified from internal evidence by their use of the present tense. Thus the preamble to *Quoniam per iniquum principem* contains the words 'Nos sepedicti principes, Raimundus et Almodis, consilio et auxilio nostrorum nobilium virorum, decernimus atque mandamus . . .' ('We, the frequently mentioned princes, Ramon and Almodis, with the advice and help of our noble barons, *decree* and *enact* . . .') Later additions make frequent use of the past tense and also refer to Ramon Berenguer as 'vetus' ('old'), a description which was not current until 1139 during the reign of Ramon Berenguer IV.

The *usatges* fall into three main groups, dealing with the sovereign, feudal customs, and criminal and civil law.

The first group, having established that the prince derives his powers from God (*non est potestas nisi a Deo*), define his legal, executive and judicial functions. His subjects are, for example, charged with supporting him in the defence of the realm and will be punished if they do not lend aid (*Princeps namque*). *Strate et vie publice* establishes that the prince does not have outright dominion over roads, running water, pastures and woods, but only for the benefit of the community as a whole. However, in mountainous areas, no one may construct a castle, church or monastery without the sovereign's express permission (*Rochas namque habeant potestates*). Another series of *usatges*, proceeding from the undeniable precept that 'the world cannot live without justice', lays its enforcement on the princely authorities (*Datum est eis justiciam facere*, etc).

The *usatges* first took shape with the purpose of codifying feudal customs and giving them the force of law. The vassal had previously acknowledged his obligations towards his feudal overlord, in virtue of which he held his land and was given protection, by a simple oath of fidelity. The *usatges* defined these obligations and made them legally binding under threat of punishment. One such obligation was to take part in the *hosts y cabalcadas* (i.e. the military operations) of his overlord; it was now enacted that if he failed to behave as *homo solidus*, he might at worst be required to indemnify his feudal superior for all the loss and damage suffered as a result of his defection (*Qui fallerit hostes vel cavalcadas seniori suo*). Another requirement was for a vassal to allow his overlord the use of his castle, if so requested.

In the sphere of criminal and civil law, the *usatges* provided for fines in less serious offences and, in the case of major crimes, for imprisonment, mutilation or death at the discretion of the sovereign authority. According to *Mulieribus etiam,* and with a brutality typical of the mediaeval period, even women might be condemned to the mutilation of nose, lips, ears or breasts, or if deemed necessary be burned alive.

The romantic view is that the *usatges* established the basis of Catalan liberties. If, as in the case of *Magna Carta,* a study of their content suggests that their compilers were less interested in the rights of common people and more concerned with preserving their own, they nevertheless mark a step forward. For the first time the rights of the individual were at least defined and the feudal customs introduced by the Franks given a basis of legality. From the modern standpoint the *usatges* were in one respect reactionary, since in Visigothic law all men were equal, whereas the *Código* recognized the social hierarchy of feudalism. On the other hand, the underlying principle of *Quoniam per iniquum principem* was that a sovereign enjoys his rights only in so far as he discharges his responsibilities towards his subjects. And in this may be seen the seeds of the 'contractual' relationship between sovereign and people which was to prove so important in centuries to come.

Ramon Berenguer I was jointly succeeded by the sons of his first and second marriages, who committed what must rank as one of the major political blunders of the century by turning down an offer of service against the Moors from the exiled El Cid. Of the personal antagonism between Berenguer Ramon II ('The Fratricide') and the all-conquering *Campeador,* the *Poema de Mio Cid* reports:

> The count is a great braggart
> > and spoke foolishly:
> 'My Cid of Bivar
> > inflicts great losses on me.
> He offended me once
> > in my own court:
> he struck my nephew
> > and gave no reparation . . .'

Catalonia was to pay dearly for the quarrel in the loss of tribute and influence when Berenguer Ramon reconciled the Moorish emirs of Saragossa, and of Lérida, Tortosa and Denia, al-Mutamin and al-Hayib, and forming a grand alliance against the Cid, struck at him at the Pinar de Tevar in the rugged country, south of the Ebro. Again in the words of the *Poema*:

'When my Cid had spoken
                    all made ready;
they have taken up their arms
                    and mounted their horses.
They saw the Catalans
            descending the slope;
when they came near the foot of the hill
                    where it joins the plain,
my Cid who in good hour was born
                    called his men to attack
his knights charged forward
                    with a will
skilfully handling
            their pennons and lances,
wounding some
            and unhorsing the rest.
He who was born in good hour
                    has won the battle.
He has taken prisoner
            the Count Ramon;
he has taken his sword Colada
            worth more than a thousand marks.'

The discomfited Count was set at liberty with a warning from the Cid against any attempt at vengeance and departed with the words:

'Be at peace, my Cid
            on that account.
I have paid you tribute
            for all this year;
I have no intention
            of coming to see you.'

Berenguer Ramon II was some years later found guilty of fratricide and ended his days in exile, fighting against the Saracens in Palestine.
    Under his successor Ramon Berenguer III ('The Great'), the son of the murdered brother, Catalonia made rapid strides; indeed it has been said that his reign 'opened windows on Europe'. If there was no spectacular reoccupation of Moorish territory, the Catalans

did well to stem the advance of a new wave of invaders from North Africa. In 1101 the Almoravid armies of Yusuf ibn-Tashufin recaptured Valencia, which had been in the hands of the Cid from 1094 until his death in 1099; and the rout of Alfonso VI of Castile at Sagrajas in 1086 was only the first of a series of Moorish victories which brought the Castilian reconquest of al-Andalus to a grinding halt.

In the face of this returning tide of Moorish aggression, and with the help of a Pisan fleet, Ramon Berenguer III actually invaded Majorca and Ibiza in 1114, but was compelled to evacuate the islands two years later. Although short-lived, the expedition was not without long-term results, since it encouraged the Catalans to build up a fleet and look east towards the Mediterranean as a future area for expansion; while the capture in 1099 of Tarragona, which was henceforth to remain in Catalan hands, gave substance to the papal decree of 1097 re-establishing the former ecclesiastical province.

Either by annexation or alliance the northern counties of Besalú, Cerdanya, Pellars, Empuriés and also Roussillon and Foix beyond the Pyrenees all came firmly within the control of the Counts of Barcelona. Ramon Berenguer III achieved an even more spectacular success in 1113 by marrying Dolça, the heiress to Provence, and so (for a time at any rate) uniting her territories with his own.

In the words of Mistral, the Count Berenguer set sail from Catalonia with a fair wind swelling the white sails of his fleet, sailed up the Rhône, and gained the hand, the crown and the diamonds of the Princess:

> *Dau comte Berenguier, fraires, ben nos sovèn,*
> *Quand de la Catalonha aduch per un bon vent*
> *Emè si velas blanquinelas,*
> *Intret dins nostre Rose e reçaupet la man*
> *E la corona e li diamants*
> *De la princesa Docinela*

There was another side to this romantic story. Ramon Berenguer III had been worsted in an attempt to gain possession of the county of Carcassonne by an alliance between the Count of Toulouse and Alfonso I (El Batallador, 'The Fighter') of Aragon, both of whom had pretensions to Provence; and it was only after a period of hostilities and by ceding Provençal territory to the Count of Toulouse and to another contender, Ramon de Baus, that he entered into undisputed possession. In the long run the threat to the union of Catalonia and

Provence was to come from the kings of France, who looked towards
the Mediterranean as a natural area of expansion; and Ramon
Berenguer III undid much of what he had achieved by the injudi-
cious separation of the territories on his death, when he left Provence to his second son, Berenguer Ramon, and the rest of his
domains to his first-born, Ramon Berenguer IV.

Catalonia and Provence were nevertheless to remain closely linked
for almost a century and a half. The ties of language, the bond of a
shared Roman heritage and the poetry of the Provençal troubadours
contributed to the cultural awakening of Catalonia; while a community of interests in trade and maritime communications led to
an expansion of commerce and opened new European horizons for
a state which had previously been inward-looking and isolated.

In spite of the success of her policies beyond the Pyrenees, on the
death of Ramon Berenguer III Catalonia faced critical problems
arising from events within the Peninsula.

Until 1119 the Almoravid armies ranged more or less at will,
penetrating to Madrid and Guadalajara and thrusting deep into
what, under the young Afonso Henriques, was emerging as the independent kingdom of Portugal. A new Christian champion now
arose in the person of Alfonso I of Aragon. In 1118, with the help
of strong contingents from the Languedoc, he captured Saragossa,
and by 1120 had reoccupied most of the Ebro basin. With Tudela,
Tarazona, Catalayud, Daroca and Alcañiz in his hands, he was poised
to secure Cuenca and Teruel and in fact mounted an even more spectacular expedition, which, over a period of fifteen months, took him
as far as Vélez-Málaga on the Mediterranean. His last encounter
with the Moors was less successful; in an attempt to take Lérida he
was gravely wounded while investing the nearby town of Fraga
and died shortly afterwards in 1134.

Relations between Catalonia and her western neighbour were not
good. There was rivalry between the two for the possession of
Lérida; and outright fighting between Aragonese and Catalan forces
had broken out in 1123. Alfonso's conquests were such as to mini-
mize any further Catalan expansion in the Moorish territories to
the south; and both Aragon and Castile had laid claim to Valencia
and Murcia. The greatest danger to Catalonia lay in the possible
union of her powerful neighbours. Castile had also made deep incursions into al-Andalus and her imperialistic ambitions were un-
disguised—both Alfonso VI and his son Alfonso VII had assumed
the title of Emperor. In the event of such a union and with an

enlarged Castile ranged along her border, Catalonia's very existence would be at stake.

For a short period after 1109 Castile and Aragon had in fact been united by the marriage of Urraca, daughter of Alfonso VI of Castile, to Alfonso (*El Batallador*). Only the fierce squabbles between the couple, arising from Alfonso's refusal to recognize the rights of her son by her previous husband, Count Raymond of Burgundy, and the Pope's final dissolution of the marriage on the grounds of incest, ended the partnership.

The problem recurred in more critical form when *El Batallador* bequeathed his kingdom to the Templars, the Hospitallers and the Canons of the Holy Sepulchre. His somewhat eccentric will was promptly set aside; of the claimants who then appeared, his brother, Ramiro II, had the best title to the vacant throne, although he was a monk and bishop-elect of Roda. Alfonso VII of Castile also had pretensions to Aragon, which he attempted to implement by entering at the head of a powerful army, and seizing Saragossa. While Ramiro fled and took refuge in Ribagorça, an impressive array of potentates converged on Saragossa from Catalonia and beyond the Pyrenees to lodge a protest. They included Saint Oleguer, Archbishop of Tarragona and Ramon Berenguer's adviser, and the Counts of Urgell, Pallars, Toulouse, Montpellier and Comminges. In the upshot, Alfonso VII withdrew from Saragossa and attempted to secure Aragon peacefully by means of a marriage between his son Sancho and Ramiro's infant daughter by Agnes of Poitiers, Petronilla.

The future of Catalonia—and of the Peninsula—was therefore to be determined by success in obtaining the hand of a two-year-old; and in this bizarre contest it was Ramon Berenguer IV who emerged the victor.

By an instrument dated 11 August 1137, Ramiro pledged his daughter to Ramon Berenguer, together with his kingdom, provided only that he undertook to respect the rights and privileges enjoyed by the Aragonese in the past. The pact was indeed exceptionally favourable to the Catalans, since in the event of Petronilla's premature death, Ramon Berenguer was still left in possession of Aragon; and should he himself die before the solemnization of the marriage, there was no obligation for one of his sons to marry her. Petronilla was to be known as Queen of Aragon, but Ramon Berenguer contented himself with the title of 'Princeps Aragonum' or 'Aragonesium regni inclitus dominator', and only after his death would his successors be entitled 'King of Aragon and Count of Barcelona'. His modesty in this respect has been put down to a desire to avoid offending the Aragonese nobility, but it also sprang from native pride. 'I,' said the Count, according to the *Chronicle* of Bernat Desclot, 'received the lady with no wish to be called king; I am now one of the premier counts of the world, and if I were to be called king, I should not be one of the greatest.'

Since Aragon was a kingdom, albeit less powerful than Catalonia, which ranked simply as a principality, the title of 'King of Aragon' was henceforth to take precedence over that of 'Count of Barcelona'. It was Catalan dynamism which later resulted in the acquisition of a Mediterranean empire and a vast expansion of trade; and Catalan historians, of whom Jaume Rossinyol is a recent example, have taken to task foreign writers for using the term 'Crown of Aragon' to describe the combined realm. It seems a rather partisan objection inspired by nationalistic fervour, for, granted that the Catalans were the predominant partners, there is no other way in which to describe the new entity.

That Aragon decided in favour of union with Catalonia and not Castile can probably be explained by a desire to link herself with a maritime, rather than a continental power, and to obtain access to the Mediterranean by way of the Ebro. Another factor was undoubtedly the bitter experience of the Aragonese when briefly united with Castile during the marriage of Alfonso (*El Batallador*) and Urraca. Alfonso VII of Castile contented himself with an undertaking that Saragossa should be regarded as under his vassalage; that he did not have recourse to more bellicose expedients was perhaps because of the peace-making influence of his wife, Dolça, a sister of Ramon Berenguer. In effect, the union of Catalonia and Aragon partitioned the Peninsula between three dominant powers: Castile, Aragon-Catalonia and the emergent Portugal of Afonso Henriques; the loser was the small Basque state of Navarre, henceforth to be a bone of contention between her powerful neighbours.

There remained the challenge of Moorish al-Andalus in the south; and although the Almoravid empire was on the wane and effectively disintegrated after the death of its last emir, Tashufin ibn-Ali, in 1145, its rivals and conquerors, the Almohads, were poised to strike from North Africa. An outcome of the new configuration of the Christian states was that spheres of influence were agreed in the fight against the common enemy. And in staking out claims to future conquests, Ramon Berenguer IV proved as astute as in snatching the hand of Petronilla from his Castilian rival. Granted that they

THE HOUSE OF BARCELONA
(from the formation of the Crown of Aragon)

RAMON BERENGUER IV = Petronilla,
Count of Barcelona   Queen of Aragon
(1131–1162)

ALFONSO II   Ramon Berenguer   Sancho
King of the Crown of Aragon   Count of Provence   Count of Provence
(1162–1196)   (1168–1181)

PETER II   Alfonso
(1196–1213)   Count of Provence

JAMES I the Conqueror   = Violante of Hungary
(1213–1276)

PETER III the Great   = Constance of Sicily   JAMES II
(1276–1285)   (Hohenstaufen)   King of Majorca
King of Sicily   (1276–1311)
(1282)

ALFONSO III   JAMES II   = Blanche of   FREDERICK II
(1285–1291)   King of Sicily   Anjou   King of Sicily
            (1285–1295)   (1296–1327)
            King of Aragon
            (1291–1327)   SANCHO I
                                King of Majorca
                                (1311–1324)
         ALFONSO IV   JAMES III
         (1327–1336)   King of Majorca
                                (1324–1348)

PETER IV the Ceremonious = (1) María of   James, Count of
(1336–1387)   Navarre   Urgell
King of Majorca   = (2) Eleanor of
(1348)   Sicily
King of Sicily
(1378)

Constance   JOHN I   MARTIN I   Eleanor
= FREDERICK III   (1387–1395)   (1396–1410)   = John I of
King of Sicily   MARTIN   Castile
(1355–1377)   King of Sicily
                       (1392–1409)

                                FERDINAND of Antequera
                                King of Aragon (1412–1416)
                                (see House of Trastámara)

were still in Moorish occupation, Castile had good claims to Valencia, Denia and Murcia. By promising to hold the cities and their dependencies as a vassal of Alfonso VII, Ramon Berenguer succeeded in gaining future freedom of action in the Levante. Possession is nine points of the law; and, as his successor, Alfonso II, was to demonstrate, ties of vassalage could later be broken.

Valencia and the lands south were to await the coming of James the Conqueror for their final liberation, but Ramon Berenguer achieved two important successes by recapturing Tortosa with the help of a Genoese fleet, and Lérida with support from Alfonso VII. The capture of these places was of more than military significance. Catalonia contained few sizeable towns apart from Barcelona; the reconquered regions were not subject to a strict feudal regime hampering social and economic development and therefore attracted large numbers of immigrants, both from the old Principality and from beyond the Pyrenees. The great demographic expansion, which was to be even more marked during the thirteenth and fourteenth centuries, was an important factor in the formation of a Catalan empire overseas.

In addition to help from the Genoese and the Castilians, Ramon Berenguer IV received aid from the military orders of the Knights Templars and Hospitallers. It was presumably to ensure their participation in the Reconquest that Alfonso I of Aragon had sought to leave them his kingdom. The Templars had first arrived in Catalonia about 1131, when Ramon Berenguer III granted them the castle of Grañena on the Moorish march; but the Order had been formed to support the crusades in the Holy Land, and it seems that at first they were unenthusiastic about fighting the Saracens on a second front in Spain. Only after complicated negotiations in 1143, when they agreed to surrender their rights in Aragon, did they enter the contest. Their price was high: the grant of the castles of Monzón, Mongay, Barbará, Chalamera, Belchite and Remolins; a tenth of the royal revenues; a further large sum from the royal dues in Saragossa and in Huesca; a fifth of all lands conquered from the Moors; and exemption from certain taxes.

The military orders constituted a better trained and more reliable fighting force than levies liable only for limited periods of service; and until the Templars were disbanded in 1308 (ostensibly because of widespread involvement in anti-Christian rites and homosexual practices—though the accusations were highly suspect), they, and the other orders, played a major part in the offensive against the

Moors, at the same time reaping vast gains in the shape of castles, lands, rents and profits from banking transactions. Catalonia and the Levante are today dotted with the shattered remains of Templar castles, ranging in size from the little fortress of Pulpis, gaunt on a hilltop, with its reservoir open to the sky and still collecting rainwater, to the noble bulk of Peñiscola, the last refuge of the Antipope Pedro de Luna, which rides the sea like a ship. Monzón, the headquarters of the order in Spain, held out against all attacks until May 1309.

In one direction Ramon Berenguer's ambitions were thwarted. After the union with Aragon, the little kingdom of Navarre remained isolated, and it was soon agreed between Ramon and his brother-in-law, Alfonso VII of Castile, that it should be partitioned between them. In the face of Catalonia's dramatic expansion, Alfonso seems to have changed his mind; and twenty-five years' campaigning on his own behalf left Ramon Berenguer without tangible gains.

In the trans-Pyrenean counties of Occitania, a more peaceable approach consolidated the ties between the two regions. The Counts of Barcelona considered Provence in the light of a benifice which reverted to the crown on the death of the beneficiary, so that when his brother, Berenguer Ramon, was killed in a skirmish with what the *Gesta comitum* calls 'robadors de la mar'—probably Genoese pirates—Ramon Berenguer IV took his young nephew into protection and himself assumed the title of Marquess of Provence until the boy came of age. The Count of Béziers and Carcassonne, whose father had successfully defied Ramon Berenguer III, swore allegiance; and by 1154 Narbonne, Montpellier and Béarn had all come within the Catalan sphere of influence.

Only the Counts of Toulouse pursued a resolutely antagonistic policy, aligning themselves with the King of France. Ramon Berenguer IV was able to contain them by concluding an alliance with Henry II of England, who had married Eleanor of Aquitaine and so come into extensive territories in Gascony, and the allies in fact laid siege to Toulouse in 1156. The English alliance was to remain a cornerstone of Catalan policy, paralleling the traditional link of Castile with France.

Ramon Berenguer IV's successors, Alfonso (El *Cast*) and Peter (Pere) II (El *Católico*), strengthened the Catalan grip on the Midi, while pursuing a policy of *détente* with Castile. Alfonso II, who married Sancha, a daughter of Alfonso VII of Castile, has been much criticized by Catalan historians for trading the claim to Murcia in

2. Title page of Jaume Roig's *Llibre de les dones* ('Book of Ladies'), 1493.

return for the Castilian renunciation of vassalage over Saragossa and Valencia. Somewhat surprisingly, Alfonso II struck the bargain with his brother-in-law, Alfonso VIII of Castile, at Cazola in 1179, after a successful Catalan expedition towards Valencia and the capture of Cuenca from the Moors. It was probably dictated by the need to make common front against the Almohads, who, moving into the vacuum left by the Almoravids, had been making alarming gains in al-Andalus since 1171. The reality of this threat was demonstrated in 1195, when the cause of Reconquest was to suffer a disastrous check by Alfonso VIII's defeat at Alarcos in 1195 at the hands of Ya'qub al-Mansur.

The first fruits of the agreement of Cazola were a joint attack on the Kingdom of Navarre, as a result of which Alfonso VIII made gains in the Rioja, which he refused to share with his ally, as had been agreed. The disillusioned Alfonso II then reverted to the traditional alliance with León and Portugal against Castile, further drawing in Navarre. Nevertheless, in the hour of greatest need, when Castile was again confronted by the Almohads at Las Navas de Tolosa in 1212, Alfonso II's son, Peter the Catholic, ranged himself by the side of Alfonso VIII and played no little part in the defeat of the Moors.

Apart from this perhaps decisive intervention in the fortunes of the Iberian Peninsula, Peter II's main endeavour was to extend the Catalan hold on southern France; yet, through a quite unforseen chain of circumstances, and largely because of his own youth and intemperateness, he was to lose both his life and Occitania in the attempt.

IV

The 'Catholic' and the 'Believers'

To visit the quiet French town of Albi, with its splendid Gothic cathedral and a museum full of paintings by Toulouse-Lautrec couched above the placid reaches of the Tarn, one would not suppose that it had given its name to a sect which provoked one of the bloodiest and most discreditable conflicts in the history of the mediaeval Church. Yet there is something a little sinister about the blank brick façade of the cathedral, pierced by the narrowest of windows, which fittingly echoes the massacre of the Albigenses and the tragic death of Pedro II of Aragon.

By a strategy of political marriages which was second nature to them, the Counts of Barcelona had succeeded in making most of Occitania between the Pyrenees and the Alps feudatory to the Crown of Aragon. Peter's father, Alfonso II, had inherited Provence on the death of his cousin, Ramon Berenguer III; most of the intervening territories, including Carcassonne and Béziers, Foix and Comminges, Narbonne and Béarn, had fallen into the orbit of the Crown of Aragon; and Peter not only married his sisters, Eleanor and Sancha, to Ramon VI and Ramon VII of Toulouse, but himself married Maria of Montpellier, heiress to the county on the death of her father.

His dominion of southern France was not merely titular, since his royal progresses through the territories were as frequent as those through Aragon and Catalonia. It is true that he was received with little overt enthusiasm by his turbulent vassals; but they were at least more reconciled to his suzerainty than to that of northern France, to which they were bitterly opposed.

The quarrels with the north arose from a difference in tradition and temperament. They were, as Charles de Tourtoulon wrote long ago in his *Études sur la maison de Barcelona*, a 'struggle between the North and the South; between the German and the Latin races, between Frank rudeness and Roman civilization.' The seigneurial courts were in keeping with the decadent Roman society which they had replaced. Luxurious and pleasure-loving, they provided a natural environment for the lyrical poetry of the troubadours so vividly evoked by Mistral:

> Provença e Catalunya, unidas per l'amor
> Mescleren son parlar, si costuma e si mor.
> E quan havia dins Magalona,
> Quan havia dins Marsilha, a-z-Ais, en Avignon,
> Quauca beutat de gran renom
> N'en parlavais a Barcelona.

> Provence and Catalonia, united by love,
> Mixed their speech, their costumes and uses.
> And whether from Magalona,
> Or from Marseilles, Aix, or Avignon,
> Any beauty of great renown
> Was the talk of Barcelona.

This sensual refinement went hand in hand with a laxity of morals, so that Azalais de Lombers had been the lover of the Count of Toulouse and also of the Count of Béziers before becoming the mistress of Peter II. And without looking further, Peter's queen, Maria of Montpellier, had been married twice previously, her second husband, the Count of Comminges, having espoused her bigamously. The clergy was little better, and simony was rife in the Midi. In these circumstances it is hardly surprising that it should have become the hotbed of an austere anti-clerical heresy.

The doctrines of the Albigenses originated in the Middle East and were closely related to those of the Cathars and the Gnostics. Although the information about their beliefs and practices is inadequate and proceeds from their adversaries and inquisitorial reports, certain tenets survive. They did not accept the Old Testament, holding that it was inspired by Satan, who is the lord and master of the temporal world, and especially of the human body with its manifold frailties and appetites. Hell and purgatory do not exist except on earth; and men are the outcome of a struggle in heaven, in which the angels, incited to revolt by Satan, were driven out and imprisoned in terrestrial bodies. It follows that the inward man can be released only by the gift of the spirit, making it possible for him to return to the true kingdom of Christ. Otherwise he will suffer another term of imprisonment in the flesh, in all probability as an animal. It was because of this that at times of fast the Albigenses were forbidden to eat flesh (or cheese, eggs and milk, as products of sexual intercourse). Only fish were excepted, since according to mediaeval belief they were born asexually in water.

The great bulk of the Albigenses, or *boni homines* as they called themselves, were *Credentes* (or Believers). Only after the rite of *Consolamentum*, or baptism with the spirit, did they enter the ranks of the *Perfecti* (or Perfect). At this point, as has been well put, man becomes 'an angel walking in the flesh, whom the thin screen of death alone separates from Christ.' Because of the extreme rigours of life as a Perfect and the punishment meted out by the Inquisition, most Believers put off baptism until the last possible moment, so that in fact it was a kind of extreme unction (the baptism of infants was not recognized by the sect).

In the eyes of the papacy, perhaps even more damaging than these heretical beliefs was the existence of an organized fellowship permanently opposed to the Roman Church because of the corruption of its priesthood. Successive Popes attempted to tackle the problem, both by reform of the clergy and decrees directed against the sect, beginning with the Council summoned at Toulouse in 1119. Innocent III sent legates to the Midi with full powers to take action in 1199, and again in 1202; but neither the bishops nor the local clergy were disposed to mend their ways.

An early outcome of the Albigensian revolt was to heal the long-standing enmity between the Houses of Barcelona and Toulouse, which had for so long been the principal obstacle to unifying the Languedoc. The county of Toulouse was the very focus of the Albigensian heresy, and its ruler, Ramon VI, no doubt felt threatened both by the papacy and King Philippe Auguste of France, who had for long been waiting for a pretext to extend his territories to the south. He therefore turned to the other interested party, Peter II, who sealed the compact by marrying his sister Eleanor to Ramon in 1200. Agreement had been reached, but at the eleventh hour and at a critical juncture in the history of the Languedoc.

Peter II was actively drawn into the struggle in 1204, when he was crowned in Rome by Innocent III, receiving the title (ironically as events were to turn out) of *El Católico*, and in return for papal recognition and support undertook to respect the priviliges of the Church and to fight against the heresy. There were heretics in Catalonia, perhaps in larger numbers than has been supposed, but it was at Carcassonne that Peter summoned a conference, which in the event did little but confirm that heresy was widespread. The Pope, despairing of peaceful means, now declared a crusade, the first of its kind to be directed against straying members of the Church, and called upon King Philippe Auguste of France to support it. Philippe was weary of crusading and otherwise occupied in the recovery of his provinces from John of England, so that the Pope turned again to Peter II, who made some perfunctory moves against the Albigenses, but soon found that to involve himself further would antagonize his vassals, particularly his brother-in-law, Ramon VI of Toulouse, and plunge the region into civil war.

In spite of the initiative of the Spanish prelate, Domingo de Guzmán, later to become St. Dominic, in forming an order to preach against the heresy, little headway was made until in January 1209, a papal legate to the Court of Toulouse, Pierre de Castelnau, was murdered in suspicious circumstances after a violent quarrel with Ramon. The Pope then took advantage of the general outcry to press his demand for a crusade and to insist upon the participation of the French king and his supporters. Largely thanks to the efforts of the Cistercians in broadcasting promises of indulgences and personal gain, adventurers and criminals flocked to join, and the crusade rapidly lost any religious purpose and became a pitched battle between the bitterly opposed north and south of France. The leadership soon devolved on Simon de Montfort, French on his father's side and third Earl of Leicester by virtue of his English mother. Ambitious and acquisitive, and an able and ruthless soldier, his overriding object was personal aggrandizement. His first major objective was Béziers, where the crusaders disgraced their cause by the wholesale murder of the inhabitants, put by some accounts at 60,000 persons. According to tradition, the soldiers turned to the Abbot Arnold for instructions and were told: 'Matad, matad a todos, que luego Dios los distinguirá en el cielo' (Kill them, kill them all, and leave it to God to distinguish between them in heaven').

De Montfort next attacked Carcassonne, which he captured after stubborn resistance. Since the crusaders were entitled to indulgences after forty days' service, he found it difficult to keep his army together and approached Peter to regularize his position and to obtain from him the title of Viscount of Carcassonne. It seems that Peter still thought that it would be possible to defeat the crusade by fomenting revolts in the occupied territories; he therefore temporized, but in 1211, in the face of the renewed threat from the Moors, was compelled to return to Spain. Before leaving, he recognized de Montfort as Lord of Béziers and Carcassonne and, reverting to the traditional policy of the Counts of Barcelona, arranged that his son James (the future Jaume I), then a child of three, should marry de Montfort's daughter, Jane, and meanwhile be left in his care.

As a result of the united efforts of all the Christian kingdoms of Spain with the exception of León, and little thanks to the disgraceful behaviour of a motley horde of crusaders, as murderous and unprincipled as their fellows in France, the Almohads, under their leader Ya'qub al-Mansur, were resoundingly defeated at Las Navas de Tolosa on 16 July 1212, a battle which presaged the end of five hundred years of Moorish supremacy in Spain and Portugal. However, when Peter II was again free to return to France, he found that de Montfort and his party had renewed hostilities against Ramon of Toulouse, who retired to his fortress at Toulouse and issued urgent appeals for help.

In the face of the crusaders' refusal to give up the territories which they had seized, Peter appealed to the Pope, pointing out that they were no longer fighting a religious war, but using it as a pretext for grabbing lands and property to which they had no conceivable claim. De Montfort countered by sending his own legates to Rome; and Innocent III, unable to decide on the rights and wrongs of the matter, instructed both parties to suspend further operations pending further investigation. Peter was now faced by a cruel dilemma : either to countenance progressive French penetration of the Languedoc and the piece meal destruction of his vassals or to take arms against the crusaders. In the words of Pascual de Gayangos,

> What could a monarch, whose orthodoxy had never been suspect, himself a dutiful son of the Holy See, who had accepted the title of 'Catholic', and had on a former occasion by his excessive complaisance towards Innocent III brought on himself the reproaches of his own subjects, do under such circumstances? How could he in the midst of the struggle forget and abandon his position as first national Prince of the South of France, and what could he do, placed as he was between the standard of the Cross, which he was heroically defending in the Peninsula, and the great national cause of the South, of which he was the natural representative?

Knowing that de Montfort could expect no help from the King of France and that there had been massive desertions from his army, Peter took action.

By August 1213 he arrived at Toulouse with an army which has been put at some 30,000, including the flower of the Catalan and

Aragonese nobility, and, having joined forces with Ramon, advanced on the small town of Muret, garrisoned by some 700 of de Montfort's men. The town was strongly fortified and lies in the angle of the River Garonne and its tributary, the Louge; to the north lies the plain of Les Pesquiès, marshy in winter but firm in summer, on which the decisive battle was to be fought.

When de Montfort reached the place on 11 September with cavalry and reinforcements, he found that Peter and his allies had already seized one of the gates and that the garrison had withdrawn into the citadel. He was nevertheless allowed to enter the town, no doubt because the besiegers were confident of trapping him there. The papal legate attached to the crusaders judged the situation hopeless and attempted to negotiate a surrender. Peter refused to listen and cut short the parley by ordering a fresh attack on the town. Ramon, aware of the parlous state of the garrison, was for continuing the siege, but Peter, with mistaken chivalry, ordained that the battle should be decided on the plain in frontal combat. De Montfort, having harangued his men in the market place, was therefore allowed to lead them out by a gate at the rear and from thence to the plain to face the main force of his attackers.

The *Llibre dels Feits* or *Chronicle* of James I supplies some picturesque details of his father's over-confidence and lack of preparedness.

I recollect hearing, and indeed know for certain, that Don Nuno Sanxes and En Guillen de Montcada[1], the son of En Guillem Ramon de Montcada and of Na Guillema de Castelvi, were not in the battle; they sent a message to the King that he should wait for them; but the King would not wait, and fought the battle with those few [sic] who were with him. The night before the battle the King had slept with a woman, as I later heard from his own seneschal, called Erf (afterwards a Knight Hospitaller), who was there on the occasion; and others who saw him with their own eyes say that [at Mass in the morning] he could not stand up when it came to the Gospel, and kept to his seat while it was read.

In spite of his exhaustion, Peter changed armour with one of his knights and took his place in the front rank, instead of stationing himself in the rear as he should have done.

As was usual in mediaeval times, the battle was decided by the

[1] In Catalan, 'En' and 'Na' correspond to the Castilian 'Don' and 'Dona'.

heavy cavalry, of which Peter possessed some 2,000 and de Montfort barely half the number. De Montfort began by charging and scattering the troops engaged in the assault on the town. The squadron then wheeled on Peter's army in the plain and, supported by a second detachment of cavalry, broke the Aragonese ranks. During the confused engagement which followed Peter was thrown from his horse and killed. Pressing home the advantage, de Montfort led a third body of cavalry against the enemy's left and completed the rout of the main Aragonese force on the plain. Ramon, under the misapprehension that it was Peter and not de Montfort who had gained the day, had meanwhile resumed the attack on the town, but was speedily disillusioned when de Montfort, breaking off the pursuit of the main force, returned and scattered the men from Toulouse who fled in hopeless confusion to the ships in the Garonne which had brought up their supplies.

It is not possible to give a reliable estimate of the number of killed and wounded; the chronicler's figure of fifteen or twenty thousand is obviously poetic licence. De Montfort gained his totally unexpected victory because he concentrated the whole weight of his cavalry in compact columns, because he was fighting his way out of a desperate situation, and because many of his men, who had received absolution from Folquet, the fanatical Bishop of Narbonne, were fired by religious fervour. As one of the victors of Las Navas de Tolosa, and faced merely by a rebellious vassal, Peter underestimated his opponent and failed to make sensible use of his superior forces.

In his Història de Catalunya Ferran Soldevila writes that 'Faced by the corpse of the king, naked, bleeding and wretched, even the grim Simon de Montfort was unable to restrain his tears.' For the Crown of Aragon, the nobles of southern France and the Albigenses, the consequences were even more lamentable. Although the war dragged on for years, the ultimate domination of the North over the South was now a foregone conclusion. As for the Albigenses, they stuck tenaciously to their beliefs, but in dwindling numbers, in face of mounting persecution. After the Council of Toulouse in 1229 an Inquisition was established and proceeded with the usual ruthlessness of such institutions: in 1245, at Montségur, 200 members of the sect were burnt in one day.

Had Peter's son, James (Jaume) I, been of age he would doubtless have struck back in revenge; but the boy was only six and under the guardianship of his father's victor, so that he could do nothing to prevent his uncle Ramon VI of Toulouse being dispossessed of his domains, and Aragon-Catalonia found herself without a leader. It is true that the Papacy, whose policies had done so much to contribute to the débâcle, promptly arranged for James to be released and returned. At an assembly of the Catalans and Aragonese held at Lérida in 1214 James was solemnly crowned, and his great uncle Sancho (or Sanç), Count of Roussillon, was appointed as procurator or regent. The boy himself was placed in the care of Guillem de Montredon, Master of the Temple in Spain and Provence, and in the Order's great castle at Monzón was at least safe from the intrigues and factions of his own nobility.

Meanwhile Simon de Montfort was free to proceed with measures aimed at eliminating Catalan and Aragonese influence in southern France, of which his earlier order of 1 December 1212, is typical:

No widow, great lady or heiress, in possession of a fortress or castle may of her own free will marry a man of this territory without the permission of the said count [de Montfort], now or for two years; but she may marry a Frenchman without the count's or other permission.

De Montfort's injunctions were reinforced by a series of bulls issued by Pope Honorius III and warning both the regent and James of the dire consequences of any attempt to intervene in France. Thus, in December 1217, he wrote to James, then only nine: 'If, on the contrary you provoke us, We and the Roman Church shall see ourselves obliged to launch a crusade against your realm.'

James was half French—according to the contemporary Chronicle of Ramon Muntaner he was born as the result of a deception, his mother, Maria of Montpellier, whom Pedro had deserted, being smuggled into the king's bedchamber in place of his awaited mistress—and it was in France that he had spent his early childhood; but during his formative years in the Templar stronghold of Monzón he came under the direct influence of Guillem de Montredon. It is therefore hardly surprising that he should have been inculcated with the Templars' own crusading zeal, and that by the time he reached manhood his thoughts should have been of the Reconquest and the fight against the Moors, rather than of intervening in the conflict in Occitania—nominally, at any rate, a crusade against the heretical Albigenses.

As the scion of the Counts of Barcelona, he could not relinquish all interest in his birthright beyond the Pyrenees, but he later confined himself to attempts to restore the situation by peaceful means. As his ancestors had done before, he turned to political marriages—but at this crucial juncture the device was destined to fail. His main hope centred on uniting Provence and Toulouse by arranging a marriage between Ramon VII of Toulouse and one of the daughters of Ramon Berenguer V of Provence. There followed a tangled saga of a divorce and dispensation for the marriage, long-postponed because of the intervening death of two Popes, of a broken engagement, and finally of the premature deaths of both Ramon and Ramon Berenguer, the last male representative of the House of Barcelona. In the upshot Provence fell to Charles of Anjou, and Toulouse to Alfonse of Poitiers, both closely related to Louis IX (St. Louis) of France.

Because of his descent from the Carolingians, St. Louis had a shadowy claim to the counties of Catalonia, and this he finally agreed to waive in exchange for James's formal recognition of the French acquisition of the territories in Provence and the Languedoc. As a result of the ensuing Treaty of Corbeil of May 1258 and an agreement over Provence later in the same year, the Crown of Aragon renounced all rights to the lands beyond the Pyrenees with the main exceptions of Roussillon, Cerdagne and James's personal patrimony of Montpellier.

It was no doubt inevitable that, because of their separation by the barrier of the Pyrenees and the demographic preponderance of northern France, the territories should sooner or later have been lost. That Catalan ambitions were brought to a summary end was the result of papal intervention on behalf of France; of Peter II's defeat at Muret; and of James I's long minority. Catalan historians argue the issue; but it is at least debatable that by surrendering the territory without a prolonged struggle James left himself free to pursue the fight against the Moors and paved the way for a Catalan expansion in the east, which in the centuries that followed was to make the Crown of Aragon master of the Mediterranean.

Of Peter the Catholic the best epitaph is perhaps Ferran Soldevila's in *La figura de Pere el Catòlic en les cròniques catalanes*:

A rough assessment of the policies of Peter the Catholic—that is to say, one that takes no account of his motives and intentions but is based solely on results—is this: abroad, he contributed to the salvation of Castile at the Battle of Las Navas de Tolosa and to the loss of Occitania at the Battle of Muret; his internal politics can be summed up in one word—bankrupt.

V

Sicilian Vespers

The century which followed the Christian victory of Las Navas de Tolosa was to see the occupations of all the former Moorish territories with the exception of the Kingdom of Granada. The Portuguese were the first to reach the south coast of the Peninsula; but the great figures of the Reconquest in the thirteenth century were Ferdinand III, who in 1230 united Castile and León, and James (Jaume) I of Aragon-Catalonia.

James early displayed the restless energies which were to win him the name of The Conqueror: at the age of nine he succeeded in escaping from the castle of Monzón, where he had been kept a virtual prisoner by the Regent Sanç, and began the uphill struggle of restoring discipline among his dissident nobility; by thirteen he was married to Eleanor, daughter of Alfonso VIII of Castile and divorced from her eight years later.

Throughout his long and turbulent career he held good to the same principle: war with the Moors and peace with Christian princes abroad, and his first major campaign was against the Almohads in Majorca. The sailing of the expedition, which was almost entirely Catalan in character, since the Aragonese refused to support it, has been described in the extract from the *Llibre dels Feits* quoted on page 28. With a force of some 1,500 horse and 15,000 foot, James first defeated the Moors in pitched battle and then advanced on the city of Majorca (present-day Palma), which was stormed and captured on the last day of 1229 after a siege of three months. Two years later he returned to the attack, subjugating Minorca; and the occupation of the Balearics was completed with the capture of Ibiza in 1235 by an expedition from the larger islands.

This success left James free to devote himself to an expedition into the Moorish territories to the south, for which his Aragonese subjects had long been pressing. His immediate pretext was that the Emir of Valencia, Zeid, had been supplanted by a rival, Zaen, who then proceeded to raid Christian territory as far as Tortosa to the north. Zeid made over his claim to the Conqueror; but the campaign took a religious character from the first, when in 1233 Pope Gregory IX declared it a crusade. By 1237 James had established a commanding position at Puig de Cebolla ('Onion Hill') overlooking Valencia; the city itself surrendered in September 1238; and by 1244–5, with the capture of the strongholds of Biar and Játiva further south, the Catalans had reached the limits of the zone of Reconquest assigned to them and were in possession of the whole rich 'garden' of Valencia.

The rapid Catalan advance led to bickering with the Infante Alfonso of Castile (shortly to become Alfonso X, 'The Wise'), especially over possession of the magnificent double castle of Játiva, described by the chronicler Bernat Desclot as *'un castell que al món no n'ha tan forts ne tan reial'* (a castle than which there is no stronger nor more regal in the world). James's famous reply to these Castilian pretensions was: *'No hi ha hom al món que vosaltres no féssets eixir de mesura, per co car fets totes les coses ab ergull a cuidats-vos que tot co que vós volets dega hom fer'* ('There is no one in the world whom you do not in time require to retreat, this because of your boundless pride—but have a care of what your demands force others to do'). As good as his word, the Conqueror met force with force; but the issues were settled amicably by the Treaty of Almiçra of 1244, by which Castile's title to Murcia was reaffirmed. James, unlike his successors, was scrupulous in observing the terms of the treaty, and when in 1261–3, Alfonso was faced by a serious uprising in the region, he was prompt to respond to an appeal for help and in fact put down the rebellion single-handed on behalf of Castile, at the same time refusing to reap any territorial advantage as pressed to do by his subjects in Aragon. Equally enlightened and of far greater significance than any immediate gains was his policy for repopulating the reconquered territories.

In Andalusia, successive Castilian monarchs left intact the *latifundias* or large estates, which in one form or another had survived from Roman and Visigothic times, redistributing them among the nobility from the north who had participated in the Reconquest. One effect of this was to reinforce the strength of the aristocracy, which was to be a thorn in the flesh of Castile's rulers for centuries to come, without at the same time encouraging the emergence of a bourgeois or mercantile class, of which the country was so sorely in need.

The other result was to prove equally disastrous for the economy of Andalusia. The hard-working Moorish peasants or skilled Mudejar artisans, who were either forced out for religious reasons or left of their own volition, were not replenished by human resources. Instead, the empty lands were repopulated with sheep, which were regularly driven north for the summer pasturage. This was the origin of the *Mesta*, the organization of sheep and cattle owners, to which Alfonso X granted its first *fuero* in 1273, and which was later to obtain a monopoly of the wool trade with Flanders and Italy. In return for taxes it obtained far-reaching privileges, including the right to pasture flocks of transhumant sheep on a seventy-yard band along the whole length of the sheep-runs from the Extremadura to Old Castile. Although the wool trade became extremely lucrative, enriched Burgos and stimulated the growth of a Castilian fleet in Basque waters, the vested interests of the cattle-owning nobility prevented the full development of a textile trade and paralysed a balanced agricultural economy.

James I, on the other hand, was from the first alive to the need for preserving an adequate labour force on the land. His reasons were part religious, part political; thus in 1270 he wrote to his counsellors in Barcelona: 'We have surveyed the Kingdom of Valencia and we find that in the whole realm there are only thirty thousand Christians' (he was evidently referring to adult males, and not to women and children), and again, 'In our opinion there should be a hundred thousand Christians in the Kingdom of Valencia . . . Seek out, therefore those men in your city who are of courage and have no heritage enabling them to live comfortably; and if there are two or three brothers, and one has an inheritance and the others not, we wish that those who are heirs should not be so in this kingdom which God has given us.'

James's measures applied not only to Valencia and the Balearics, but also to Alicante, Murcia and Cartagena within the Castilian zone, so that Ramon Muntaner, who began his celebrated chronicle in 1335 reports that 'all those in the said city of Murcia and in the other places already mentioned are true Catalans and speak their native tongue with the best.'

Unlike their Castilian counterparts, the nobility received few concessions from the redistribution of the conquered territories, being limited to the grant of lands in the unproductive mountain areas of Aragon on the route of the sheep-runs from the Pyrenees to the Mediterranean. The main beneficiaries were the Catalan knights—as James remarked to Alfonso the Wise in criticizing the arrangements in Castile, every hundred brave men who had been well endowed would rally to the Crown in hour of need—and farmers from the north, many from Lérida. The latter were quick to adapt to the specialized methods of the Moors in cultivating the rich Valencian *huertas*, with their crops of sugar, rice, fruit and wine, and were imbued with the democratic spirit of the communities from which they came. These had for long enjoyed liberal *fueros*; and the monarchy wisely continued the tradition by extending autonomous government to the neo-Valencians. As a result, the Moriscos worked side by side with the newcomers, and the Catalan merchant marine was by now well placed to transport the produce.

Even before the invasion of the Balearics James had in 1227 conceded that all merchandise transported to and from the port of Barcelona should be in Catalan vessels; and the conquest of the islands and ensuing trade with them was another fillip to Catalonia's growing sea power. Before the end of his reign consulates had been established as far afield as Tunis and Alexandria. Occitania had been lost; but by his wise measures for securing an economic base at home and encouraging sea-borne commerce abroad, James had laid secure foundations for Catalonia's future and much more important role as the major power in the Mediterranean.

It has sometimes been affirmed that Catalonia was enabled to found her Mediterranean empire on the basis of the gold brought into the country by Albigensian refugees; but this seems altogether too narrow a view. Quite apart from the fact that such refugees were not entirely welcome—James actually inaugurated an Inquisition for their especial benefit—Catalonia had been benefiting for years from the massive tribute paid by the Moors. And as Ferran Soldevila has written: 'Up to the death of Pere el Catòlic (Peter II of Aragon) at Muret, it may be said that the history of our country, under the descendants of Guifré el Pilós (Wilfred the Hairy), had been one of steady growth, without the occurrence of any irreparable damage or sudden changes in direction.' Although Peter II brought the state to the verge of bankruptcy, mercantile enterprises continued to prosper, and James I's agricultural, demographic and naval policies made possible the dazzling achievements of the fourteenth century.

Tall and commanding in presence, James the Conqueror was a man of powerful passions, and his defects were the complement of his virtues. The list of his illegitimate children is legion; nevertheless his infatuation for his second wife, Violante of Hungary, led him to be unduly influenced by her in political decisions, notably in the

3. Woodcut from the *Llibre de cosolat*, 1502, an historic book on maritime law.

4. Catalan merchants, from the *Consulado del Mar*, 1539.

disastrous provisions of his will. It is said that he cut out the tongue of a bishop of Gerona, whom he suspected of betraying the secrecy of the confessional—only to repent by building and endowing a monastery. He evidently considered that his crusading activities more than atoned for his many moral lapses and cruelties.

He has been condemned as an illiterate barbarian, yet his *Llibre dels Feits*, which, if he did not actually write, he must certainly have dictated, was the first of the four great Catalan *Chronicles* (the others were those of Ramon Muntaner, Bernat Desclot and Peter the Ceremonious), of which it has been said by H. J. Chaytor that they will collectively 'bear comparison with Villehardouin, Join-ville, Froissart or any similar company of contemporary historiographers in Western Europe'. By making Catalan the official language of the country—the great *Llibre del Consolat de Mar*, a compendium of maritime law, was, for example, written in the vernacular during his reign—James paved the way for writers such as Ramon Llull and the flowering of Catalan literature in the decades following his death. And he was undoubtedly loved by his subjects: '*nunqua rey era tant amat per son poble com aquest.*'

James's death in 1276 marked the end of an era. Catalonia was clearly reaching the limits of expansion within the Peninsula and was now set to play a larger role on the European stage; and in this wider context two decisions taken by the Conqueror were to have far-reaching repercussions. One was the marriage of his first-born, the future Peter (Pere) III ('The Great'), to Constance, daughter of Manfred, the last Hohenstaufen king of Sicily; and the other, an unfortunate throwback to the earlier policies of the House of Barcelona, the partitioning of the kingdom between Peter and his brother, James. By the terms of the Conqueror's will, Peter inherited Catalonia, Aragon and Valencia; and James, the Balearics and the remaining territories beyond the Pyrenees, comprising the Roussillon, Cerdagne and Montpellier.

The marriage to Constance had been a logical step, taken in accord-

5. James the Conqueror, from Ramon Llull, *Aureum opus*, 1515.

ance with the wishes of the Barcelona merchants and maritime community and aimed at extending island bases for Catalan shipping and commerce in the Mediterranean (James also had ambitions in Sardinia, but had been refused permission by the Pope to occupy the island). The marriage was consummated in the teeth of stubborn opposition by the Pope, and when Peter the Great set about claiming the island in the name of his wife he was at once involved in armed conflict with the two major powers of the time, the Papacy and France.

In brief, the quarrel originated during the break-up of the Holy Roman Empire on the death of Lothaire II, when the Imperial Crown was contested by Conrad of Hohenstaufen and Henry the Proud, Duke of Bavaria. Their family names of Waiblingen and Wölf were Italianized; and the Ghibellines and the Guelfs were to form warring factions throughout the struggles between the Empire and the papacy in the twelfth and thirteenth centuries. In general, the Popes felt that their claims for temporal dominion over Italy were better served by the Guelfs.

By his will of 1250, the Emperor Frederick II appointed his natural son Manfred Hohenstaufen governor of the Kingdom of Naples and Sicily, an arrangement bitterly contested by the French-born Pope Urban IV, who turned to his compatriot Charles of Anjou to drive out the Germans. Charles, a brother of St. Louis of France, who already held Provence by virtue of his marriage to Beatrice, the daughter of Berenguer IV, had boundless ambitions in the Mediterranean. In 1266 he routed and killed Manfred at Benevento and imprisoned his wife and children, the only member of the family who escaped being Constance. The Ghibellines counter-attacked, but were again decisively beaten at the Battle of Tagliacozzo in August 1268, and Charles, with the blessing of successive Popes, was enabled to hold Naples and Sicily as their vassal. His autocratic conduct made him extremely unpopular, and the outbreak of the rebellion known as the Sicilian Vespers gave Peter III the opportunity to recover the island in the name of his wife.

On Easter Monday 1282, a scuffle broke out as the people were leaving church in Palermo. With shouts of '*Muoiano i Francesi*', they turned on the French soldiery, beginning a twenty-four hours' massacre, during which 4,000 French were killed. Coincidentally or not, Peter was engaged with an army of 15,000 men and 140 ships along the North African coast, when the Sicilians asked him to intervene. He was prompt to respond and landed at Trapani on

30 August 1282, and was greeted with great enthusiasm at Palermo, where he received the homage of the Sicilians and proceeded to confirm their laws and privileges.

So began a twenty-year period during which all attempts to regain the island were beaten off; Catalan influence was steadily extended; and, although Sicily and the Crown of Aragon were at first ruled by separate branches of the House of Barcelona, Sicily in fact became an advance base for Catalan mercantile enterprise along the African coast and in the Near East. Peter the Great's expedition cannot, in fact, be described merely in terms of dynasty rivalry or kingly ambition; Feran Soldevila goes to the heart of the matter when he writes:

> Could a nation of mariners, sailors and merchants with the degree of maritime power they had now developed, lose an opportunity such as that afforded by the occupation of Sicily, a base of the first importance in the central Mediterranean, a stepping stone to the Levant and close to the markets of North Africa? King Peter, in pursuing his own ambitions, his desire for revenge and the repossession of the heritage of his wife and children, far from embroiling Catalonia in a struggle concerned solely with dynastic interests or questions of prestige, was entering into a battle essential in the interests of the nation as a whole. Provençals, Genoese, Pisans and the other traditional maritime peoples of Italy in large part dominated the Mediterranean markets of the Near East: the latest arrivals, the Catalans, had to establish themselves in one way or another. This is how the Catalans of the time saw it, and for this reason they supported their king's Sicilian adventure with enthusiasm.

Although the long-term consequences were economic, the immediate repercussions were personal and furious. The Pope excommunicated Peter III; and Charles of Anjou, who had been soundly drubbed by the great Catalan admiral Roger de Llúria along the Calabrian coast, issued a personal challenge, which Peter, a redoubtable warrior, accepted with alacrity. The two were to meet in single combat at Bordeaux, with Edward I of England acting as umpire. In the event Edward stood down, and Peter, hearing that Charles had no intention of fighting, but was rather preparing to ambush him and his following, returned to Aragon, giving the slip to his French pursuers.

Here, he found that the Pope, pursuing the vendetta, had de-

c*

creed that he be deprived of his kingdom and had conferred it on
Charles of Valois, son of Philip III of France, who was preparing
a crusade against him. The Aragonese nobility, far less enthusiastic
about the Sicilian venture than the merchants of Barcelona, resented the fact that they had incurred a papal indictment over an
enterprise to which they had not given their consent and formed an
armed 'Union' to demand concessions, known as the *Privilegio General*, as the price of their continuing support. In spite of granting
their demands, Peter received little help from Aragon in meeting
the huge French force of 100 ships, 16,000 knights, 17,000 crossbow-
men and 100,000 infantry, which, with active support from his own
dissident brother, James II of Majorca, was massing in the region
of the Pyrenees. An attempt to hold Sancho IV of Castile to his
alliance with the Crown of Aragon proved unsuccessful; and in
the last resort Peter was supported by only the Catalans.

It proved impossible to hold the Pyrenean passes; and on 21 June
1285, the French army laid siege to Gerona, which fell at the
end of August. Its stubborn defence had nevertheless gained the
Catalans a breathing space; and the sudden appearance of the in-
vincible Roger de Llúria and his destruction of the French fleet in
the Bay of Rosas effectively ended the invasion. The French, abandoning baggage and supplies and harried by Peter's men, straggled
back across the Pyrenees with heavy loss. Philip III had fallen victim to an epidemic which had broken out in Gerona during the
siege, and died in Perpignan. An enormous booty fell into the hands
of the victorious Catalans; thus the anonymous author of the *Gesta
Comitum* writes: 'It is not possible to give any idea of the gold and
silver which fell into the hands of our knights and foot soldiers: precious stones, collars embroidered with gold and silken gowns relieved the poverty of all Catalonia.'

The short reign of Peter the Great had seen the emergence of
Catalonia-Aragon as a major Mediterranean power well able to
defend herself against the most formidable attack from abroad, and
Peter well merited Dante's description, '*D'ogni valor portò cinta la
corda*' ('Today he wears courage like a belt'). At the same time, as
the price of allowing him freedom of initiative abroad, his subjects
demanded concessions at home, which were to have profound political and social consequences.

The *Privilegio general* granted to the Aragonese nobility was
further to be extended during the reign of his successor, Alfonso III
('The Liberal'), when the 'Union' established that the monarch must

consult its counsellors over all questions relating to Aragon, the county of Ribagorça and Valencia and that he might not take unilateral action against any of its members without the prior consent of the *Justicia* and the agreement of the Corts. Already in 1283, shortly before Peter's death, it was agreed at a meeting of the Catalan Corts that they should henceforth be held every year (in fact, the annual convocation was soon discontinued in favour of a triennial one) and that no statutes should be passed without the approval of a majority of its three Estates, the clergy, the nobility, and the cities and royal towns. It has been claimed that these provisions were unique in Europe at the time and they undoubtedly reflected a climate of liberty. It was, however, liberty only for the upper classes; and with the passage of time the peasants, too, were to resort to force for the loosening of their bonds.

Without the éclat of their father, his sons, Alfonso III (1285–91) and James (Jaume) II (1291–96), were to continue his policies and to consolidate the country's position both at home and abroad. Just before his death Peter the Great had despatched an expedition to the Balearics to bring to book James II of Majorca for his participation on the French side during the crusade. As a result, Majorca and Minorca were speedily subjugated and annexed to the Crown of Aragon. Sancho IV of Castile had also played an unfriendly role during the invasion, and in retribution James II not only sheltered the pretenders to the Castilian throne, the Infantes of Cerda, but invaded Murcia and took possession of Alicante and the surrounding area.

Under Peter the Great's will, James had originally succeeded to the Kingdom of Sicily, Catalonia, Aragon and Valencia going to his elder brother, Alfonso. On Alfonso's death in 1291, James accepted the invitation of a delegation of Catalan nobles to assume the Crown of Aragon as the eldest surviving son of Peter III, and at the same time appointed a third brother, Frederick, governor of Sicily. This was by no means in accordance with the wishes of the Papacy or of its most powerful supporter, Charles of Valois. Prolonged and tortuous negotiations ensued, involving James II, the Pope, Charles of Valois, Sancho IV of Castile and Edward I of England, and covering not only the question of Sicily, but the succession to the throne of Castile and Charles of Valois's pretentions to the Crown of Aragon. As an outcome, James not only gave up his claim to Sicily, but actually lent support to attacks on his brother by the papal party.

Frederick, with firm backing from the Sicilians and with naval aid from the brilliant Roger de Llúria, held firm; and the confused and prolonged conflict was eventually terminated by the Peace of Caltabellotta. Concluded in August 1302, this provided that Frederick should reign over Sicily during his lifetime as independent king and embraced clauses about the succession, which in the upshot were conveniently ignored and in no way prevented the ultimate integration of Sicily with the Crown of Aragon.

As a side-product of this devious horse-dealing, and in return for yielding up his claim to Sicily, James II was in 1297 granted the sovereignty of Sardinia and Corsica by Pope Boniface VIII. The islands, which had been captured from the Moors in 1050 by the joint forces of Genoa and Pisa, were not in the Pope's possession; and it was not until 1309 that James took the first steps to gain Sardinia from its occupiers, the Pisans. In that year he received a somewhat singular offer from Pisa to become part of the Crown of Aragon. This was promptly vetoed by the papacy; and it was only by mounting a large expedition under the command of his son, the future Alfonso IV, and at the cost of some 1,200 soldiers, that he captured the larger part of the island in 1321. Although the subsequent rebellions of the Sardinians were to prove a thorn in the flesh of his successors, James II had moved a further step towards Aragonese hegemony of the Mediterranean.

VI

To the Iron Gates

Among the most colourful characters who helped Frederick of Sicily to beat off the attacks of Charles of Valois was Roger de Flor, appointed admiral of the fleet during the last years of the war. The son of a German falconer to the Hohenstaufen Emperor Frederick II by an Italian mother, he was christened Rutger von Blum; and the name was Italianized as Ruggero della Fiore, hence Roger de Flor. After the death of his father at the Battle of Tagliacozzo in 1268, he and his mother were left in penury, and at the tender age of eight he took service with a French sea captain in command of a vessel belonging to the Templars. He subsequently became a sergeant-brother of the Temple, was promoted to the command of his own ship, the *Falcon*, and after questionable behaviour at the siege of Acre, when he was accused of having sold fellow Christians to the Saracens, was expelled from the order. Prior to joining Frederick of Sicily he had acquired a large fortune by the indiscriminate pillage of the coasts of Spain, France, Italy and North Africa.

The no doubt prejudiced Greek chronicler, George Pachymeres, describes him as 'a man in the prime of life, of terrible aspect, quick in gesture and impetuous in action'; and the troops whom he commanded during the Sicilian campaign were the formidable and savage Catalan and Aragonese mercenaries known as the Almogàvers. They were men who lived by war and rapine, so that it evidently came as a relief to Frederick when Roger de Flor proposed an outlet for their bellicose energies.

The story is taken up by Ramon Muntaner, the chronicler of the legendary Catalan expedition to the East, in which he himself played a distinguished, and perhaps the most creditable part:

Frey Roger was full of thought, considering what he would do later on, and he was the wisest man in the world for foresight. He reflected thus: 'This lord is lost to us and I see he will not be able to give anything to the Catalans and Aragonese and that they will be a great hindrance to him. They are like all men, and cannot live without eating and drinking; and so, getting nothing from the Lord King, they will keep an enforced Lent, and in the end they will destroy all the land and will die one after the other. And so it is necessary, as you have served the Lord King so long, who has shown you so much honour, that you deliver him from these people, for his honour and for the advantage of them all.'

Muntaner, who was Roger's Procurator General in Sicily, says of his account of the expedition that 'you must believe me rather than anyone else'—a claim substantiated by his French translator, Buchon, when he wrote:

Facts, places, men are portrayed to the life in their true aspect. I have carefully compared his account with those of the Greek authors of the day and I have always found in Muntaner the superiority, not only of a more judicious spirit and a firmer character, but of a more impartial judgement of his enemies and a more thorough and resolute respect for the truth . . .

His chronicle, after explaining that Roger de Flor was *persona non grata* with the Pope, the Templars and King Robert of Naples, continues with a dramatized interview with Frederick of Sicily:

'Then, Lord,' said Frey Roger, 'by your leave, I shall send two knights with an armed galley to the Emperor of Constantinople, and shall let him know that I am ready to go to him with as great a company of horse and foot, all Catalans and Aragonese, as he wishes, and that he should give us pay and all necessaries; that I know he greatly needs these succours, for the Turks have taken from him land to the extent of thirty journeys . . .'

The current troubles of the Byzantine Empire stemmed from the Fourth Crusade, declared by Pope Innocent III in 1198. Far from fighting the infidel, its mercenary warriors—mainly from France, Burgundy and Flanders—with the active assistance of the Venetians, had sacked and occupied Constantinople and Athens and installed themselves as the new rulers of the larger part of the Empire. In their wake, the Genoese, the great trading rivals of the Venetians in the eastern Mediterranean, had moved into the area and by assisting in the recovery of Contantinople from the degenerate descendants of the crusaders had gained most favoured nation treatment, establishing a base on the Golden Horn opposite Constantinople.

Roger de Flor's offer to the Byzantine Emperor, Andronicus II, came at a most opportune moment, since the Ottoman Turks, a nomadic tribe of hardy fighters from Asia Minor, were moving west on the Empire and had occupied its southernmost portion, Anatolia, utterly defeating Andronicus's son, the future Michael IX, in 1301.

Roger drove a hard bargain over pay for his troops and also demanded for himself the title of Megaduc and the hand of the Emperor's cousin, Maria; and, in Muntaner's words, 'the Emperor sent the charter of his title of Grand Duke to Frey Roger in a handsome gold casket, signed by him and his sons, and he sent him the baton of the office and the banner and hat (all the officials of Romania have a special hat, the like of which no other man may wear). And so likewise he granted that they should find provisions of pay at Monemvasia [a fortress in the Peloponnese] and all they would need on arrival.'

The Grand Company which arrived in Constantinople in September 1303 consisted of 1,500 cavalry, 4,000 foot and 1,000 sailors, making a total of 8,000 with their accompanying women and children (the figures are Muntaner's and have not been contested by Greek historians—though he was apt to swell the tally of enemy dead when writing of the subsequent Catalan victories). The Catalans were received with open arms and Roger was married to Maria with due ceremony; but on the very night of the wedding a riot broke out, which was to give the Byzantines a foretaste of Almogàver savagery, still remembered in Thrace, where to this day the ultimate curse is: 'May the Catalan Vengeance overtake you!'

Of the inhabitants of Constantinople, the least pleased to see the Catalans were the Genoese, who suspected a threat to their commercial interests. A scuffle broke out between the rival factions; Andronicus was content enough for the overbearing Genoese to be taught a lesson; but when eventually he sent one of his senior officers to quell the riot, it was only to see him torn to pieces by the Almogàvers. Before Roger de Flor, summoned from his wedding bed, intervened to call off his men, 3,000 Genoese had been massacred.

Andronicus hastily shipped his savage allies across the Sea of Marmara to Cyzicus at the northern extremity of Anatolia, which was under siege by the Turks who had not long before routed a supposed 12,000 cavalry and 100,000 infantry under the co-Emperor Michael. The 5,500 men of the Grand Company, reinforced by some thousand Greek and Alan mercenaries, surprised the sleeping Turks at dead of night; it is said that some 10,000 of the enemy were killed, quarter being given only to women and children.

After wintering in Cyzicus, Roger de Flor resumed operations against the Turks in April 1304, being delayed by the fighting which had broken out between his own men and the Alan mercenaries. Moving south, he inflicted a heavy defeat on the Turks at Tira near Ephesus and finally scattered the remnants at the Iron Gates in the Taurus Mountains on the verge of Syria. There was talk of pushing on into Palestine, but Roger decided that he was far enough extended and began the return journey north.

These successes were first received with acclamation in Constantinople, but it was not long before reports came back that the Almogàvers were treating the Greeks whom they had been sent to liberate like conquered enemies and that their barbarities were worse than any committed by the Turks. The first Byzantine report of these excesses by Nikephoros Gregoras, quoted by Alphonso Lowe in his *Catalan Vengeance*, was to become a constant refrain:

> It was dreadful to see the goods of the unfortunate Romans [i.e. heirs to the Roman Empire] snatched away, girls and women violated, old men and priests carried off into captivity, victims of punishments, ever new, to which the impious hands of the Latins [i.e. westerners] subjected them; and seeing the sword poised continually over their necks, to kill them if they did not reveal their treasures and wealth. Those who gave up everything were reduced to beggary; those who had not the means to buy their freedom had their hands or legs cut off and were exposed in the streets as a lamentable spectacle, that they might beg an obol or a crust, without other means of support than their tongues or their flowing tears.

In the autumn of 1304, when on the point of laying siege to the city of Magnesia, Roger de Flor received urgent instructions from Andronicus bidding him proceed to Bulgaria to support the co-Emperor Michael in a war against a usurper to the throne. Michael and the Genoese had always been antagonistic to the Catalans, and it would seem that Andronicus was now anxious to rid himself of his unruly allies and that from the start this was a manoeuvre to split and weaken the Grand Company. The original understanding had been that Roger and his men would stay for nine months; but with their task largely accomplished and the Turks on the retreat, there must now have seemed every possibility that they would remain in Anatolia and carve out an independent kingdom for themselves.

Roger duly moved his army north, only to be greeted by the news that Michael had composed his differences with the Bulgarians and had no need of his services. He nevertheless proceeded to Constantinople, where, in spite of an overtly enthusiastic welcome, relations with Andronicus further deteriorated when he put in a claim for back pay for his troops. Andronicus eventually responded by making good the arrears in depreciated coinage, thus occasioning an uproar in which Berenguer de Entenza, a nobleman from Ribagorça and friend of Roger de Flor, newly arrived from Catalonia with reinforcements, threw his insignia of office into the sea and Roger was obliged to sell his personal property and his wife's jewels to pacify the troops. Matters were finally patched up when the Emperor agreed that, in return for being relieved of most of his financial obligations, the Catalans should hold Anatolia in vassalage to the Byzantine Empire, rendering military aid when so required—an arrangement which would keep them as far as possible from Constantinople.

The movement of the Company from their winter quarters in Gallipoli had already begun in April 1305, when, according to the ingenuous Muntaner, Roger felt it incumbent on him 'for the great loyalty he had in his heart, and the love and correct considerations he bore the Emperor and his son' to pay a farewell visit to Prince Michael, then stationed with his army at Adrianopolis in Bulgaria. Princess Maria, now carrying his child, and her mother, the ex-Empress of Bulgaria, implored him not to make the journey; and since it involved the splitting of the Catalan force, already depleted by the defection of the Greek and Alan mercenaries, it would seem that Roger must have had some strong motive—possibly to further his ambitions by reaching an agreement to place his brother-in-law on the Bulgarian throne.

Ignoring all warnings, he set out with 300 cavaliers and 1,000 horsemen, a quarter of the Grand Company. A week went by in feasting and entertainments, while Michael secretly reinforced his army, already amounting to 5,000 men. On 5 April, a farewell banquet was held to mark Roger's intended departure the following day; at the height of the celebrations Michael withdrew. It was the signal for a horde of Alan mercenaries to burst in and fall on the unarmed Catalans. Roger was stabbed and cut to pieces; and in the ensuing shambles all but three of the unsuspecting 1,300 Catalans were murdered. The three survivors retreated step by step up a church tower and, in Muntaner's words, 'defended themselves so well that the son of the Emperor said it would be a sin if they were killed; and so he gave them a safe-conduct, and they alone escaped.'

That same night Michael despatched a force of Alans and Byzantine mercenaries to Gallipoli, where they surprised the garrison and killed a further 1,000 men, reducing the combined strength of the Catalans to 3,307 men and 206 horse—the figures are Muntaner's. But if the plot had come within an ace of success, the survivors were far from giving in. An embassy was sent to Constantinople with a formal declaration of war. Andronicus, while protesting himself innocent of Roger's murder, responded by ordering the killing of all Catalans resident in the city, including Ferdinand d'Aónes, the admiral of the Company's fleet; while the ambassadors were assassinated on their return journey. Desperate as their situation was, the Catalans in Gallipoli beat off a further attempt by an army sent against them by Prince Michael and said to have amounted to 30,000 foot and 10,000 horse. The attempt to rid the Empire of the Catalans by treachery and murder had miscarried; and if the depredations of the Almogàvers had been savage enough already, they were now to pursue a course of relentless and cold-blooded retribution.

At this low ebb in their fortunes they were placed at a further disadvantage by a feud between their leaders, which was ultimately to end in tragedy. The command had devolved upon Berenguer de Entenza; but almost equally important was the seneschal, Bernard de Rocafort. The fact that Entenza was an aristocrat and Rocafort a rough-hewn captain who had risen through the ranks only accentuated their differences. Neither for one moment contemplated a retreat to Sicily; but whereas Entenza was in favour of sallying out into the Hellespont in galleys and carrying the war along the northern shores of the Sea of Marmara towards Constantinople, Rocafort argued heatedly against the proposed sortie: 'Our fame would diminish and be lost when we return to our country if our vengeance is not as terrible as the treachery of the Greeks. But I must join issue with Berenguer de Entenza in regard to his tactics. Dividing our forces strikes me as a cardinal mistake, seeing that as we stand we are already far inferior in numbers and strength.'

The majority was with Rocafort, but Entenza, overruling the decision as supreme commander, proceeded to ravage the shores of Thrace, until, falling in with a squadron of eighteen Genoese galleys, he fell victim to a ruse like Roger de Flor before him. Accepting a friendly invitation from the Genoese admiral, he went aboard the flagship, only to be taken prisoner with his escort. The Genoese then destroyed his small fleet; and despite offers of ransom, including one of ten thousand gold hyperpers from Muntaner, he was sent captive to Genoa.

Rocafort now took command of the remaining 1,200 infantry and 200 cavalry, with Muntaner as governor of Gallipoli. In a desperate gesture the survivors decided to scuttle their ships and to sally forth and attack the besiegers. The Byzantines were thrown back and even more decisively beaten in June 1305 at Apros on the road to Constantinople, when a huge force assembled by the co-Emperor Michael was routed and he himself badly wounded in the face. The Byzantine mercenaries now began defecting to the Catalans, and Rocafort decided that the time was ripe to take revenge on the Alans, with whom he caught up near Mount Hemos on the borders of Bulgaria. Here, they encountered the stiffest opposition they had yet met, but with comparatively small losses slaughtered all but 300 of the 9,000 Alans, including their leader, Gircon, who had murdered Roger de Flor.

To achieve this victory Rocafort had stripped Gallipoli of all but 200 foot and about 20 horse—of whom 140 subsequently followed the main expedition—and left Muntaner in charge of the women, children and sick. He was, as he drily comments 'poorly provided with men, but well found with women'. At this juncture a Genoese fleet arrived at Constantinople, and their commander, Antonio Spinola, proposed to Andronicus that he should seize the opportunity to wipe out the Catalan base. Muntaner attempted to gain time by pointing out that the Republic of Genoa was at peace with Aragon and Sicily, but Spinola pressed on with preparations for an attack from his twenty-five galleys. The subsequent events are graphically related by Muntaner:

I made all the women who were there put on armour—for of armour there was plenty—and ordered them to the walls, and over each division of the wall I ordered a merchant of those Catalan merchants who were there to be commander of the women. And I ordered half-casks and bowls of well-tempered wine and much bread in every street, and who liked might eat and drink, for I knew well, they would not let us eat indoors . . . And I made every man put on armour and had the posterns of the *barbacana* left open (for all the *barbacanas* were stockaded) in order that I might hasten to where it was most necessary. And I also ordered physicians to be ready to assist when any man was wounded, so that he could return to the battle at once . . .

Muntaner himself sallied out with a handful of cavalry to prevent the landing of the galleys, but was forced to retire into the fortress 'with five wounds I had, which I felt but little except one, a sword cut along my foot'. Meanwhile the castle came under a hail of crossbow fire:

A cook of mine was in the kitchen, cooking fowls for the wounded, when a bolt came down the chimney and entered his thigh, full two fingers deep. What should I tell you about it? The battle was very hard, and our women defended the *barbacana*, with stones and pieces of rock which I had placed on the wall, in so masterly a manner, it was marvellous. Indeed a woman was found there who had five wounds in her face from quarrels and still continued the defence as if she had no hurt. And so this fight lasted until the morning hour.

Spinola now moved in for the *coup de grâce*; and Muntaner, nothing daunted, got ready the seven horses remaining to him.

I summoned a hundred men of the best in the castle, and made them all take off their armour, as it was very hot, for it was the middle of July, and I saw the quarrels had stopped, none were being shot, they had all been used . . . And when the commander, namely Antonio Spinola, with all his good men with their five banners had come to the iron gate of the castle and had been attacking it vigorously for a long while, so that the greater number had their tongues hanging out with thirst and the heat, I commended myself to God and to Our Lady Saint Mary and I had the gate opened and with the six armed horses and with the men afoot who had come thus lightly equipped, we attacked the banners. At the first blow we cut down four. And they, seeing us attack thus vigorously, horse as well as foot, saw they were defeated, so that they soon turned their backs to us. What should I tell you about it? Antonio Spinola had his head cut off in the place in which he had made the changes, and with him all the noblemen who had come out with him, so that altogether six hundred Genoese were killed there . . .

The Company had meanwhile been petitioning James II of Aragon to secure Entenza's release from the Genoese, at the same time offering to become his vassals. James, while declining the offer in favour of Frederick of Sicily, intervened on Entenza's behalf, with the result that he recruited 500 men at his own expense and returned to Gallipoli early in 1306. The quarrel with Rocafort broke out anew; for a time both leaders led separate raiding expeditions on Thrace, until in the summer of 1307 the King of Sicily sent out Prince Ferdinand, a younger son of James, King of Majorca, with further reinforcements to take command of the expedition. The Catalans had made little attempt to exploit their victories commercially and had completely devastated the country around Gallipoli, so that it was decided to evacuate the peninsula and to seek booty further afield in Greece.

Rocafort, who by now regarded himself as the architect of the Company's successes, was hardly more pleased by Ferdinand's arrival than Entenza's: 'Had the king offered his help when it was so sorely needed? No, but only when it suited him and was of no service to us. And then, at long last, did he send arms, fighting men, supplies or money to carry on the war? No, only a general and commander to govern us, who need no other leader.'

When the Catalans evacuated Gallipoli and began an overland march into Macedonia, it was agreed that Rocafort and his party should keep one day's march ahead of the rearguard under the *infante* and Entenza. Muntaner was meanwhile left to convey the women, children and stores to the island of Thásos in the thirty-six vessels at the Company's disposal.

The tragedy which Ferdinand had sought to avoid by this manoeuvre followed swiftly. Two days' march short of the Thracian boundary, Entenza's column caught up with the vanguard under Rocafort. Under the impression that they were being attacked, Rocafort's men charged their compatriots. Then, in Muntaner's words,

'En Berenguer de Entenza quickly mounted his horse, with only a hauberk on without any armour, with his sword girded on and a hunting spear in hand, and he proceeded to head off and drive back his men and make them return. And whilst he was thus rallying them as well as he could (for he did not know whence the noise arose and headed them off, like a wise rich hom [gentleman] and expert knight) there came, on his horse, fully armed, En Gisbert de Rocafort, younger brother of En Berenguer de Rocafort, and likewise En Dalmau Sant-Marti, their uncle, on his horse and well armed. And together they came towards En Berenguer de Entenza heading off his men, but they thought he was urging on the company. Both together rushed at him and En Berenguer de Entenza cried: "What is this?" But both attacked him and found him unarmed, and thrust their lances right through him, so that, then and there, they slew him, and this was a great wrong and a great loss, that they, when he was acting rightly, killed him.'

As a result of this sorry affair some 750 men were killed; the *infante*, as Rocafort had probably intended, threw up his command in disgust and, joining Muntaner at Thásos, took ship for Sicily. Both were captured near Chalcis by one Thibaut de Chepoy, a minion of Charles of Valois, whose ambitions extended to Byzantium as well as Aragon. They were delivered to the Duke of Athens in Thebes, but were shortly released—Ferdinand to return to Majorca, and Muntaner to be handed over to Rocafort.

Rocafort, now in undisputed charge of the Company, had advanced as far as Cassandria in Macedonia and was actually negotiating with Chepoy to put the Company at the service of Charles of Valois. Muntaner, who was universally popular with the men, was however well received and rewarded before returning to Sicily. The best-loved and certainly the most human of the expedition's leaders, he subsequently held office as Governor of the Island of Jerba until 1315, when he retired to Valencia to begin his *Chronicle*, dying in the Balearic Islands in 1336 at about the age of seventy.

Having offended the rulers of Aragon and Sicily by his high-handed treatment of Ferdinand, Rocafort probably had little choice in throwing in his hand with Charles of Valois; but his action was deeply distasteful to the Catalans, who had scornfully christened Charles, with his indiscriminate pretensions to Aragon and other kingdoms, '*el rei del xapeu e del vent*'—for he was as erratic as a hat snatched by the wind. Rocafort, like Napoleon after him, had all the virtues and defects of a self-made man. Arrogant and unscrupulous as he was, he had made many enemies among the Almogàvers and soon fell out with Chepoy. The two parties got together; and Rocafort and his brother were shipped in chains in one of Chepoy's galleys to King Robert of Naples, who had a private score to settle with them. They were subsequently bricked up in a dungeon at the Castle of Aversa, near Naples, and left to die of starvation.

With the exception of Muntaner, all the Company's original leaders had now died violent deaths; and Chepoy soon abandoned the Catalans to their own devices. In the spring of 1310 they struck a bargain with the ambitious Duke of Athens, Walter de Brienne, to campaign on his behalf in Thessaly. Fighting with their accustomed tenacity, and with the support of the Athenian army, they succeeded in reducing most of the strong-points in the area; but Andronicus had meanwhile signed a treaty with the Venetians forbidding any of their subjects 'to trade with the Catalan Company, while it forcibly occupies any part of the Empire'. Rather than antagonize his powerful neighbours, de Brienne summarily ordered the Company to leave at the end of its six-month engagement.

The Duke of Athens was to find it as impossible to rid himself of his turbulent allies as Andronicus before him : the Catalans were cornered and had nowhere to go. The last of their great battles was fought on the banks of the River Kephissos. The result seemed a foregone conclusion : 4,000 Almogàvers were confronted by a host which has been put at 3,000 horse and 12,000 foot; but by diverting the river and transforming the battlefield into a quagmire, the Catalans were able to bog down and decimate their heavily-armoured opponents. The Turkish mercenaries, who had stood aloof while the issue was in doubt, now joined in the slaughter; and the flower of the Frank nobility, de Brienne among them, perished.

The Greek population offered no resistance to their new masters; Thebes and Athens were speedily occupied; and in Muntaner's words, 'they divided amongst themselves the city of Thebes and all the towns and castles of the Duchy and gave the ladies as wives to the men of the Company, to each according to his importance, and to some they gave so distinguished a lady that he was not worthy to hand her a bowl to wash her hands'.

The plundering Almogàvers had at last found a resting place. Relations with King Frederick were eventually restored; rulers of varying capabilities were sent to govern the Sicilian Duchy of Athens, which survived until 1387; and shortly before its demise envoys were sent to King Peter IV of Aragon to request that it be joined to the Crown of Aragon. Successive kings of Aragon, and later of Spain, in fact bore the title of 'Duke of Athens and Neopatras' until the Hapsburg dynasty came to an end in the seventeenth century.

Spectacular as was the achievement of a few thousand rough warriors in holding in thrall Asia Minor, Constantinople and Greece, it had few lasting political or economic repercussions. The Almogàvers were congenitally unsuited to develop the territories they had won, which were too far north of the main route to Alexandria to enable them to benefit from the trade in spices with the Middle East. The Catalan merchants displayed little interest in the area, leaving its exploitation to their rivals, the Venetians and the Genoese. As a result, the fortunes of the Duchy declined continuously until Athens fell prey to the Florentine Nerio Acciajuoli and the whole Empire was finally overrun by the Turks.

It was perhaps too much to expect that a foray mounted by a body of unoccupied mercenaries should achieve results any more permanent than those of the crusades, many of whose participants were equally unprincipled; but the Catalan expedition to the East remains one of the strangest episodes of mediaeval history. The best epitaph is perhaps A. E. Housman's:

> These, in the day when heaven was falling,
> The hour when earth's foundations fled,
> Followed their mercenary calling
> And took their wages and are dead.
>
> Their shoulders held the sky suspended;
> They stood, and earth's foundations stay;
> What God abandoned, these defended,
> And saved the sum of things for pay.

VII

Queen of the Mediterranean

Consolidation of the Catalan-Aragonese empire in the Mediterranean proceeded apace during the reign of Peter (Pere) IV, the
Ceremonious (1336–87). The Balearics had been reincorporated in
the Crown of Aragon in 1287 (see page 75); but on Peter's accession the King of Majorca, James (Jaume) III, proved reluctant to re-
affirm his oaths of fealty and took a similar high-handed line with
his other powerful neighbour, Philip VI of France over the county of
Montpellier, relying on help from Edward III of England, now
engaged in the Hundred Years War with France.

He miscalculated in both instances. Philip struck back on the
mainland and Peter occupied Majorca without difficulty, sternly re-
calling the Majorcans to their allegiance: 'Sou catalans e naturals
nostres. Catalans sou, e catalans tostemps foren lleials.' ('You are
Catalans and our countrymen. Catalans you are, and Catalans will
always be loyal.') In an attempt to retrieve the situation, James sold
Montpellier to the French, using the proceeds to equip an expedition to Majorca, but was routed and killed at the Battle of Llucmayor
in 1349. Shortly afterwards Peter set the seal to the reintegration
of the Kingdom of Majorca in the Crown of Aragon by occupying
the other islands and also the Roussillon and Cerdagne.

The pacification of Sardinia was to prove a much costlier and
lengthier business, but with help from Venice Peter was able to
inflict a series of damaging naval defeats on the Genoese, who, as
his principal rivals in the Mediterranean, were constantly stirring up
trouble with the native dissidents. Sardinia remained a running sore,
immensely taxing in terms of Catalan lives and resources; but in
the face of opposition from Genoa and the papacy and mounting
criticism at home, the Ceremonious at least maintained the Catalan
presence on the island.

An issue of even greater importance was the integration into his
kingdom of Sicily, which remained under the rule of a junior branch
of the Counts of Barcelona; and here Peter reverted to the traditional

policy of matrimonial alliance with a persistence worthy of his ancestor James the Conqueror.

His first step was to marry his daughter Constance to the King of Sicily, Frederick IV, and as insurance Peter himself, on the death of his wife, married Frederick's sister, Eleanor. When Frederick died without issue, Peter might therefore have pressed his claim to the throne, but encountered bitter opposition not only from the Sicilians, but from the Pope and the Kings of Naples, who invoked the terms of the Treaty of Caltabellotta (see page 76). Frederick had left a daughter, Maria, and bending to the storm, Peter now sought to marry her to his son, John (Joan). The *infante's* affections were otherwise engaged and Peter's other son Martin (Martí) was already married, but possessed a son, also named Martin (Martí el Joven), to whom Maria, snatched from under the noses of her rival suitors, was duly married. Peter did not live to see the fruition of his plans, but twenty-five years later Sicily was formally united with the Crown of Aragon.

Biographers of Peter the Ceremonious rightly lay stress on his boundless ambitions, his intelligence and his shrewdness in political manoeuvre; the reverse side of the coin was an almost complete lack of moral scruple and a revolting streak of cruelty. All of these qualities came to the fore in the campaign to expand the boundaries of his kingdom at the expense of Castile, which mushroomed into a conflict involving not only the two sister realms, but Genoa, Navarre, the papacy, France, England and Portugal.

It is difficult to say whether, in the first place, it was he or Pedro I of Castile who was the aggressor. Despite his nickname of 'The Cruel', Pedro remains considerably the more sympathetic character in modern eyes. (As regards this sobriquet, Peter the Ceremonious yielded nothing to his rival. It is on record that, after an uprising of the Valencian nobility during the early years of his reign, Peter melted down the bell used to summon his opponents and forced them to drink the molten metal. The legend of Pedro's cruelty was largely fabricated by his usurpers, the Trastámaras, to justify what they had done, and was actually repudiated by their own descendants, Isabel the Catholic and Philip II.)

The conflict was sparked off by the seizure early in 1356 of two vessels belonging to Pedro's allies, the Genoese, at Sanlúcar in the Guadalquivir estuary by a Catalan naval force under the Francophile Fransesc de Perellós while on a mission against England. Underlying the outbreak of hostilities was a Catalan nervousness about the

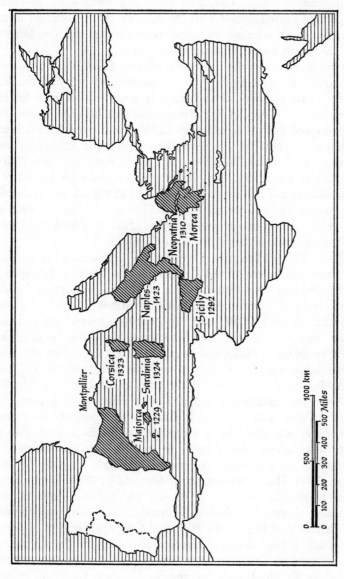

The Crown of Aragon and the full extent of Catalan conquests in the Mediterranean.

exposed position of Valencia and Castilian aspirations to an outlet on the Mediterranean. Territorial losses and gains were, however, unimportant in comparison with the dynastic change brought about in Castile, which wreaked profound social changes and was later to affect the whole future of Aragon-Catalonia.

On his accession at the age of twenty-two Pedro I had embarked on a policy of checking the unruly nobility, so bringing the less privileged into positions of authority. It was therefore easy for his bastard brother, Henry of Trastámara, one year his senior, who had never accepted Pedro's accession to the throne above his own head, to whip up support for his pretensions among the aristocracy and further to involve the Church in his crusade, especially since Pedro, though in fact a devout Catholic, was well known for his interest in Moorish art and culture (it was he who had the Alcázar at Seville reconstructed by Mudejar craftsmen). After an abortive rebellion in 1354, Henry fled to France, but made his appearance in Aragon soon after the outbreak of hostilities with Castile.

The war had not been going well for the Ceremonious in the face of superior and better-trained Castilian forces. He now hit upon a plan for dividing his opponents by a declaration of support for the bastard Henry of Trastámara against his half-brother. Henry accordingly took an oath to the King of Aragon, undertaking to make war on 'any man in the world excepting none', so breaking his bond of vassalage to Pedro, and in return for his overthrow promised to cede large areas of Castilian territory. His intervention was nevertheless ineffective, and in the face of further damaging defeats Peter the Ceremonious signed a peace treaty in May 1361.

Neither Peter, smarting from its humiliating terms, nor the opportunist Henry was prepared to accept this as the final word. Preparations went ahead for Henry to recruit Free Companies of mercenaries, with financial support unwillingly granted by the Catalan Corts. Their offensive was pre-empted by Pedro I, who made further large gains in western Aragon and around Valencia, and Peter, now thoroughly alarmed, entered into devious negotiations with Charles V of France, the Pope, and King Charles II of Navarre. As a result, a large army of mercenaries under the French adventurer Bertrand du Guesclin, with further parties of English mercenaries led by Sir Hugh Calveley and Sir Matthew Gournay, crossed into Castile by way of Aragon and Navarre in the early spring of 1366, plundering and ravaging on their way, and by the summer of [that year had compelled Pedro's retreat to Galicia. Henry of Trastámara meanwhile had himself crowned King of Castile in Burgos on Palm Sunday.

Peter the Ceremonious had intervened with certain misgivings, since he had got wind of the Treaty of Mutual Aid under discussion between Pedro I and Edward III of England. The object of the English was to detach Castile from her traditional alliance with France and so to deny the French the co-operation of the powerful Castilian fleet during the hostilities of the Hundred Years War; and the treaty was in fact signed in 1362. After his reverse, Pedro therefore took ship to Bayonne and called upon the Black Prince, then English governor of Aquitaine, for military assistance. The Prince had been influenced by Trastámaran propaganda and, as Froissart relates in his *Chronicle*, was evidently in two minds, but finally decided that:

It is not proper nor right nor reasonable that a bastard should hold a kingdom where the law of inheritance prevails, nor that he should drive a brother, king and heir to the land by a legitimate marriage from his lands and heritage. No king or son of a king should, in any way, desire or consent to such a thing . . .

The hard bargaining that followed paralleled that between the supporters of Henry of Trastámara, Pedro proving equally willing to sign away tracts of Castile of which he was not actually in possession. The turncoat Charles II of Navarre was promised a slice of the Basque country in return for unhindered passage through Navarre, while the Black Prince's reward was to be a principality centred on Bilbao. The doubtful promises made, the English mercenaries were recalled from Castile and enlisted in the opposite cause; and on 3 April 1367, a mixed force composed of English, Gascons, Navarrese and a detachment under the pretender James (Jaume) of Majorca, who had joined the expedition on the understanding that his father's kingdom should be restored to him, confronted the Castilians under Henry and the Free Companies of du Guesclin near the little town of Nájera in the Rioja. Thanks to superior tactics and equipment, the outcome was a decisive victory for the Black Prince; Pedro I was restored to his throne, and Henry of Trastámara once again sought refuge in France.

In the final resort all the parties to this mercenary venture were paid in their own coin. Neither the Black Prince nor Charles II of Navarre received the promised grants of land, and the Prince was indeed compelled to melt down his own plate to meet the expenses of the expedition. The apprehensive Peter the Ceremonious promptly changed colours and entered into abortive negotiations for a joint English-Catalan invasion of Castile, from which he was to benefit by seizure of large areas of Castile, and the Prince by acceding to her throne. The threat to Majorca disappeared with the premature death of the pretender in 1375; and the only eventual winner was the time-seeking Henry of Trastámara, who by a further descent on Castile with du Guesclin and by the murder of his brother at Montiel in 1369 achieved his own selfish objective and by playing into the hands of the nobility set back the cause of economic reform in Castile for the foreseeable future.

Needless to say, the Ceremonious received none of the promised concessions from Henry of Trastámara; and the only other and somewhat unexpected outcome was the cementing of the historic Anglo-Portuguese Alliance as an indirect result of the Black Prince's younger brother, John of Gaunt, marrying Pedro I's daughter, Constance, and pursuing his brother's pretensions to the throne of Castile with military assistance from Portugal.

As has been pertinently observed by Professor P. E. Russell (*The English Intervention in Spain and Portugal in the Time of Edward III and Richard II*), Peter the Ceremonious was 'a person of complicated psychology and subtle intellect . . . who, in the end, found himself irretrievably imprisoned in diplomatic webs of his own weaving . . .' Apart from fussiness over etiquette and ceremony, he was a distinguished orator, read French with ease, and his interest in history, astronomy, poetry and architecture (as well as supervising the writing of his *Chronicle* he was the author of a eulogy on the Acropolis at Athens) reflects the flowering of literature, the arts and sciences, which accompanied Catalonia's territorial and economic expansion during the thirteenth and fourteenth centuries.

As early as the tenth century, when Gerbert of Aurillac, later to become Pope Sylvester II, studied mathematics at the monastery of Santa Maria de Ripoll, Catalonia had played a role in transmitting knowledge to Western Europe—though from 1125 onwards this was overshadowed by the outstanding work of the Toledan School of Translators, whose Latin and Spanish versions of Greek, Roman and Arabic authors profoundly influenced the whole course of mediaeval thought.

From the middle of the twelfth to the end of the thirteenth century, Catalan troubadour poetry was more than an extension of the

Provençal. Such famous poets as Guillem de Bergadà, Ramon Vidal de Besalú, Alfonso I, Peter (Pere) II and Cerverí de Girona used a profusion of Catalan words and expressions. But, if James I, by insisting on the use of the Catalan language and by the example of his *Llibre dels Feits*, may be called the father of Catalan literature, it was Ramon Llull (1232–1315), perhaps the greatest of the country's writers, who ushered in its Golden Age.

Llull came of an aristocratic Majorcan family and spent a profligate youth at court, until, as the story goes, his mistress showed him a terrible cancer affecting her breast, after which he devoted himself to religion and philosophy. During the course of his studies and missionary activities, he ranged Europe and the Mediterranean and was stoned to death when more than eighty on a crusade to Bougie in North Africa. Such was his mastery of Catalan prose that it has been said that he did for Catalan what Dante did for Italian. Apart from his famous romance *Blanquerna*, partly autobiographical and written more than a century before Chaucer's *Canterbury Tales*, his books are mainly mystical and philosophical, like the *Llibre d'Amic e Amat*, the *Llibre de contemplació*, the *Llibre de meravelles* etc.

In the *Desconhort* ['The Lament which Master Ramon Llull made in his old age, since he saw that the Pope and other secular lords would not arrange for the conversion of the infidels, as he urged'], he sums up his life and beliefs:

When I began to consider the state of the world, how few are the Christians and how many the unbelievers, then in my heart I conceived the idea of going to prelates, also to kings and religious, showing them that they should advance and preach in such wise that with fire and sword and true argument our faith should be so high exalted that the infidels would come to true conversion. And in this way I have been busy for thirty years and indeed I have achieved nought, for which reason I am so grieved that I often weep and am in despondency.

Llull was perhaps less than fair to himself in this passage, for one of his cardinal tenets was that the Muslims could not be converted by brute force alone, but only through the spiritual gifts of the missionary and a knowledge of their speech; and his college at Miramar in Majorca was one of the first in Europe for the study of Oriental languages.

He also wrote scientific works and was credited by contemporary

6. The martyrdom of Ramon Llull at Bujía in North Africa, from Ramon Llull, *Ars inventiva veritatis*, 1515.

commentators with some thousand on alchemy alone! Modern scholars have, not unnaturally, come to the conclusion that most, if not all, the alchemical texts with which he is credited are spurious. The little-known *Testament* of John Cremer, a reputed Abbot of Westminster, recounts how Llull, working at Westminster Abbey and the Tower of London, transmuted twenty-two tons of base metal into gold for King Edward III, 'who received him kindly and honourably, and obtained from him a promise of inexhaustible wealth, on condition that he (the King) should in person conduct a Crusade against the Turks, the enemies of God, and that he should thenceforward refrain from making war on other Christian nations.'

The King failed to keep his word; and according to Ashmole's *Theatrum Chemicum*, 'King *Edward* the *third* . . . clapt him up in the *Tower*, where he . . . began to study his *Freedom*, and to that end made himself a *Leaper* [or early master of space travel], by which meanes he gained more Liberty, and at length an Advantage of escaping into *France*.' Since Cremer's name does not appear on the roll of the Abbots of Westminster and Llull probably never visited England, the story is more than suspect—but seems worth preserving!

Llull nevertheless made solid contributions to science by the thoroughly modern method of direct observation and had realized long before Columbus that the earth was spherical, a conclusion which he reached in his *Liber de Contemplatione*:

> When my thought imagines the surface of the earth opposite to the one we are on, it appears to my intelligence and reason that all the stones and waters which are on the surface should fall into the vacuum. But to those who dwell on that surface of the earth which lies opposite to ours, it will appear to the contrary, for they will think that we, together with the stones and water on our side, must go up, because 'up' will appear to them as 'down', because their feet will be placed in a direction opposite to ours.

In this same book he describes the use of the magnetic needle, well in advance of its mention by the Italian Flavio Gioa in 1302; and his account of charts and astrolabes for navigational purposes in the *Arte de Navegar* is evidence of the proficiency of Catalan seamen. The book remained unbettered even at the time of Columbus.

Another acute observation was as to the rise and fall of the tides, which he put down to 'the fact that the earth being spherical, the water of the sea equally takes the shape of an arc' and that 'the arc formed by the waters must have an opposite basis on which it finds the support without which they could not be maintained'. Carrying the argument a step further, he concluded that there must be land on the far side of the Atlantic, 'a Continent against which the water strikes when displaced, as happens on our side, which is, with respect to the other, the eastern one.'

Another formidable figure in the annals of science was Llull's contemporary Arnold (Arnau) de Vilanova (*c.* 1240–1311), also an alchemist of repute, who studied at Montpellier University and was

D

in fact one of the most remarkable figures of mediaeval medicine, being the first modern exponent of the Hippocratic method of keeping careful case histories. He is best known for his use of alcohol in sterilizing wounds (although he did not, as is sometimes mistakenly said, discover it). His *Regimen Sanitatis ad Inclitum Regem Aragonum*, composed for James II, was the first mediaeval book to be written on public hygiene and stresses the importance of fresh air, baths, physical exercise and the value of a balanced diet.

At a time when Pope Boniface VIII was the most implacable opponent of Catalan expansion in the Mediterranean, Arnold of Vilanova visited Rome and was at once imprisoned. However, the Pope was suffering agonies from stones in the bladder; Arnold was called in and by designing a special truss and other means succeeded in relieving the condition. The grateful Pope said of him, 'At last I have found a Catalan who does good', and it seems that it was thanks to their subsequent friendship that Boniface changed his policy towards the Catalans and signed a peace treaty with Frederick of Sicily in 1302 (see page 76).

Arnold of Vilanova's books were written in Latin, with the exception of the famous *Raonment d'Avinyó*, which was in Catalan and dedicated to Pope Clement V. It was while on a journey to treat the Avignon Pope, who had fallen seriously ill, that Arnold contracted pleurisy and died in Genoa.

Reference has already been made to the four great Catalan chronicles (see page 70); and an idea of their graphic and factual style may be gained from the passages of James I's *Llibre dels Feits* reproduced on pages 28 and 61, and Muntaner's *Chronicle*, extensively quoted in the preceding chapter. It derives from the fact that their authors either took part in the events which they record or consulted eye-witnesses; and two of them were kings, who were free to write as bluntly as they chose. It is true that Muntaner, inspired by a romantic loyalty towards the House of Barcelona, sometimes suppresses events discreditable to his patron, James II of Majorca; but if, on occasion, he does not tell the whole truth, he does not invent.

Taken together, the *Chronicles* cover a period of about two hundred years. That of Bernat Desclot, written in the clear-cut manner of Xenophon's *Anabasis*, overlaps the *Llibre dels Feits*, but is primarily concerned with the reign of Peter III. The narrative is taken up by Muntaner and continued in the *Chronicle* known as that of Peter IV, but actually written by Bernat Dezcoll and other collaborators employed by the King. Nevertheless, it is clear that Peter exercised strict editorial control; and his influence is clear in the detailed accounts of troop movements during his campaigns.

During the classical age of Catalan literature, roughly corresponding to the fifteenth century, the *pus bell catalesc* ('the loveliest Catalan'), in Muntaner's phrase, echoed down the Mediterranean coast and throughout its shores and islands. The purest model of Catalan prose, later enriched by Italian and Latin words and turns of expression, was perhaps the great *Lo Somni* by Bernat Metge (1350–1410). Outstanding works of fiction were *Tirant lo Blanc* by Joanot Martorell, a chivalrous romance much praised by Cervantes in *Don Quixote*, and the anonymous *Curial e Guelfa*.

If, because of the dominance of the Provençal lyric, prose took pride of place over poetry and preceded it in the development of Catalan literature, Catalonia gave birth to some notable poets during the fifteenth century. Among the best were the Valencian Jaume Roig (d. 1479), whose *Llibres de les dones* (see fig. 2) was a satire on women written in four-syllable metre, and Auziàs March (1397–1459), the author of numerous subtle love poems and also religious and moral verse. Poetry received a stimulus through the establishment of the *Jocs florals* ('Floral Games') in Barcelona in 1393, of which Enrique de Villena has left a vivid account in his *Arte de Trobar*:

> On the appointed day the mantenedors [judges] and the troubadours assembled in the royal palace where I was staying, whence we proceeded in order . . . The floor was carpeted, and the troubadours sat upon two rows of seats in a semicircle, while upon a platform in the middle, as high as an altar and covered with cloth of gold, lay the books of art and the prizes. To the right of this was a seat for the king, who often attended . . . Each poet then rose and read in a clear voice his composition, which was written on Damascus paper in different colours in gold and silver letters . . . After this, we returned in procession to the palace, the prize-winner walking between the mantenedors, while a page, accompanied by minstrels and trumpeters, carried the prize before him. Sweets and wines were then served in the palace . . .

Although Saint Vicens Ferrer (1355–1419) wrote some miracle plays, Catalonia produced no drama of note; but many historical and political works were written, and also translations of the Bible

and of important Latin and Italian writers, which were thus introduced to the Peninsula for the first time.

After the union of the Crowns of Aragon and Castile in 1479,
Catalan fell out of fashion as a literary medium and was to be
revived only as a result of the *Renaixença* of the nineteenth century—but not before Joan Lluís Vives had given expression to all
that was best and most typical of Catalan thought.

Vives, related on his mother's side to Auziàs March, was a man
of the Renaissance. Born in Valencia in 1492, he was educated at
Paris University and spent most of his life in Bruges, where he
became a friend of Erasmus. During a stay of some years in England
he was tutor to the future Queen Mary, daughter of Catherine of
Aragon by Henry VIII—though in later life she does not seem
to have been much influenced by his wise advice. During 1525 and
1526 he worked at the University of Oxford, but came under a
cloud as a result of Catherine's divorce and returned to Bruges in
1528, where he died in 1540.

The quality of his teaching can best be illustrated by a few short
quotations:

On the Inquisition, from *De Concordia et Discordia in Humano
Genere* (1529):

> Today the clergy too has its jurisdiction, procedure, method of
> accusation; its witnesses, judges, police; its prisons, hangmen,
> sword, fire, poison . . . And in the hands of this clergy is the
> sacerdocy of that same Christ who, being the judge of the quick
> and the dead, yet answered one who wanted Him to advise his
> brother to divide their heritage: 'Who has made me judge be-
> tween you?'

From *De Tradendis Disciplinis* (1531):

> Princes are, for the most part, so corrupt of heart and so intoxi-
> cated by the magnitude of their good fortune that by no skill
> can they be reformed for the better, since they show themselves
> harsh and unperceptive to those who would cure them . . .

And finally from his *Subventione Pauperum* (1526), perhaps the
most eloquent and moving of his books, in which he sets out
his views on sociology and the dignity of man, arguing that the
care of the sick, the needy, the blind and the mentally disturbed is
a public duty:

The causes of poverty are wars with the ensuing economic distress; continuous increase of population; a wrong basis in our economic system; and above all, insufficient education . . .

To all outward appearances the fourteenth century was a period of spectacular expansion for the Crown of Aragon. In the wake of naval victories, Barcelona maintained consuls in all the Mediterranean ports and in the market-places of the Atlantic. Catalan merchants rivalled those of Genoa and Venice in the traffic of spices from Alexandria, and her sailors ranged from the Sea of Azov to England and Flanders. Indeed, in Bruges, then the mainspring of northern European commerce, Catalan merchants played a dominant role in the traffic in Mediterranean products. Nevertheless, the outbreak of the Black Death in 1348 and it repercussions in 1362, 1371 and 1375 signalled a period of economic depression throughout Western Europe. Over-extended as the kingdom was, the appalling death toll put the Crown of Aragon at a demographic disadvantage in comparison with her much larger neighbour, Castile, and the scarcity of labour to work the land led to unrest among the agricultural workers, which was soon to erupt in violence.

The signs were plain to read during the last years of Peter IV's reign. During 1381 a string of private banks collapsed in Barcelona, Gerona and Perpignan; and by 1365 the golden florin, introduced by Peter in 1346 in imitation of Florence, had depreciated by 75 per cent in value.

The first organized protest from the *pagesos de remença*, peasants tied to the land, who were subject to the *mals usos* (or 'evil practices') of their lords and could achieve freedom only by a monetary payment, occurred in 1388 during the first year of the reign of John (Joan) I, successor to Peter the Ceremonious. As a result of the widespread epidemics, many of the peasant farmsteads, the so-called *masos ronècs*, were abandoned and left empty. Such was the shortage of labour that the proprietors had to hire help from further afield to gather the harvests, while the occupants of the remaining *masos* were left with more land in their care and were able to improve their bargaining position at the expense of the owners. The position was complicated by urban landlords, who had bought land as a hedge against the depression and attempted to instal new *pagesos* in the abandoned *masos ronècs*.

The conflicting attitudes are summed up in the battle-cry of the peasants '*El temps de la servitud és ja passat*' ('The period of slavery has passed') and the rebuttal of their lords. 'The law of nature is that all men are born equal, but according to human law it stands to reason that they are widely different: thus some are talented and free and others menial and slaves.'

In face of a turbulent and divided aristocracy, John I and his successors were increasingly to take the part of the *remences*, so that in time a loose alliance was formed between the peasants and the Crown as a counterweight to the other powerful echelons of the community with their vested interests. In fact, the most oppressive of the large proprietors were the clergy, who carried their hostility to the *pagesos de remença* to the extreme of forbidding them to enter holy orders. It was no doubt this intransigent attitude which prompted the famous letter written by Maria de Luna, wife of John's brother and successor, Martin (Martí) the Humane, to her illustrious relative, Pedro de Luna, the Avignon Anti-pope. Since they formed the basis for the famous Sentence of Guadalupe promulgated by Ferdinand the Catholic in 1402, the Queen's strictures on the *mals usos* are worth quoting:

> And this, Most Holy Father, in the sight of God and of men, is a thing singularly detestable and monstrous, which basens and depraves men submitted to the aforesaid burdens and sufferings. It is also, to some extent, a blot on our country and its people. It causes the other nations of the world to think the less of the Catalan nation and more and more gravitates against natural justice and human liberty, which God in the beginning granted to all human beings.

If the last two kings of the House of Barcelona were unable to reconcile the differences between the landed proprietors and their peasants, they were also faced with an almost equally intractable problem in the unruliness of the nobility and local feuds which at time approximated to a state of civil war. So, Aragon was split between the rival factions of the de Lunas and the Urrea, and Valencia between those of the Centelles and Soler-Vilaragut. Martin summoned Corts in both regions, but with short-lived effect, and in 1408 appointed his nephew James (Jaume) of Urgell *lloctinent* or viceroy of Aragon in an attempt to restore order. James's involvement in this vicious in-fighting was soon to bear tragic fruit during the crisis of the succession precipitated by Martin's death less than two years later.

Although the reigns of John I and Martin the Humane were in

general peaceful and gave the country much needed respite after the foreign campaigns of their father, Peter the Ceremonious, it proved necessary to mount an expedition to Sicily to install Martí el Joven and his bride Maria (see page 90), and rebellion flared up yet again in Sardinia. In the face of jingoist enthusiasm and against his own better judgement—in vain the gentle and pacific king reminded his countrymen of the existing toll of Catalan lives and described the venture as 'fishing with a hook of gold'—Martin allowed his only son and heir to the throne, Martí el Joven, to head the expedition. The prince's resounding victory of Sant Luri was deliriously acclaimed by the deputies of the *Generalitat* in Barcelona : 'Oh, what an abundance of grace is today lavished on the Catalan nation and on the vassals and supporters of the king and on you, endowed with such a successor and *senyor*!' But only days after his triumph Martí el Joven fell gravely ill and died on 25 July 1409.

The shock was traumatic. So a contemporary writer, Tomic, lamented: 'All that great victory has turned to anguish and grief . . . The whole nation weeps, and not without good cause, because all its hope for the future lay in that king . . .'

The five centuries which had passed since Wilfred the Hairy (page 36) founded the House of Barcelona had seen Catalonia progress from a struggling principality to become the dominant maritime power in the Mediterranean, and in the eyes of the Catalans, especially the mercantile classes, who had most benefited, the country's health and prosperity were dependent on the survival of the dynasty. Years before, the chronicler Muntaner had prophesied disaster, should there be strife between the different branches of the family. Even today, Catalan historians, foremost among them Ferran Soldevila, attribute the country's subsequent decline and 'Castilianization' to the events surrounding the succession at the time of Martin's death. This is to underestimate economic, social and demographic factors, but undoubtedly this was a crucial moment in Catalonia's history; and behind the events of the next few years looms the figure of one of the most forceful characters to emerge from the mediaeval Crown of Aragon, the Anti-pope Pedro de Luna.

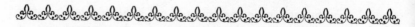

VIII

Casp and Afterwards

The Great Schism of the mediaeval Church had repercussions all over Europe, but the Crown of Aragon was particularly involved since the last of the Anti-popes was of the influential Aragonese family of de Luna.

The origins of the split dated from the feuding of the great Roman families of Orsini and Colonna, which had rendered Rome unsafe as the Holy See. In the Christian world at large, the Pope was Pope and universally revered as such; in Rome he was one of a number of warring princes. As a result, successive Popes since Clement V, elected in 1305 with the backing of Philip IV of France, had spent more time abroad and travelling than in the Eternal City itself; and Clement established his court at Avignon in territory ceded to the Church a century before by the Counts of Toulouse.

The Romans had, however, by no means resigned themselves to the permanent domicile of the Papacy in this New Babylon. In this they were helped by an outbreak of plague in Avignon and by the death of Gregory XI in 1378 during his temporary residence in Rome. Under threat of violence from an angry mob, the Cardinals hastily elected the Archbishop of Bari. Of these prelates, so used to the *dolce vita*, only the ex-soldier Pedro de Luna, who had earlier fought by the side of Henry of Trastámara at Nájera (page 93), had the courage to face the rabble; and Urban VI soon proved himself intolerant and brutal, torturing and murdering some of the cardinals he had himself named; so much so that the others, including even the Italians, soon revoked their decision, elected a Frenchman, Clement VII, in his place and made their escape to Avignon.

Henceforth there were to be two separate lines of Popes: those of Rome and those of Avignon. On Clement VII's death in 1394 the Cardinals at Avignon elected de Luna his successor, and he took the title of Benedict XIII. Before his election de Luna had pledged himself to do everything in his power to end the Great Schism of Christianity. It was over the means of doing so that the conflict arose that was to last until his final exile in Peñisicola and his death in 1422 at the advanced age of ninety-four. To begin with, the former professor of Montpellier was supported by the French Crown, but Paris was no less jealously partisan than Rome, nor less aware of Petrarch's prophecy: 'The papal seat, which was always on the banks of the Tiber, is now on the Rhône; and our grandchildren will find it on the Tagus.' In the upshot, the French court, happy enough with an Avignon Pope so long as he was a Frenchman, now declared for cession: both Popes were to abdicate so as to leave the way clear for a mutually acceptable successor.

De Luna refused to give way and for almost four and a half years withstood an onslaught on his palace at Avignon by an army of French mercenaries. After a cloak-and-dagger escape from the castle, he was finally rescued through the intervention of a naval expedition despatched to Marseilles by his friend Martin the Humane. The remainder of his long life—during which he survived no less than five short-lived would-be Popes—was devoted to rallying his waning supporters, among them the Crown of Aragon, and to the stubborn defence of his own legitimacy.

On the premature death of Martí el Joven in 1409, it was to de Luna that the ailing Martin the Humane turned for advice and help. There was no shortage of candidates for his throne, although two of the better-favoured, Louis of Anjou and the Castilian Ferdinand of Antequera, were *prima facie* ineligible under the terms of Peter IV's will, because they were his descendants by the female line. The strongest contender was Martin's nephew, James (Jaume) of Urgell, a direct descendant by the male line of Alfonso III, who had already proved himself as viceroy of Aragon; and if he had been promptly named, there seems little doubt that he would have been widely accepted. It seems, however, that Martin had set his heart on the succession to the throne of his grandson, Frederick de Luna, the illegitimate offspring of Martí el Joven of Sicily. With this in mind he sought de Luna's help in legitimizing him, and as the ambitious old prelate was the boy's relation and no doubt envisaged himself as regent, he pledged his support. But Martin acted too slowly, first summoning 'solemn and scientific ambassadors' from the different regions of the kingdom to approve his plans. The 'ambassadors' were slow in assembling, and in the meantime Martin died on May 1410 with the issue unresolved.

The story goes that on his deathbed he was visited by a deputation representing itself as from the Catalan Corts, but in fact composed of delegates opposed to James of Urgell. Asked to signify his wishes

D*

in regard to the accession, the dying king made no reply, until the delegation's spokesman, Ferrer de Gualbes, put to him the loaded question: 'Senyor, does it please you that after your death the succession to your kingdom and lands should go to the one who prevails through justice?' The dying man signified his assent with the single word 'Hoc'; and his deathbed affirmation now resulted in a free-for-all of all the interested parties.

In the upshot the field was effectively narrowed to two candidates, James of Urgell and Ferdinand of Antequera. James commanded overwhelming support in Catalonia, but Ferdinand of Antequera (who derived his claim from being the second son of John I of Castile and Eleanor, daughter of Peter the Ceremonious) was in the advantageous position of being Regent of Castile and of threatening Aragon with his troops. At the same time he was the possessor of the large private fortune of his wife Eleanor of Alburquerque, and perhaps most important of all, had enlisted the support of Pedro de Luna, who saw in Ferdinand's succession an opportunity to swing Castile behind him in the struggle to maintain his own position as Pope.

The Catalan Corts, with conspicuous fairness, proposed that *Parlaments* should be convoked from all three divisions of the kingdom—Catalonia, Aragon and Valencia—to decide between the claimants. From this point the proceedings degenerated into a maze of intrigue, fed by the rival factions of the nobility (see page 102); and the cause of James of Urgell suffered a decisive set-back, when one of his partisans murdered the anti-Urgellist Archbishop of Saragossa, García Fernández de Heredia—in his lifetime denounced by Martin the Humane as the defender of criminals and miscreants, and on his death proclaimed an overnight martyr.

In February 1412 a *Parlament* convened at Alcañiz and dominated by the Aragonese faction opposed to James of Urgell, named nine *compromissaris*, who later met at the town of Casp to name Martin's successor. The composition of this body is of interest as demonstrating the overwhelming influence of Pedro de Luna on its final decision. Aragon was represented by Fransesc d'Aranda, an agent of the Anti-pope; Domingo Ram, who owed the bishopric of Osca to de Luna; and Berenguer de Bardaxi, an advocate in the pay of Ferdinand of Antequera. The delegates from Valencia were Saint Vicens Ferrer, de Luna's confessor; his brother, Bonifaci Ferrer, who had argued de Luna's case at the Council of Pisa; and Gener Rabassa, who was unable to attend. From Catalonia, Pere Sagarriga had been

appointed Archbishop of Tarragona by de Luna and had also attended the Council of Pisa on his behalf, while Bernat de Gualbes was
another of his familiars and an avowed enemy of James of Urgell.
Only one of the *compromissaris*, the eminent Catalan advocate
Guillem de Vallseca, was a supporter of James, so that when Saint
Vicens Ferrer formally declared Ferdinand of Antequera king,
the outcome was a foregone conclusion.

The Compromise of Casp was immediately denounced by a large
section of opinion in Catalonia, thus the Councillor Berenguer d'Oms
spoke out against 'the multitude of manners and practices which we
have seen and continue to see in our kingdom and government, entirely contrary to the beneficent, likeable, liberal and trustworthy
customs of your glorious predecessors, the Kings of Aragon, which
endeared them to their vassals and constituted the greatest treasure
possed by a monarch. . . .' Feeling in the Principality ran so
high that James of Urgell was encouraged to revolt against the new
king, but with help from strong Castilian reinforcements Ferdinand
soon pinned him down to his castle at Balaguer, where James surrendered in October 1413. He had first obtained a pledge that he
would neither be killed, mutilated nor exiled, and spent the remainder of his life confined to dungeons, first in Castile and later at
the castle of Játiva; Ferdinand was almost equally ruthless in his
treatment of the Count's mother and sisters.

That doyen of Catalan historians, Ferran Soldevila, squarely states
that 'The dynasty of Trastámara was firmly enthroned in Catalonia,
with all the foreseeable consequences that followed the introduction
of a Castilian dynasty. From this moment began the denationaliza-
tion of Catalonia.' Jaime Vicens Vives sees the events rather differently in terms of a choice between 'a contractual state with its
ultimate consequence of an aristocratic republic, or royal authori-
tarianism with its inevitable sequel of social, political, and administrative reforms.'

It was the contractual state which was reinforced by the election
of Ferdinand of Antequera. Its principles were later set out very
clearly in a declaration by the *Generalitat*, or standing committee of
three *diputats* drawn from the different Estates of the Corts and
charged with representing the Catalan nation in its dealings with
its prince:

The affairs of the Principality of Catalonia are not to be judged
by reference to those of other kingdoms and provinces, where the

kings and lords are sovereign lords, with such power that they make and unmake laws and rule their vassals as they will; and where, after making laws, they themselves are not bound by them . . . In Catalonia, the supreme power and jurisdiction over the province belongs not to His Majesty alone, but to His Majesty and the three estates of the province, which together possess supreme and absolute power to make and unmake laws, and to alter the machinery and government of the province . . . These laws we have in Catalonia are laws compacted between the king and the land, and the prince can no more exempt himself from them than he can exempt himself from a contract . . .[1]

The powers of the *Generalitat* and the Corts were further defined and extended by Ferdinand in 1413, when the executive powers of the Crown were separated from the functioning of the judiciary, and also during Corts convoked by his successor, Alfonso 'The Magnanimous', in 1420 and 1421–3. Another significant outcome of the Compromise was that the establishment of the same ruling dynasty in Castile and the Crown of Aragon brought nearer the day when the two kingdoms were to be amalgamated, although for the time being there was to be no conscious effort to unite the monarchy.

In so far as the architect of the Compromise was concerned, Pedro de Luna fared little better than the supporters of Ferdinand's forebear, Henry of Trastámara. None of the diplomatic overtures of the king or of Saint Vicens Ferrer could induce the indestructible old man to renounce his claim to the Papacy. At the Convocation of Perpignan, held in 1415 and attended by all the interested parties, Saint Vicens Ferrer, speaking on behalf of Ferdinand, now mortally ill, and prefacing his address with a text from Ezekiel, 'O ye dry bones, hear the word of the Lord', urged his lifelong friend and ally to abdicate. Without giving an inch, de Luna beat a retreat to the castle of Peñiscola, where he survived until 1422—but not before delivering the scathing rejoinder: 'Tell your king, I have made him what he is, and now he casts me out into exile!'

Although Alfonso V, 'The Magnanimous', (1416–58) was criticized for installing his Castilian following in positions of authority, he

---

[1] Fuller Bonsoms, No. 12. *Per los Diputats del General de Catalunya* (Barcelona, 1622), quoted by J. H. Elliott, *The Revolt of the Catalans*, Cambridge, 1963.

THE HOUSE OF TRASTÁMARA

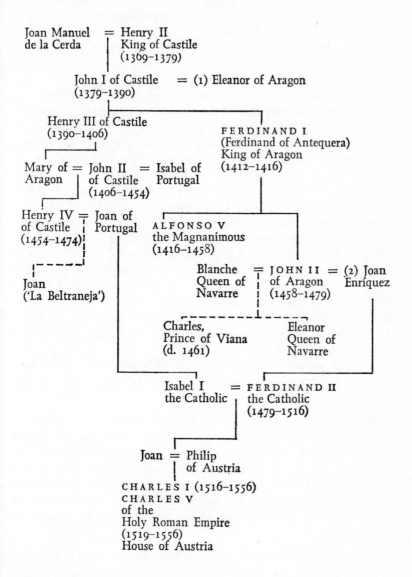

Kings of the Crown of Aragon are printed in small capitals.

can hardly be accused of furthering the interests of Castile at the expense of the Crown of Aragon. His life was devoted to the traditional aim of expansion in the Mediterranean to the neglect of domestic affairs, which he left very largely in the hands of his able first wife, María of Castile. Shortly after his accession Sicily was formally incorporated in the Crown, and naval expeditions stabilized the situation in Sardinia and Corsica.

Alfonso was then free to undertake what was to be his major preoccupation, the conquest of the Kingdom of Naples. In answer to an appeal from Queen Joan II, who was at the time beset by the forces of Louis III of Anjou and his allies the Genoese, Alfonso sailed from Messina with his fleet and raised the siege in June 1421. Queen Joan had declared Alfonso her adopted son and heir, but soon changed her mind, suspecting that he wished to supplant her, and called in that formidable *Condottiere*, Francesco Sforza, at whose hands Alfonso suffered a resounding defeat. It was to require twenty years of bitter campaigning, during which Alfonso at one point fell into the hands of the Duke of Milan, before he finally possessed himself of Naples in June 1442, where he spent the rest of his life, dividing his time between patronage of the arts—his chef, Rupert de Nola, wrote one of the first cookbooks to achieve European circulation, the famous *Llibre de Coch*, published in Barcelona in 1477—and grandiose projects for military expansion in the Balkans and eastern Mediterranean.

The achievements of Alfonso 'The Magnanimous' have been summed up astringently, but perhaps not unfairly, by Ferran Soldevila :

A kingdom conquered by dint of huge sacrifices and separated from the Crown of Aragon after his death [Alfonso left Naples to his bastard, Ferdinand of Calabria]; an eastern empire in the making, but so insecurely founded that it disintegrated on his disappearance from the scene; a series of conflicts with Castile without advantage to his realms; and the impoverishment of both Aragon and Catalonia as the result of his Mediterranean campaigns.

All of Catalonia's internal problems were accentuated by Alfonso's constant demands for money. The landed proprietors renewed their demands on the *pagesos* (see page 101) and they in turn, through their newly-formed 'syndicates', protested to the Queen in Alfonso's absence. She and her counsellors proved sympathetic and referred the *síndics* to her husband in Naples, who in 1448 authorized the *pagesos* (but not the *foráns*, or Majorcan peasantry) to band together and to collect money for the defence of their cause in the tribunals of justice. This decision occasioned bitter opposition, not only from the nobility, clergy and the bourgeoisie, but also from the *Generalitat* of Barcelona.

The ruling oligarchy was still further incensed when in 1455, after the Catalan Corts had raised difficulties over raising 400,000 florins for Alfonso's foreign adventures, he retorted by decreeing the participation of artisans and guilds in the city government and further suspending the payment of moneys by the *pagesos* under the terms of the *mals usos*. His action was seen as a surrender to subversive elements of the labouring classes and an infringement of contractual government; and the brunt of the pactists' fury was borne by his brother, the future John (Joan) II, deputed to carry out the measures and very shortly to succeed him.

John II (1458–79) had married Blanche, daughter and heiress of Charles III 'The Noble' of Navarre, to whose kingdom he succeeded on Charles's death in 1425. Thereafter, his consuming preoccupation, in partnership with his younger brother Henry (together, they were known as the 'Infantes of Aragon') was to intervene in the affairs of Castile to the detriment of her sovereign, John II, of the senior branch of the Trastámara family. His ambitions suffered a check after his defeat at the hands of the Constable of Castile, the redoubtable Alvaro de Luna in 1445 and the confiscation of his Castilian holdings in 1454 soon after the accession of Henry IV to the throne of Castile.

During this period the administration of Catalonia had been left to Queen María so that John was not familiar with the Principality's problems at first hand. Even if he had not been otherwise occupied in Navarre and Castile, it is doubtful whether he could have done much to avert the catastrophe that followed in Catalonia as the inevitable outcome of the internal dissensions that came to a head during Alfonso's prolonged absence in Naples. The idea that the crisis sprang solely from John's treatment of his son, the popular Prince of Viana, is a romantic myth.

The fundamental division in Catalonia was between the landed proprietors, including the major and minor nobility, bishops, clerics and townspeople who had acquired country properties—in fact, about 90 per cent of the ruling hierarchy—and the *pagesos de remença*, on whom they depended for the larger part of their income. Although the privileged were united in their support of pactist government, they were themselves much divided. Of the two most powerful noble families, as at the time of James of Urgell, the Counts of Cardona were firm in their support of the king, and those of Pallars considerably less so; among the clergy, royalist sympathies were not unnaturally strongest among those who had received bishoprics and benefices; and the mercantile community was split down the centre by the wealthy and patrician *Bigaires* and the smaller entrepreneurs or *Busceiras*, who differed radically over economic and monetary policies.

The *pagesos* and manual workers stood together in their universal distrust of the nobility, ecclesiastics and bourgeoisie, and institutions such as the Corts, *Generalitat* and municipality of Barcelona, which perpetuated the *status quo*. 'Of what good,' as the saying went at the time, 'are Corts, when we are no part of them?' But they too were split, between the *pagesos* who had profited from the *masos ronècs* to become small proprietors in their own right, and casual labourers entirely at the mercy of the landowners.

These differences explain the conflicting and often contradictory positions taken up when civil war broke out and the country was polarized between supporters of the monarchy and the Corts.

Since 1451 John II and the Prince of Viana, his son by Blanche of Navarre, had been at loggerheads, a prime reason being that John, at the insistence of his second wife, Juana Enríquez, daughter of the Admiral of Castile, had refused to name the Prince heir to the throne of Navarre as laid down in Blanche's will. In 1460 the Prince of Viana indiscreetly engaged in negotiations with Henry IV of Castile to marry his half-sister, Isabel; and what sparked off the Catalan revolution was the Prince's subsequent arrest and imprisonment by his father.

The immediate reaction of the Catalan Corts was that the Prince's arrest was a challenge to their own rights and authority, and since the king refused to yield, an army was recruited and sent against him under the command of the Count of Mòdica. The Catalans were at this stage supported by the Valencians and Aragonese; and bowing to *force majeure*, John released the Prince of Viana, who had been held captive at Morella since February 1461.

The problem was now to resolve the constitutional issue. Was Catalonia to become a patrician republic in the style of Venice or Genoa, or was it still possible to revive pactist government with suitable guarantees? In the upshot, moderate views prevailed, and the king agreed to sweeping concessions—including a veto on his own entry into Catalonia—by the Capitulation of Vilafranca del Penedès, signed on 22 June 1461. The central problem remained: *'quin rei havia d'ésser rei deixant d'ésser rei?'* ('how to be a king without being king').

A solution was found in the appointment of Charles of Viana as viceroy of Catalonia, and he took up office with the acclamation of all sections of opinion in the Principality. But Charles died a few months later—soon to be revered as a saint—and Catalonia was immediately involved in a new and much severer crisis.

Under the terms of Charles's appointment it had been agreed that, in the event of his death, the viceroyalty should devolve on his half-brother, the *infante* Ferdinand (later to become Ferdinand II of Aragon and Castile). Ferdinand was only nine at the time, and his mother, Queen Juana Enríquez, had been the lifelong enemy of Charles of Viana and had bitterly opposed the Capitulation of Vilafranca del Penedès. When she arrived in Barcelona with her son, against the express orders of her husband and in an attempt to rally royalist support, the Corts took immediate counteraction, and in May 1462 war broke out between the two sides, continuing with unparalleled savagery and loss of life for the next ten years.

Loyalties were confused and divided. Some of the nobility, most of the clergy and the majority of the peasants sided with John II, while the minor nobility, the mercantile oligarchy of Barcelona and the artisans took the part of the Corts. Neither side was strong enough on its own to win a quick victory: at the time the population of Catalonia was only 300,000 and support was not forthcoming from Valencia, Aragon or Majorca.

John II, in the face of early reverses, sought aid from Louis XI of France, who promptly improved the occasion to seize the counties of Roussillon and Cerdagne. The Corts thereupon disowned John and proclaimed Henry IV of Castile King of Aragon. When he stood down as a result of French pressure, the crown was next offered to Peter, Constable of Portugal, and finally, as an act of desperation after the defeat at Prats del Rei and the surrender of Tortosa in 1466, to René of Anjou, Count of Provence and uncle of Louis XI.

What had begun as an internal struggle for power had developed into an international dog-fight for possession of Catalonia. Louis XI now deserted John II, and all the signs were that he would exploit the situation to partition the Crown of Aragon and to appropriate Catalonia and the Balearics. John II reacted with involved diplomatic moves to enlist the power of England, Brittany, Burgundy and Naples, and played his last card by enlisting the help of Castile and negotiating the marriage in 1469 of his sixteen-year-old son Ferdinand to Henry IV's half-sister, Isabel.

In 1472 the Catalan Corts surrendered, signing an honourable peace with John (The Capitulation of Pedralbes), which began by stating that Catalonia had fought in defence of her liberties and which salvaged most of the Principality's traditional rights. There was a further declaration that neither side had won or lost; but the true loser was Catalonia itself, which after the blood-letting and disruption of the war, was left in a position of demographic and economic inferiority to Castile. Isabel was only recognized as heir to Castile after prolonged dissension and in the teeth of opposition from Henry IV, who favoured the cause of his supposedly bastard daughter, Juana la Beltraneja; but in the event the marriage of the two *infantes* was to ensure the future paramount role of Castile in ordering the affairs of the Peninsula.

IX

Union with Castile

At the centre of the arcaded Plaça Real in Barcelona, where the *tertulias* sit late into the night over their glasses of beer, there once stood a plinth destined for an equestrian statue of Ferdinand the Catholic. It was demolished in 1869 by order of the City Council, and to this day Barcelona remains without a memorial to the last of its Trastámaran rulers. This is no doubt because the Catalan writers who contributed to the *Renaixença*, the romantic and nationalistic literary movement of the nineteenth century, laid at his door the lion's share of the blame for the depressed and decadent state of the Principality during the sixteenth century; and their accusations are echoed today by the more perfervid Catalan historians. The charges include the Castilianization of government, the whittling away of traditional rights, the appeasement of the landowners at the expense of the *pagesos*, the introduction of the Inquisition and the ruin of the economy by debarring Catalan participation in exploiting the newly-discovered territories in America. To what extent are they justified?

At the outset it should be explained that Ferdinand's marriage to Isabel of Castile did not, as is often thought, imply the amalgamation of the two countries, but their association under a common dynasty: although they worked in close unison, Isabel remained Queen of Castile and Ferdinand ruler of the Crown of Aragon. On Isabel's death in 1504, Ferdinand did not become King, but Regent of Castile; and it was only after the accession of their Hapsburg grandson, the Emperor Charles V, that the kingship was combined in one person. Even then, Ferdinand's pluralistic concept survived: the ruler became not 'King of Spain', but 'King of the Spains', and Catalonia, Aragon and Valencia continued to enjoy a much greater degree of regional autonomy than the overseas possessions of the ruling dynasty, such as Naples or the provinces in the New World, which were strictly controlled from Madrid.

After succeeding his father, John II, in 1479, and swearing the laws and constitution of the country, Ferdinand's first task was to heal the gaping wounds of the civil war. Having first declared a general amnesty (which excluded only the anti-royalist Count of Pallars), he next addressed himself to the task of restoring goods and properties which had changed hands, sometimes more than once, during the confused course of hostilities. This was resolved by re-establishing the *status quo* of 1462; and during their session of 1480–1 the Corts of Barcelona voted a credit of 100,000 florins to indemnify those who now found themselves obliged to return property seized during the war.

The problem of the *pagesos de remença* was to prove even thornier. During the war most of the *pagesos* had fought on the side of the royalists. Nevertheless, many of the landed proprietors and clergy had also sided with the king and now demanded restitution of their ancient rights. It was in vain that Ferdinand urged more moderate policies; and to avoid disruption of other useful measures under discussion by the Corts, he unwillingly agreed to a decree of 1481, 'Com per lo Senyor', which annulled the concessions granted to the *pagesos* by his uncle, Alfonso 'The Magnanimous'.

The immediate outcome was the murder of a collector of taxes and dues in 1482, and by the next year the *pagesos* of the Muntanya (the mountainous district north of Barcelona) were on the brink of open revolt. Their leader, Pere Joan Sala, refused to accept royal assurances of a legal solution, and in September 1484 the rebels defeated a force sent against them under the command of the viceroy of Catalonia, Henry of Aragon, and advanced on Barcelona. The authorities sent to Ferdinand, who was in Seville at the time (during the whole of his long reign he spent only five years in Catalonia). Astute and politic as he was, Ferdinand was a confirmed authoritarian and at once ordered the punishment of Sala, who was duly apprehended, executed and quartered in Barcelona in 1485. But the problem of the *pagesos* did not admit of a solution imposed by force; new leaders sprang up hydra-headed; and Ferdinand finally undertook to arbitrate between the two parties.

After a painstaking study of the issues by his vice-chancellor, Lluís de Cavalleria, Ferdinand summoned the representatives of the owners and the *pagesos* to the Monastery of Guadalupe and there delivered his verdict on 21 April 1486, the historic *Sentència Arbitral de Guadalupe*. Under its terms the *pagesos* were granted personal liberty and the use of the land which they occupied; at the same time the *mals usos* and certain other bonds of servitude were suspended. In return, the proprietors retained possession of the *masos* and the right to receive the homage of their tenants and certain fixed dues. The Crown paid 50,000 lliures to the proprietors in settlement, and they received another 6,000, payable over five years, from the peasantry as an indemnity for the damage suffered during the revolt. It was an equitable settlement, which, with good will on both sides, was in the long run to lead to a revival of the rural economy.

The charge that Ferdinand imposed a centralist and absolutist regime on Catalonia cannot be sustained. With his assent, the Barcelona Corts in 1481 agreed a *Constitució de l'Observança*, providing that any royal measure considered in breach of the laws and usages of Catalonia should forthwith be declared null and void and referred to the *Audiència Real* (or Supreme Tribunal), which was required to pronounce on its legality within a space of ten days.

7. The Catholic Monarchs, Ferdinand II of Aragon and Isabel I of Castile.

Since the king, whose energies were, to begin with, so largely absorbed in overcoming the last pocket of Moorish resistance in the Kingdom of Granada, was rarely in the Principality, a decree of 1479 named a viceroy to exercise his royal functions; and this was followed by the establishment in 1494 of the Council of Aragon, which remained in permanent attendance on the monarch during his long absences. It is of relevance that all its members—a

Treasurer-General, Vice-Chancellor and five *Regentes*—were, with the exception of the Treasurer, natives.

Ferdinand's other most important innovation was the substitution of a triennial system of ballot in place of elections for choosing the deputies of the *Generalitat* and *Consell de Cent* (the 'Council of One Hundred' or city council of Barcelona). The names were henceforth drawn at random from a silver bowl by a boy of under eight years of age, thus providing a degree of protection against graft or bribery. However, in the case of the *Generalitat*, only some five hundred persons, drawn from the nobility (the *Braç militar*), the higher-ranking clergy (*Braç eclesiàstic*)—parish priests were not represented—and *Ciutadàs honrats* or most distinguished of the citizenry (*Braç reial*), were eligible for the draw of three *diputats* and three *oidors*. Although the peasants and artisans were not represented at all, the reform at least militated against the perpetuation of the same oligarchic clique and was later to be stubbornly defended by the Catalans themselves, when Philip V introduced his autocratic *Nueva Planta* in 1716.

All the facts go to show that in matters of government, Ferdinand, while firm in exercising his royal authority, was genuinely imbued by the traditional principles of pactist rule. Further evidence for his belief in regional autonomy under the umbrella of a united Spain was his respect for the Corts and institutions of Navarre, when the kingdom was incorporated into Castile in 1512.

It is a different story in regard to the enforcement of an Inquisition on a country rootedly opposed to it, and here Ferdinand was perhaps unduly influenced by his more bigotedly Catholic wife and the very different situation in Castile. In Castile, the Jews and *conversos* (converts to Catholicism) were numerous and often rich. The nobility, clergy and even the kings themselves had come to depend on them for finance; in consequence they were heartily disliked, and the racial question had reached explosive proportions.

Especially in Aragon and Valencia the position was radically different, since the numerous *conversos* had been assimilated and formed a most useful section of the community. In Catalonia most of the Jews had left after the pogrom of 1381 and the small minority that remained posed no threat. Cases of back-sliding *conversos*, who were the principal target of the Inquisition, were dealt with leniently and without difficulty by the episcopal tribunes of the different dioceses, first set up in the early thirteenth century to combat the Albigenses (see page 58).

In spite of the foreseeable and subsequently disastrous reper-cussions on the economy, the Catholic Monarchs petitioned the Holy See to set up an Inquisition under their own personal jurisdiction, with powers in both Castile and the Crown of Aragon that overrode all local statutes. After much hesitation, Pope Sixtus IV finally granted the dispensation, and in 1481 a first *auto-da-fe* took place in Seville with the burning of six of the city's most influential *con-versos*.

In Barcelona, the authorities fought tooth and nail to avoid the extension of the Inquisition to Catalonia. At Ferdinand's very threat to introduce it, in 1484, there had been a mass emigration of *con-versos*, and in the parlous condition of its affairs this was some-thing the city could not afford.

After the civil war production and commerce had declined by more than a quarter; inflation was rampant and the florin had slumped; whilst the population had declined to some 20,000—the lowest figure since the eleventh century. 'How can the city and country survive such a blow?' the councillors demanded of the king. His reply was simple and forthright: what he proposed was *'al servei de N.S. Déu'* ('in the service of God'), though he added that the Tribunal would, in his own words, be conducted *'sense fúria ni crueltat, sinó amb molta moderació'* ('without fury or cruelty, but with great moderation'). Such an assurance hardly carried weight in view of what was happening alsewhere; and his motives must be suspect, since, apart from the religious aspect, the Inquisition consti-tuted a formidable new weapon in controlling the country.

Neither prayers nor embassies moved him, but served only to stave off the moment when the Inquisitor, Alfonso Espina, formally entered Barcelona on 5 July 1487. The results were predictable: it has been estimated that during the twenty years of its functioning, 38 people were burned, 149 imprisoned and many more interrogated, while some 600 *conversos* left for good. These figures, which cor-respond to about a thirtieth of the population, may not seem over-large; but it must be remembered that those concerned formed a most important element in the social and economic life of the city.

The low watermark of Barcelona's fortunes occurred about 1487, when the economic consequences of the civil war were reinforced by the rising of the *pagesos* and the first fruits of the Inquisition. By then the population had still further fallen to about 18,000, and as a further barometer of depression Pierre Villar, in his *La Catalogne dans l'Espagne moderne*, quotes figures for the *Dret de Peritatge* (professional dues), which had fallen to a thirtieth of the sum levied forty years before.

The upswing began in about 1490, when Catalonia benefited from a general economic revival throughout Europe. Ferdinand made his own contribution by encouraging agriculture, by attempts to stamp out the piracy rampant in the Mediterranean, and above all by protecting Catalonia's basic industries. The Principality was granted a monopoly in the export of cloth to Sardinia, Sicily and Naples. The spice trade with Alexandria was resumed in 1502 and trafficking with North Africa in 1511. This improved state of affairs was reflected by a growth in population to 26,000 in 1497 and 29,000 in 1515. Catalan historians are nevertheless vociferous in accusing Ferdinand of holding up a more marked revival by denying Catalonia a fair share of the trade with the Indies.

Christopher Columbus, who had opened up vast new horizons in the New World by his first voyage of discovery in 1492, occupies a special place in Catalan affections. Unlike Ferdinand, he is commemorated by an imposing, if florid, column near Barcelona's harbour, where a replica of one of his ships lies at anchor. It was in Barcelona that he first reported to the Catholic Monarchs on his discoveries, and although it is generally accepted that he was born in Genoa, his origins are somewhat obscure and there is a strong local tradition that he was in fact a Catalan.

The thesis, so baldly stated in most history books, that the trade with the Indies was from the first a Castilian prerogative is not the whole truth. Since Columbus was authorized to undertake his voyages jointly by Isabel, as Queen of Castile, and Ferdinand, as King of Aragon, both claimed equal shares in exploiting the new territories. The right of the Crown of Aragon to participate in the trade was repeatedly affirmed by Ferdinand, especially when he became Regent of Castile after Isabel's death in 1504. The fact that the trade *did* rapidly become a Castilian monopoly was largely through default. Captains of the ships engaged in the trade very soon found that the most convenient port was Seville, where a *Casa de Contratación* was established to handle the merchandise. The position was crystallized when the merchants of Seville petitioned for and obtained a decree that all ships on the transatlantic route must sail from and berth at Seville. As the trade grew, the Emperor Charles V (Charles I of Spain) recognized the inconvenience of concentrating it on one port and in 1529 decreed that ships might sail from a variety of other ports, but must call in at Seville on the return journey. But by then the practice was so well established that until the middle of the eighteenth century, Seville and, to a lesser degree, Cadiz, enjoyed an effective monopoly.

J. Vicens Vives' analysis (in *Moments crucials de la història de Catalunya*, Barcelona, 1962) of the *technical* reasons for the absence of Catalan shipping on the Atlantic route is so illuminating as to be worth quoting at length:

Why, then, if Ferran [Ferdinand] II contributed to the economic recuperation of Catalonia, did he not offer her a large participation in the trade with America, as befitted a people who had traded so successfully in the Mediterranean? This is one of the charges which is debated with most heat, on the basis of Catalonia's success in trading with the New World in the eighteenth century.

But to understand what happened it is essential to avoid comparisons between the sixteenth century and the eighteenth. There was a technical factor which made commerce between the Mediterranean coast and Columbus's newly-discovered America an impossibility. It was the following: it was not feasible for a caravel to make the passage of the Strait of Gibraltar from west to east, against current and winds, without losing much time and risking men and ships. It required the nautical revolution of the early eighteenth century, especially the introduction of sails known as *focs* and an enlarged cruising range before the Mediterranean peoples could hope to participate in the American trade. Málaga, an important part of the Kingdom of Granada, with a hinterland rich in wheat, wines and silk, did not take part in commerce with America until 1778, although expressly awarded the privilege of free trade by Charles V in 1529.

Technical considerations apart, the real reason why Catalonia did not engage in trade with the Americas from the outset lay in her economic exhaustion and lack of capital to embark on the new venture. As matters stood, her merchant navy was fully extended along the routes to the Balearics, Sardinia, Sicily and Alexandria, and in coastal trading with Provence, the Languedoc and North Africa. Taking a wider view, it was inevitable that the Principality should henceforth take second place to Castile, both because of the demographic disparity and because the Mediterranean, which was to be increasingly dominated by the Turks and the Barbary Corsairs, was to lose its historical importance as the focus of European commerce and communications.

If Ferdinand II, born in Navarre and fluent in Aragonese and Catalan, took a lively interest in the affairs of the Principality and admired its administrative and social organization to the extent of applying some of its techniques to Castile, the position changed radically during the period of his Hapsburg successors. With the advent of his grandson, Charles I of Spain, the country became a European and world power, of which Catalonia, Valencia and Aragon were only a small unit.

Charles's mother, the mad Queen Joan, daughter of the Catholic Monarchs, had married Philip of Austria; and on the death of his grandfather Maximilian I (his father died prematurely), he was elected Holy Roman Emperor as Charles V, the name by which he is usually known. Born in Ghent, his first interest remained the defence of Catholicism in the Low Countries and Germany against the rising tide of Protestantism and, beyond that, consolidation of his domains in Italy against attack from France and the buttressing of Europe against the expansionist Ottoman empire of the Turks. An absolutist by upbringing, he mounted his campaigns from Castile, where he was untrammelled by the restrictions on royal power obtaining in the Crown of Aragon, and which was in any case a much greater reserve of manpower and, because of the ever-increasing flow of precious metals from America, the indispensable source of finance for his foreign adventures.

Catalonia became increasingly inward-looking and aloof from the religious struggles of the sixteenth century, which were tearing the rest of Europe apart—although even she suffered from the backwash of the Huguenot uprisings in France, as will appear. Historians such as Fernand Braudel have interpreted these conflicts as the masked protest of the underprivileged against the division of society into rich and poor in the face of overpopulation, failure of production and a consequent rampant inflation and rise in the price of food. But even on this level the Principality failed to respond to appeals for help from her sister states.

The trouble began when Charles, after his first arrival in Spain in 1517, began installing his Flemish favourites in positions of authority, notably appointing the twenty-year-old nephew of his *alter rex*, William of Croy, to the premier see of Spain, Toledo. Between 1519 and 1521 this provoked the war of the Comunidades, in which the bourgeoisie and urban gentry of the incorporated municipalities of Spain fought against the Emperor and nobility, eventually suffering outright defeat at the Battle of Villalar in 1521. Beyond this, the rebellion, like those of the Valencian and Majorcan *agermanats* at the same period, reflected a much wider-spread protest against the monopolization of agricultural land by the Grandees, thanks to the concessions of the Catholic Monarchs.

That Barcelona, traditionally a bastion of civil liberties, turned a deaf ear to all pleas from the rebels in Castile and Valencia is a measure of the Principality's exhaustion and self-centred isolation. With pactist government firmly underwritten by Ferdinand II and the settlement of differences between *pagesos* and landowners, and *Bigaires* and *Busceiras*, the Catalan authorities were no more willing to intervene than when Philip II was later to attack Aragon in 1591. Their refusal, understandable enough in view of demographic and economic weakness, nevertheless went a long way to sever the remaining links between the partners in the Crown of Aragon.

Deprived of her former proud role of mistress of the Mediterranean by the ordering of foreign affairs from Madrid, Catalonia was only stirred into action by a new threat from the sea. During the fourteenth century the Ottomans had dismantled the Byzantine Empire and under Suleyman the Magnificent (1520–66) had overrun eastern Europe, laid siege to Vienna and advanced into Germany, where they were finally checked by an Imperial army under Charles V. Although defeated by Charles at Tunis in 1535, the Turks were no less menacing at sea, and the Castilian fleet was able to do little more than police the quadrilateral Barcelona–Genoa–Palermo–Cartagena.

The main threat to Catalonia was the depredations of the Barbary Corsairs, operating from the North African coast, and Algiers in particular. In the past the Counts of Barcelona had ensured the freedom of the seas by their suzerainty of the Berber kingdoms; Ferdinand II had resorted to a different strategy, installing Spanish garrisons in strong-points along the coast; but the defence line lay in ruins when the formidable Barbarossa (Khair-ed-Din), so-called because of his fiery red beard, overwhelmed Algiers in 1521.

As Fernand Braudel points out, piracy was by no means the sole prerogative of the Muslims, but was an ancient and honoured industry in the region. When, for example, Ibiza was sacked in 1536, its despoilers carried away sides of salt pork and were very probably French. Nevertheless, the Levante coast suffered cruelly at the hands of the Corsairs, who landed more or less at will from about

1545 until the Battle of Lepanto in 1571, plundering, setting fire to *masos* and carrying off captives by the hundred for enslavement or subsequent ransom. The presence of some 300,000 Moriscos in the region, many of them restless and unwilling converts, did nothing to allay anxiety; and matters came to a head with an attack of unparalleled ferocity on Minorca in 1558 by a fleet of some hundred Turkish ships, during which it is said that more than 6,000 people were taken captive.

Barcelona was at last shaken from its years-long torpor. A force of 600 soldiers was summoned from Aragon; heavy artillery was bought; and, on the orders of Philip II, a series of watchtowers was constructed the length of the coast from Valencia to the French frontier. Meanwhile oak logs were brought down from the Pyrenees, and the city's shipyards rang to long-forgotten activity. It seems that the Catalans were fired with something of the old crusading zeal, since large contingents enlisted in the army which defeated the rebellion of the Moriscos in the Alpujarras mountains near Granada during 1568–71 and also helped to man Don Juan of Austria's ships at the Battle of Lepanto—though it is uncertain to what extent the volunteers were enrolled under the viceroy's promise of a free pardon to bandits and miscreants. The resounding victory of Lepanto in 1571, resulting in the death of 20,000 Turks at the cost of 8,000 Christian lives, did not put an end to Turkish sea power. It proved necessary as late as 1493 to form a joint Catalan–Valencian–Majorcan squadron to police the western Mediterranean; but from the time of Lepanto the Ottoman Empire progressively declined and the danger was much reduced.

During the sixteenth and much of the seventeenth centuries banditry was as great a problem on land as on sea, and it was not confined to Catalonia, but was prevalent all over the Mediterranean area. Its basic cause was over-population, a failure of harvests and widespread poverty, which led to an army of vagrants and 'vagabonds' taking to the roads and countryside.

In Catalonia the effects were exaggerated by other factors. The revolt of the *pagesos* and the civil war left in their wake numerous uprooted peasants and scores of unresolved feuds and rivalries among the nobility. J. H. Elliott has further related the internecine fighting to 'the virtual exclusion of Catalan nobles and gentry from offices of profit under the Spanish Crown', with consequent loss of income and injury to their pride and self-respect. An overriding conflict was that between the *nyerros* and *cadells*, who originally took their names from the feuding families of Neró and Cadell from the mountainous north, but the labels soon took on a derogatory sense, since in Catalan *nyerro* means a pig and *cadell* a small dog; and it was not long before the whole country was split between rival factions with no very clear affiliations or aims.

Matters had reached such a pitch in 1535 that Charles V instructed his viceroy to quell the disturbances. Although the Duke of Gandia, with the support of Francisco Borgia, the future General of the Jesuits, took firm action, many of the bandits slipped through his fingers, finding sanctuary in the churches or in the castles of their aristocratic patrons; and unrest was, in fact, to continue until the end of the War of the *Segadors* in the next century.

Catalonia was only a minor concern of Charles's son and successor, Philip II, deluged as he was in his monastic apartments in the gloomy Escorial with diplomatic despatches from Naples, France or England, the accounts of silver mines in America, or demands for yet more money and troops from his generals in the Low Countries. But Philip had saddled Spain with championing the cause of Catholicism in Europe and viewed with some alarm reports on the penetration of the Principality by Huguenots from the Midi. This human flotsam and jetsam, the victims of religious persecution in France, were known in Catalonia as *Gascons*, although most came from the south of France. Especially between 1565 and 1570, they infiltrated the Roussillon and Cerdagne, recovered for Spain by Ferdinand the Catholic, and crossed the Pyrenees in appreciable numbers, either as seasonal workers to help gather in the harvest or to despoil churches of their treasures and to swell the growing number of *bandolers*.

The Inquisition celebrated a number of *autos-da-fe*, during which French Lutherans were either burnt or sent to the galleys. Both in Rome and Madrid there was apprehension that Catalonia was being undermined by Protestantism; and in 1596 the Viceroy, Hurtado de Mendoza, actually arrested and imprisoned the deputies and *oidors* (financial officers) of the *Generalitat*, together with members of the clergy and aristocracy, on suspicion of heresy. Philip followed up by forbidding Catalans to study abroad and by imposing a rigid censorship, thus further augmenting a feeling of claustrophobia and detachment from the larger affairs of Europe inside the Principality.

The moneys which financed Philip's grandiose campaigns against the Protestants and the Turks had their origin in the silver mines of Potosí in Peru. Either in the form of bullion or minted coin, the silver was first transported to Seville and thence to Antwerp, the banking centre of northern Europe, or to Genoa. The great convoys early became the target for pirates and later for bandits. In the first place, the silver was sent overland by Burgos to the Bay of Biscay and thence by ship to the Netherlands to defray the bottomless expenditure on the Spanish armies.

With the decline of the wool market in Antwerp and in the face of mounting attacks by English privateers in the Channel, there was then a major change of route, dating from about 1578. The silver, sometimes in amounts of as much as 200,000 ducats, was instead despatched under armed escort along the primitive roads to Saragossa and Lérida and thence to Barcelona for shipment to Genoa and further distribution in northern Europe or Italy, or to reimburse the Genoese bankers for the ruinous loans, to which Philip had increasingly to resort.

Not unnaturally the convoys became a prime target for the *bandolers*, whose members included the gentry, students and *Gascons*, and even attracted adventurers from abroad, such as the notorious Barbeta from Italy, whose gang carried out a spectacular attack on a convoy of 108 cases of silver, part bullion and part coin, destined for the Genoese banker, Niccolo Balbi, in December 1613. In his *Revolt of the Catalans*, Cambridge, 1963, J. H. Elliott quotes from a plaintive letter written to Balbi by the Genoese Commissioner on 30 December 1613:

> This is to bring you the worst news you have ever heard. Today, at one o'clock in the afternoon, the convoy was between the village of Hostalets and a place called Montmaneu (on the road from Lérida to Barcelona), guarded by more than eighty men from Cervera. Suddenly, more than a hundred bandits emerged from the mountains, each armed with four arquebuses and accompanied by horsemen. They looted the silver and the money, and only fifty-nine crates are left. The rest is missing; and of all the guards, not one man remained—they all fled, and the bandits forced open the boxes at their leisure . . .
>
> The bandits themselves carried off only ten or twelve crates, and all the rest was stolen by the local inhabitants whom we had called to our help. They were in league with the bandits, who said to them: 'Take as much money as you want, friends. Now's the time to make yourself rich—this money belongs to the Genoese. And if you don't open those boxes, we'll break your heads open.

If you can't carry off the silver bars, hide them—they'll come in useful in time . . .'

Banditry had therefore become a way of life in Catalonia. It would be pleasing to interpret it as an assertion of Catalan independence and a precursor of the stirring events of the next century, when Catalans were again to assert their rights and individuality; but in sober fact it is much nearer the truth to see it as an impotent reaction to enforced isolation and conformism. Hemmed in behind the Mediterranean and a boundary of which the defence could safely be left to Castile and the father figures of Charles V and Philip II, the great events of sixteenth-century Europe passed Catalonia by, and her outlook extended no further than Perpignan and Narbonne. Nevertheless, if Catalonia was lapped by a false sense of security, her economic position was slowly improving and her institutions had survived intact—one is tempted to say 'fossilized'—and when once those institutions were menaced by Philip IV, all the country's dormant energies were at last to be released.

X

The Revolt of the Harvesters

We have no money, gold or silver in Spain because
we have it; we are not rich because we are rich.

Memorial de la política necesaria y
útil restauración a la Republica de
España, Valladolid, 1600.

After the death of Philip II in 1598 and during the first decades
of the seventeenth century, there was to be a major change of attitude on the part of Castile and its Hapsburg rulers towards the peripheral provinces of Portugal and the Crown of Aragon. Shored up
by American gold and silver the Castilians had on the whole not
unsuccessfully succeeded in imposing a hegemony on a large part
of Western Europe; but in 1599 Castile and Andalusia were over-
taken by plague, labour shortage, famine and a rampant inflation.
Why, it was argued in Madrid, should Castile continue to bear
the whole burden of Empire? Was it not time that practical form
should be given to the loose union and that the Crown of Aragon,
for example, should play its fair share in repealing outdated laws
which forbade the raising of troops for service beyond its boundaries
and in contributing to the expense of campaigns abroad? During
the whole of his twenty-three years as king, Philip III had obtained
1,100,000 ducats from Catalonia in 1599, 400,000 from Valencia and
nothing at all from Aragon, while in Castile the nominal annual
yield from direct taxes during the early years of his reign was
6,200,000 ducats.

Seen from Catalonia (or the other provinces) the position was very
different. The religious and dynastic wars in Europe were not of
the Principality's seeking and had been undertaken by the Monarch
on his own account. Catalonia had been denied participation in the
great venture in the Indies and had shared none of the riches from
the mines, except incidentally as payment for cloth supplied to the
troops or in the course of treasure shipments via Barcelona to

Genoa. The treasure had been squandered in Flanders and Italy, and why, at this late stage, when shipments of silver were failing and the war was going badly, should she be involved?

The *Constitucions* forbade the grant of money to the king except when he personally convoked Corts in the Principality, and he had seen fit to make an appearance only once, in 1599. Only one of his viceroys, the energetic Duke of Alburquerque, had proved popular with the Catalans, for his ruthless and effective methods of putting down banditry, although these had involved suspension of some of the *Constitucions* which hampered him. His successor, the Duke of Alcalá, continued to act in breach of the *Constitucions* without the same justification, antagonizing the nobility by forbidding the use of *pedrenyals* (muskets) and arousing the deepest suspicion by placing over the *dressanes*—the Barcelona dockyards—the coat of arms, not of Catalonia, but of Castile and León. It could only mean that, in distant Madrid, the king and his counsellors were plotting to overturn cherished laws and liberties and replace them by *un rey, una ley, una moneda*—the king, laws and (by now debased) coinage of Castile.

It is more than doubtful whether the pleasure-loving Philip III or his chief adviser, the indolent Duke of Lerma, had any such clearcut ideas; but matters changed dramatically when his successor, Philip IV, appointed the Count Duke of Olivares chief minister in March 1621. A member of the influential Guzmán family, Olivares soon gained the complete confidence of the king and was in effect to direct the government of Castile for the next twenty years. His portrait by Velazquez conveys something of the force and determination of a man who was up by five o'clock to make his confession and worked unremittingly until late at night, in private audience with the king, himself granting audiences, attending the numerous Councils and Juntas and drafting state papers; even when accompanying the king on a boar-hunt, he would continue to give audiences in the open air.

Throughout his career Olivares remained convinced of the necessity for welding the scattered domains of the Spanish Hapsburgs into an effective whole, if the Spanish empire was to survive. It is an irony of history that the means he adopted for doing so came close to causing wholesale ruin and disruption, since in effect it meant enforcing the law of Castile on provinces which jealousy preserved their own rights and liberties and were prepared to fight for them.

E

Olivares set out his aims in the famous secret memorandum of 1624, prepared for the king:

> The most important thing in Your Majesty's Monarchy is for you to become king of Spain: by this I mean, Sir, that Your Majesty should not be content with being king of Portugal, of Aragon, of Valencia and Count of Barcelona, but should secretly plan and work to reduce these kingdoms of which Spain is composed to the style and laws of Castile . . .

Debating three possible ways of achieving the desired result, he continues:

> The third way, although not so justified, but the most effective, would be for Your Majesty—assuming you have these forces—to go in person as if to visit the kingdom where the business is to be done; and there to bring about some great popular tumult. Under this pretext, the troops could intervene. And in order to restore calm and prevent any further recurrence of the troubles, the laws could be reorganized (as if the country had been newly conquered) and brought into conformity with those of Castile.

In the eyes of most Catalan historians this cynical blue-print constitutes sufficient evidence for damning the subsequent actions of the Count Duke out of hand; but it is worth quoting another passage from the same memorandum:

> What reason is there that these [non-Castilian] vassals should be excluded from honour or privilege in these kingdoms? Why should not they equally enjoy the honours, offices and confidence given to those born in the heart of Castile and Andalusia . . . There is the greatest justification for discontent in those other kingdoms and provinces, which have not only put up with government for so many years without the presence of the king, but are also regarded as unfitted for honours and unequal to other vassals . . .

There seems no reason to doubt that Olivares was sincere in these sentiments, which he repeats elsewhere, but in the distressed state of Castile it was obviously out of the question to implement such a policy in the teeth of opposition from an already discontented aristocracy. However, it is an over-simplification to say that Olivares at once proceeded to his 'third way'; in the face of military disasters abroad and his desperate search for reinforcements, he was finally caught up in a net of his own making.

His first step was to propose a Union of Arms by the creation of a large common reserve of troops, paid for and supplied by the different provinces of the empire for deployment in whichever of them might come under attack. From the standpoint of Madrid this was a fair and reasonable measure in view of the military and financial crisis (even during the euphoric era of Philip II the state had been declared bankrupt in 1557, 1575 and 1596, and again during the reign of Philip III in 1607), but Olivares soon found that whatever slender hopes there were of obtaining acceptance of his ideas in Aragon, Valencia and Catalonia hinged on a royal visit and convocation of the Corts.

By rights, Philip IV should have visited the Principality on his accession to swear the rights and *Constitucions* and to authorize the appointment of a new viceroy in place of the hated Alcalá, and the Catalans had been clamouring for a royal visit since 1621. It had been put off on the score of the king's pressing preoccupation with the affairs of the other provinces of his far-flung empire; but one practical reason for his delay was that, in the parlous state of the royal finances, the king could not afford the large expense of a visit accompanied by a royal suite some 2,000 strong. By 1626 the situation was so desperate that he belatedly took to the road, first summoning Corts in Aragon and Valencia. The proposal for a Union of Arms at once ran into strenuous opposition, and the best that he could obtain from Valencia was a grant of 72,000 ducats a year to maintain a force of 1,000 infantrymen for fifteen years.

When the session of the Catalan Corts began on 28 March 1626, it immediately became obvious that a wide gulf divided the two sides. In Catalan eyes the primary object of the Corts was to obtain redress for all the grievances which had arisen since their last convocation in 1599; and if the *Constitucions*, which expressly forbade the levying of troops for service abroad, were to be amended, the Principality expected a substantial gesture on the part of the king in the form of *mercedes* or royal favours. Olivares and the king, on the other hand, clearly regarded Catalonia as a land flowing with milk and honey, which had evaded its responsibilities and must now contribute to the common cause. In Philip's own words (no doubt drafted by Olivares), 'My Catalans, your count comes to your doors, besieged by his enemies, in order to request money not to be spent on vain display, but on obtaining satisfaction against them . . .

To serve with paid men, as is proposed to you, is not to infringe your constitutions nor to do anything contrary to custom, but to revive the glory of your nation, and the name that for so long has been forgotten, but was once feared throughout Europe. . . .'

A strange feature of the ensuing wrangle was that both sides based their arguments and the financial resources of the Principality on an assumed population of 1,000,000 inhabitants. The census of 1553 had enumerated 71,690 *focs* (or hearths), and reckoning an average of four persons to a household, this would give a figure of some 300,000. It is difficult to believe that the population had trebled during the ensuing period. However, when the hard bargaining began, the Corts, while pleading poverty, took their stand over the question of the *quints*, the fifth part of municipal revenues traditionally payable to the royal treasury. The custom had long since fallen into disuse and the City of Barcelona was specifically exempted from it, but if concessions were to be made, the Corts made it plain that they expected a formal renunciation of the *quints* in return. Far from renouncing its rights, the Crown was increasingly to insist on the payments, even requiring them from Barcelona; and this was the rock on which this and all subsequent attempts at negotiation were to founder.

The procedure of the Corts was not such as to allow of quick decisions. Any proposed measure had to be agreed by each of the three estates, the *Braç eclesiàstic*, the *Braç militar* and the *Braç reial* (see page 118) sitting in separate session; and for a financial measure to be approved, unanimous agreement, not a simple majority, was necessary. In the *dissentiment*, the Corts also allowed unlimited powers to the filibusterer. During all debates an individual member might rise from his seat and state a grievance, whether related to the subject in hand or not, and until it had been settled to his satisfaction, all other business was suspended. Not unnaturally the practice lent itself to blackmail and goes some way to explain the prevalence of bribes, often in the form of appointments in the royal patrimony, to induce influential *síndics* to vote one way or the other.

In the circumstances, it is not surprising that the Corts of 1626 dragged on interminably. After displaying considerable patience in the first place, the king began dropping hints that he would have to return to Madrid for reasons of health and to prorogue them. Although Catalonia's premier noble, the Duke of Cardona, threw his weight behind the king, there was complete deadlock over three cardinal points : the *quints*, the powers of the Inquisition and the implementation of the *Observança* (see page 117), a corner-stone of Catalan liberties. By the end of April the king burst out: 'Take note that I have been here five weeks, and my service has not yet been discussed. I have to leave on Monday . . . and I warn you that I have seen into your hearts and know the manner of your proceeding. . . .'

On Sunday, 3 May, Olivares decided to force the issue and a formal motion was put to all three *Braços*, proposing a grant of 3,300,000 ducats to the king. Dismayed by the size of the sum, the Corts rose in turmoil; Olivares now came to the conclusion that there was nothing to be gained by further discussion; and Philip left abruptly at six o'clock next morning.

In spite of their differences with him, now as later the Catalans displayed a touching faith in his good intentions; and news of his unheralded departure was received with consternation. On behalf of the City of Barcelona, the leader of the Council of One Hundred, the *Conseller-en-Cap*, rode after him post-haste with the offer of a loan of 50,000 lliures to meet the expenses of his journey and begged that he should return to resume the Corts. The Corts themselves got down to serious discussion of the grant, and it seems that a sum of 2,000,000 ducats might well have been agreed, if the king had been induced to return; but Philip's curt reply to the *Conseller* was : 'I thank the city for what you have said to me on its behalf. I shall remember this all my life and will deal swiftly with your petitions.'

The king was not to return for another six years; and in the meantime, despite the grant of 12,000 lliures in 1631 towards providing troops for Italy, relations became increasingly embittered—and were not improved by an ill-judged proposal to separate the counties of Roussillon and Cerdagne from the Principality.

By February 1632 the military position in Italy and Flanders was critical, and the simultaneous loss of the treasure fleet from New Spain compelled Olivares to swallow his pride and to accompany the king and his two brothers to Barcelona for the convocation of new Corts. They got off to a bad start, because Olivares, profiting from earlier experience, had decided that they must be allowed to run their full course and that the king's place should be taken by his brother, the Cardenal Infante Don Fernando, who was to act both as President and Viceroy. The proposal was finally accepted with ill grace, and the young Cardinal, who had been briefed by the notorious *pronotario* of the Council of Aragon, Jerónimo de Villanueva, that he must at all costs extract a subsidy of 3,000,000 ducats, never got the proceedings off the ground.

On 27 May, the day before the opening of the Corts, the Cardenal Infante was to be sworn in as viceroy in the Cathedral. It happened that the *Consellers* of the City of Barcelona claimed a long-standing right, in common with the Grandees of Spain, to remain covered in the royal presence. This they were determined to exercise; and they were only induced to forgo the privilege when, after the Cardenal Infante's entrance, the Duke of Cardona, the only person with an unassailable right to wear his hat, ostentatiously removed it.

Public reaction to their climb-down was immediate and furious, and bowing to the storm, the Council of One Hundred lodged a *dissentiment* in the Corts, which effectively held up all other business.

The issue may seem trivial. Olivares might ask: 'Do not the *Consell de Cent* realize that this affair keeps the whole world in suspense and that all the kingdoms of the Monarchy have their eyes fixed on what is happening?' But of all its privileges it was this that was most important to Barcelona. It was enjoyed by no other city in Spain; and for its people, its withdrawal symbolized a policy aimed at the progressive destruction of Catalan laws and liberties. Both parties, taking their stand on considerations of status and prestige, refused to budge; and proceedings came to a sorry end, with nothing achieved, when Olivares wrote to the Cardenal Infante on 24 October, instructing him to prorogue the Corts once again.

It was the French declaration of war on Spain in May 1635 which made a head-on conflict between Olivares and the Catalans more or less inevitable. Both Richelieu and Olivares were doubtful about their countries' capacity to sustain long hostilities; but a cardinal principle of the Count Duke's strategy, which had already involved him in costly fighting in Italy, was that the road between Milan and Flanders must at all costs be kept open. What Olivares regarded as a lifeline, Richelieu saw as a stranglehold on France. The French had been seriously affected by an economic crisis and civil disturbances, but the country was at least in better shape than Spain, which had been at war continuously since 1621. The crying need in Madrid was for more money and more troops, and Olivares was determined that Catalonia should supply them.

As a diversion, Olivares planned an attack on the fortress of Leucata in the Languedoc in the summer of 1637 to relieve pressure on Flanders and Italy. He was now prepared to brook no excuses and invoked the *usatge of Princeps namque* (page 44), calling to arms all able-bodied men in defence of the Principality. However, the Catalans were quick to retort that *Princeps namque* was applicable only when the king himself was in the Principality. The viceroy, now the Duke of Cardona, had the utmost difficulty in raising even five hundred men, and before they reached Leucata the siege had been raised. Disgust in Madrid knew no bounds, and feelings ran even higher when in the summer of 1638 Catalonia alone refused to send troops to participate in the heroic defence of the Spanish frontier post of Fuenterrabía against the onslaught of the *Prince de Condé.*

Relations between Barcelona and Madrid were further disturbed by an acrimonious dispute about customs. The Principality's prosperity depended very largely on the trade with France, which had been officially suspended on the outbreak of war. Nevertheless large amounts of contraband still found their way into the port of Mataró, where they were seized by officials of the *Generalitat* and impounded in its warehouses—ostensibly because customs dues had not been paid, but in fact to prevent the viceroy from appropriating the goods. The new viceroy, the Count of Santa Coloma, who had recently been appointed to reassert royal authority, did just this and, while offering to refund the *Generalitat* the dues, had the goods forcibly transferred to the royal warehouse. For some twenty years the *Generalitat* had taken a back seat and left active resistance to the Crown's demands to the City of Barcelona as represented by the Council of One Hundred. Although the issue was a dubious one, it now declared in round terms that Santa Coloma's action was illegal and unconstitutional.

At this juncture it happened that the ballot for the new *diputats* fell due, and by the luck of the draw the senior office of *diputat eclesiàstic* fell to Pau Claris. A canon of Seu d'Urgell and a bitter critic of its royalist bishop, Pau Duran, he was a man who epitomized the determination of the seventeenth-century Catalans not to deviate a hair's breadth from the laws and customs handed down by their predecessors. To make matters more difficult, Fransesc de Tamarit, chosen as *diputat militar*, was equally opposed to the viceroy and pledged to the defence of traditional liberties. Although the Council of One Hundred did not at first see eye to eye with the *Generalitat* over the issue of the customs, it too was in conflict with Madrid, and the arrest of two of its *Consellers* and an important official of the *Braç militar* was soon to cement a firm alliance between the most powerful institutions in the Principality. It was in these un-propitious circumstances that Olivares embarked on what was to amount to the 'third way' of his famous memorandum of 1624.

He now decided that the only method of involving the Catalans in the war against France, as the 'common welfare of the Monarchy demanded', was to launch the 1639 offensive from the Principality. Santa Coloma was ordered to recruit 6,000 Catalans, and 'If,' as Olivares was to burst out later, 'the constitutions do not allow this, then *the devil take the constitutions* and whoever observes them, myself included !'

The campaign began disastrously with the fall on 11 July of the important frontier fortress of Salces to a besieging French army of 16,000. By this time there were 7,500 Catalan troops in the area, but most were engaged in frontier defences; and Olivares now in-structed Santa Coloma that an all-out effort must be made to recruit more troops and commandeer supplies, so as to recapture Salces before the summer was out. The onus of obtaining these reinforce-ments was placed on the judges of the *Audiència*, who, besides form-ing the supreme judiciary, acted as the viceroy's advisers in the Principality. That they should be asked to stump the countryside, haggling for men and supplies in breach of *Constitucions* which they were sworn to defend, immediately cast doubts on their impartiality, and conscientiously as they struggled to fulfil their double role, they were henceforth to be regarded as traitors and were in fact to be the first victims of insurrection. Meanwhile, as the summer dragged on, the Spanish forces at Salces were decimated by illness and desertion; Santa Coloma was in despair; and it was only the belated arrival in the Roussillon of the *Conseller-en-Cap* of Barce-lona in December which called out the Catalans in their thousands.

Salces surrendered to the Spanish on 4 January 1640, but at a cost out of all proportion to its value. It has been estimated that some 40,000 Catalans took part in the operation, and their casu-alties have been put at between 4,000 and 10,000 dead, mostly from disease. The municipalities and *Generalitat* had exhausted their re-serves and the country had been denuded.

If the Principality expected recognition from Madrid for its sacrifices, it was speedily to be disillusioned. Its effort was dismissed as belated and unwilling; nevertheless, Olivares was well on the way to achieving his Union of Arms and decided to apply the next turn of the screw. His prime consideration was to keep together the army; the obvious place to quarter it was in Catalonia in readiness for next year's campaign, and where its presence would bring pressure to bear on the Corts in forcing through the unpopular reforms that he considered necessary. Even in Madrid there were dissentient voices: did the exhausted Principality possess sufficient resources to quarter an army of 9,000 men and was it prudent to risk another head-on clash over the legality of requiring householders to feed the men, when the *Constitucion of Nous vectigals* expressly laid down that they could be expected to provide no more than a bed, a table, light and service, and to furnish salt, water and vinegar?

Olivares was obdurate and indeed stepped up his demands as the months went by. Billeting was to be carried out in the much more lavish 'Lombardy style' and 6,000 Catalans were to be recruited for service in Italy. In the face of united opposition from the *Audiència*, the Corts and the Council of One Hundred, Olivares retorted by ordering the billeting of troops in Barcelona itself, although the city was specifically exempt. Finally, losing all patience, he instructed Santa Coloma to arrest Tamarit, the *diputat militar*. The viceroy, though aware of the likely repercussions, was not the man to question a royal order; and when Tamarit was arrested on 16 March, the Corts were immediately summoned by trumpet and the Council of One Hundred by the ringing of the city bell. But popular feeling was now running far ahead of the Catalan authorities, and when the showdown came it was as the result of a spontaneous explosion.

Up and down the rural areas of the country, the inhabitants were seething from the depredations of the half-starved and ill-disciplined troops, many of them mercenaries. As early as 1638, the people of the little town of Palafrugell had clashed with the troops; ten cavalry companies thereupon embarked on systematic pillage and loot; and the inhabitants had either fled or been murdered. During the spring of 1640, such incidents multiplied on a smaller or greater scale. On 27 April, the town of Santa Coloma de Farnés near Gerona was called upon to billet a large body of troops; the viceroy's agent, the *agutzil* Monrodón, an arrogant and drunken bully who had personally carried out the arrest of Tamarit, arrived to make arrangements and promptly provoked a riot. He then took refuge with his servants in the inn, which was surrounded and burnt to the ground.

Under instructions from Madrid, the viceroy mounted a punitive expedition, razing the now deserted town to the ground and for

E*

good measure burning down the neighbouring village of Riurdare-nes. Reaction was electric. Massed bands of armed peasants appeared overnight and, with the blessing of the Bishop of Gerona, who ex-communicated the entire *tercio* responsible for the burning and sacrilege of the church at Riurdarenes, were soon in command of the whole area, forcing the troops to retreat to the garrison town of Blanes. Gathering strength, the rebels now advanced on Barcelona itself and, very possibly with the connivance of the *Generalitat*, gained entrance through one of the city gates on 21 May and made straight for the prison, where they demolished the gates and lib-erated all its occupants, including the *diputat militar*, Tamarit. By now there were some 3,000 armed peasants surging through the streets, and the authorities appealed to the bishop for help. With the Bishop of Vich, he called on the rioters to leave, which they did peaceably with cries of 'Long live the Holy Mother Church and the King our Lord.'

If the descent on Barcelona had been without bloodshed, it was not long before insurgent bands were breaking into towns up and down the Principality, looting, setting fire to houses and killing those whom they regarded as traitors and collaborators—their full fury being reserved for the judges of the *Audiència*. The distur-bances were so widespread that Santa Coloma found himself power-less to check them: it was with difficulty that he succeeded in withdrawing the troops in the northern part of the country from Blanes, where they had found temporary shelter, to the strongly fortified garrison town of Rosas.

Matters reached their bloody climax at the beginning of June, when it was the custom for the *segadors*, the casual labourers who hired themselves out for the harvest, to assemble in Barcelona. At the best of times the descent of this rough-and-tumble crowd was a matter of anxiety for the city authorities. There were thoughts of denying them entry, but with the populace already thoroughly aroused, Santa Coloma was reluctant to intervene. Refusing sanctu-ary aboard the Marquess of Villafranca's galleys, which were about to leave the harbour for Cartagena, he decided to stand by his post and await what might come.

On Corpus Christi day, 7 June 1640, some 500 *segadors*, infiltrated by groups of insurgents, entered the city. Fighting first broke out near the house of the *agutzil* Monrodón, killed at Santa Coloma Farnés, and the mob then converged on the viceroy's palace, where they began piling wood against the doors so as to set fire to it. They were interrupted by the hasty arrival of the *Consellers*, the *diputats* and the Bishops of Barcelona, Vich and Urgell, who succeeded in calming them; but the respite was short-lived, and a break-away group entered the house of Dr. Berart, one of the judges of the *Audiència*, and set fire to his effects. Berart himself escaped to a convent, later to be discovered and murdered. During the next five days all the judges were compelled to go into hiding, and their houses, like those of the king's other ministers in the city, were systematically looted or destroyed.

Meanwhile the *Consellers* provided an armed guard for the viceroy and he was escorted to the harbour, where a Genoese galley had just docked. Still loath to leave with the city in tumult, Santa Coloma delayed the moment of departure and by the time he finally signalled the galley, it was too late. The insurgents had broken into the dockyard and brought the ship under artillery fire. Separated from the civic officials, the viceroy, with his son and one or two others, took to their heels and scrambled out on to the rocky shore. His son and a few others managed to board a skiff, but Santa Coloma, fat and out of condition, fell behind, stumbled and collapsed. Shortly afterwards the rioters caught up with him and he was summarily despatched, when they set on him with their daggers.

The first news of general insurrection reached Madrid in late May, and then, as later, the authorities entirely underestimated the gravity of the situation. The first reaction of the Council of Aragon, led by its inflexible *pronotario*, Villanueva, was a recommendation that the king should 'bridle the province'. However, Olivares would not accept what was now becoming obvious—that his cherished Union of Arms lay in ruins. He still believed that a policy of *blandura y rigor* might save the day and therefore wrote to the viceroy, instructing him to put down the insurrection without delay, at the same time indicating that the king was disposed to grant a royal pardon to the rebels, that billeting requirements would be relaxed and that more opportunity would be given to Catalans to participate in offices of state; punishment could follow later.

These conciliatory measures were so belated as to be irrelevant, and even the murder of Santa Coloma, while reducing the Court to stunned incredulity, only led to further argument and indecision. While Madrid dithered, the *Generalitat* was forced to the decision that definite and drastic action must be taken if the Principality was to be saved. The position had been exacerbated by the bombardment and destruction of Perpignan in response to riots fomented by the disgraceful behaviour of the billeted troops, but what was undoubtedly uppermost in the minds of Pau Claris and his colleagues was that the Catalan revolution had got entirely out of hand.

It was not simply a matter of the Principality standing up to the Crown to retain its traditional rights and liberties, but also of a social revolution of the poor against the rich and privileged. Declarations by rebel leaders, such as the self-styled 'Captain-General of the Christian army', had not only demanded the root-and-branch removal of royal officials, but in the same breath attacked the Catalan authorities in Barcelona itself. If the Principality was not to degenerate into anarchy and if its institutions were to be preserved, help must be sought from outside.

In the past the Corts would have turned to the king, as they had when the Principality was threatened by banditry and had been saved by the prompt action of the Duke of Albuquerque. Since Claris could expect no help from Philip while he remained under the thumb of his ill-disposed advisers, the only alternative was an appeal for assistance from France. There was no overt affection in Catalonia for her traditional enemy; even the numerous French immigrants do not appear to have been disloyal. The new initiative was simply one of expediency, arising out of the alienation of every branch of Catalan society—the mercantile oligarchy, the nobility, the bulk of the clerics, the bourgeoisie and the peasantry—by the ruling clique in Madrid. There are historians who have seen Claris and his associates as a self-interested group of conspirators who surrendered the Principality because they had been denied royal favours and rewards. The issue was more fundamental; although some of the revolutionary leaders did undoubtedly feel that they had received less than their just deserts, among them Fransesc Vilaplana, who made the first approaches to the representatives of Cardinal Richelieu.

Long before the *Generalitat*, in consultation with the Council of One Hundred, had come to the agonizing decision to present a formal petition for aid to the King of France on 24 September 1640, Olivares had got wind of the negotiations. He now had every pretext for putting into execution the long-mooted plan for marching into Catalonia and abolishing its institutions by force, but he meanwhile found himself faced with similar unrest in Portugal, where his attempts to impose a Union of Arms and raise money for use outside the country had run into equally stubborn opposition. Even at this eleventh hour, he therefore continued to negotiate with the *Generalitat* before taking the fateful decision to send an army against the Principality.

Both sides now began active preparations for an autumn campaign. If Olivares was unsuccessful in persuading Portugal to provide troops to quell the revolt in Catalonia—on the score that it would then be possible to despatch a strong force to Brazil to recover Portuguese territory lost to the Dutch—the *Generalitat* soon found that it was almost as difficult to find men for self-defence as for service with the king.

Neither the Castilian army, described by the English ambassador as consisting 'of married men who long to be at home, and of gentlemen, the most part whereof have hardly means to set themselves on horseback,' nor its commander, the Marquess of los Vélez, inspired confidence. Nevertheless, the Marquess entered Tortosa on 23 November and began an advance on Barcelona along the coast, scoring an early success at Cambrils in mid-December, when some 600 Catalans surrendered and were promptly massacred. This atrocity at once stiffened Catalan resistance and lent renewed urgency to negotiations for French participation. About the same time Olivares suffered a crushing blow when, profiting from his involvement in Catalonia, the Portuguese staged a rebellion which he was powerless to put down, and on 1 December proclaimed the Duke of Bragança king, as John IV.

Richelieu had so far been dragging his heels, unwilling to implicate himself too deeply while, on the one hand, the Catalans, who drew a sharp distinction between Philip IV and his advisers, stopped short of renouncing their oath of allegiance, and on the other, made so little effort to defend themselves. On 24 December his commander, the Duke of Espenan, actually came to terms with the Marquess of los Vélez to withdraw from Catalonia and thereupon abandoned Tarragona. The news of its fall provoked wholesale riots in Barcelona, during which three of the surviving judges of the *Audiència* were hounded to their deaths.

Claris and the other *diputats* now saw no alternative to making a personal appeal to Richelieu and agreeing with his legate, Duplessis Besançon, the declaration of a Catalan republic. It lasted for only a week, after which the Principality acknowledged the sovereignty of Louis XIII—with the sole proviso that its constitutions should be respected as in the past. Energetic measures were now undertaken for the defence of Barcelona, and a joint Catalan-French army defeated los Vélez on the slopes of Montjuic on 26 January 1641. Olivares had gambled and lost.

Catalonia had, in fact, simply exchanged one autocratic master for another. Even if Pau Claris had not died prematurely in February 1641, possibly poisoned on orders from Madrid, there was no real prospect that Richelieu and his successors would altruistically buttress the Principality's traditional liberties. The affairs of Barcelona were more strictly controlled than at the time of the Count Duke by the simple expedient of 'vetting' the lists of candidates for the ballot and removing the names of any likely to cause trouble. It was clearly of strategic importance to France to maintain a bridgehead across the Pyrenees; what was in effect an army of occupation remained there in breach of agreement; and the French were no more willing to pay for the upkeep of the troops than were the Castilians or their mercenaries before them.

Olivares had lamentably failed in his efforts to hold together the disunited parts of the monarchy; and after his enforced retirement in 1643, his nephew and successor, Don Luis de Haro, deployed considerable skill in repairing the damage, as far as this was still possible. Philip IV was, of course, in no way resigned to the permanent loss of Catalonia; the French were slowly forced back on the defensive; and the great plague which swept the land in 1650–54, in combination with a recurrent shortage of corn and a steep fall in the value of the currency, so weakened the Principality that its recovery by the Spanish Crown was only a matter of time. The surrender of Barcelona in October 1652 effectively marked the end of the Catalan revolution; and three months later, Philip IV, profiting from past mistakes, proclaimed a general amnesty and pledged himself to respect the Principality's constitutions and liberties. The Treaty of the Pyrenees, which followed in 1659, brought to an end hostilities between France and Spain, but peace was bought only at the price of ceding to France the Catalan counties east of the Pyrenees.

If the Spanish Monarchy emerged from the Thirty Years War mauled, but largely intact, the tide of European politics was fast overwhelming the loosely-knit Hapsburg empire. Elsewhere, energetic centralist governments were asserting their authority at the expense of entrenched pressure groups and small self-contained regions.

The most drastic repercussion of the Catalan revolution took place outside the borders of the Principality, in that the timing of the

GAZETA
VINGVDA A ESTA
CIVTAT DE BARCELONA, PER
lo Ordinari de Paris, vuy à 28. de
Maîg, Any 1641.

Traduida de Frances, en nostra llengua Catalana.

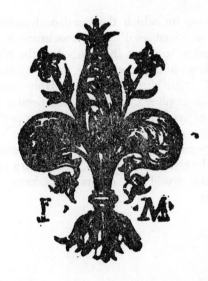

F · M

AB LLICENCIA,

En Barcelona ; en la Eſtampa de Iaume Romeu,
deuant S. Iaume, Any 1641.

8. Title page of one of the first Barcelona periodicals.

revolt enabled Portugal to cut free from Spain. Catalan writers, of whom Jaume Rossinyol (*Le problème national catalan*) is only one of the most recent, have suggested that it was purely fortuitous that Portugal was able to achieve independence in 1640 while Catalonia did not, and to deploy this as an argument for separatism today. This is a misinterpretation of the facts for a variety of reasons: Portugal had been briefly united with Castile within living memory; the country did not suffer from the same internal and social divisions; and perhaps most important, she looked towards the Atlantic and was in a position to trade profitably with Brazil and indeed to expel the Dutch by her own efforts, when Castile failed to do so. A fundamental weakness of Catalonia was that, while beginning to recognize the inadequacy of trade with the Mediterranean, she could not, except as part of a larger Spain, participate in viable markets farther afield.

The constitutions for which the Catalans fought in 1640 have been described as 'mediaeval' and 'anachronistic'—which they undoubtedly were, in so far as they embodied the traditional rights of a privileged class—and in the upshot the revolution did no more than buy time. Catalan historians are justifiably proud of the Principality's success in standing up to a Castilian dictator, who so grossly mismanaged the affairs of the Peninsula, but have perhaps placed the wrong emphasis on the outcome. The Count Duke had disastrously failed to impose union by force, but ironically enough the most lasting result of the clash was to drive Catalonia to a reluctant awareness of the outside world and of her dependence on the rest of Spain in particular.

XI

Phoenix from the Ashes

When Philip IV died in 1665, he left a sickly, half-imbecile son, Charles II, who was to prove quite incapable of defending the prostrate empire against foreign depredations. Under the regency of the Queen Mother, María Anna of Austria, a rudderless and misgoverned Castile plumbed the depths. The strong-points in Flanders and Spain's other European possessions were successively detached, and the country increasingly became the target for the ambitions of the great powers, headed on the one hand by Louis XIV and on the other by Leopold of Austria and William III of England. After the costly and disastrous attempts of the Count Duke of Olivares to tamper with provincial liberties, the peripheral regions were left to themselves. Inertia became the order of the day; and Charles II was the first monarch in history neither to visit the Principality nor summon its Corts.

While Catalonia suffered from the repeated incursions of Louis XIV's armies, she was nevertheless to show signs of marked economic growth and to take a new interest in the government of Spain as a whole. A prime architect of this economic and political revival was the writer and historian, Narcís Feliu de la Penya, author of two important books, *Politico discurso en defensa de cierta verdad* (1681) and *Fenix de Cataluña* (1683), who took energetic steps to put his theories into practice as president of a newly-created action committee. Feliu saw the regeneration of Catalonia in a renewal of manufactures and commerce. He encouraged the textile industry, drew up long-term plans for trade with the Indies and the establishment of Barcelona as a free port, and embarked upon the construction of frigates and galleys to protect merchant shipping from the Barbary corsairs.

The new-found interest in Hispanic politics manifested itself in support for John Joseph of Austria, a bastard son of Philip IV by the actress María Calderón, in his coup of 1669. John Joseph had ambitious plans for legal and tax reform and the participation of

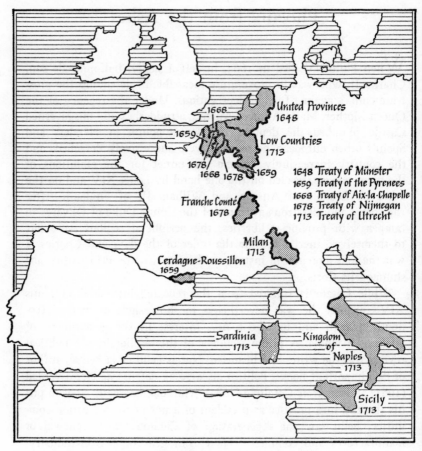

The loss of the Spanish domains in Europe.

the peripheral provinces in the trade with the Indies, but was out-
witted by the wily Queen Regent and proved insufficiently forceful
to carry through his plans when he eventually gained power during
1677–9.

Charles II was unable to father an heir by either of his two wives,
and during the last years of his reign, not only Spain, but the rest
of Europe, in search of easy pickings, became obsessed with the
problem of the succession. Both France and Austria wanted the
fabled inheritance for themselves, while England and Holland on
the sidelines were determined to prevent the establishment of a new
hegemony in Europe. Nearer home, the Catalans, still smarting from
the loss of the Roussillon and Cerdagne, and exposed to repeated
military aggression from France and competition in the important
textile trade, favoured the Austrians.

The wretched king, whose death was so eagerly awaited, above all
by Louis XIV of France, died on 1 November 1700. He had spent
the last week of his life stone deaf; the Queen fed him with milk
of pearls; and his doctors put cantharides on his feet and freshly-
killed pigeons on his head to prevent dizziness, finally applying the
steaming entrails of animals to his stomach to keep him warm. His
will had been drawn up on 2 October but left blank for Charles to
make the all-important choice between the Archduke Charles of
Austria, great-grandson of Philip III, and Philip of Anjou, a great-
grandson of Philip IV. For Charles, the operative clause was that
his inheritor must not allow 'the least dismemberment nor diminish-
ing of the Monarchy founded with such glory by my ancestors', and
with this uppermost he finally opted in favour of the Bourbon can-
didate.

To begin with, his decision was not contested inside Spain itself,
even by the Catalans. Louis XIV had counselled his grandson : 'You
will need all your patience. When peoples are naturally restless and
jealous of their privileges, it must be seen that there is no intention
of suppressing them. Their trust will inspire all the more zeal in
Your Majesty's service; and it is no less true that you require the
co-operation of all your subjects.'

Whether or not because he had a revolt on his hands in Naples
and also foresaw the inevitable clash with the Austrian Empire,
Philip followed his grandfather's instructions to the letter. Once in
Madrid, he announced a prompt visit to the Principality; and Corts
were convoked in his presence in 1701–2. Of their outcome, his
secretary, Melchor Rafael de Macanaz, wrote that 'The Catalans have

gained all that they wanted, since there remains nothing else for them to ask or for the king to concede; they are therefore more independent of him than the Parliament of England', while Feliu de la Penya described the constitutions as 'the most favourable ever obtained by the province'. Apart from confirming all the traditional rights and privileges of the Principality, Philip went even further in declaring Barcelona a free port and granting permission for two vessels a year to be sent to the Indies, in recognition of which he received an outright grant of a million and a half lliures and a further service of twelve million payable over six years.

In the upshot, Spain was not left alone to decide her destiny. The Grand Alliance of England, Austria and Holland, the creation of William III of England, was determined to avoid a future union between France and Spain, and approaches were made to the Catalans to join the Allies. In spite of Philip's generous concessions, the majority of Catalans—but not the *Generalitat*—still remained sympathetic to the House of Austria, which had, after all, lent them support against the recent incursions of the French; and in the divided state of Spain, the Allies seemed more likely to ensure territorial integrity than a beleaguered France. Envoys were therefore sent to Geneva, where the British plenipotentiary, Mitford Crow, promised troops and arms and gave cast-iron guarantees, whatever the vicissitudes of the war, as to Catalonia's traditional liberties: 'Neither now nor in the future, need the inhabitants and natives of the Principality entertain the least doubt that all their Privileges and Laws will be fully maintained and preserved.'

Matters were clinched by the arrival of a British fleet off Barcelona; the viceroy, Velasco, thereupon formally surrendered to the city, and the Archduke Charles made a triumphal entry on 7 November 1705. The Corts were immediately convoked and proceeded to declare the House of France perpetually excluded from the succession to Catalonia or the other realms of the Spanish monarchy. Aragon, Valencia and Majorca soon followed suit; and Minorca was to be captured by an English fleet and to remain in British possession for the best part of a century.

The battle was now on, and though the French suffered a series of disastrous defeats in the Low Countries at the hands of the Duke of Marlborough, the tide of war followed a much more chequered course in Spain itself, with Philip commanding increasing popular support in Castile, so that on the two occasions when allied armies entered Madrid they were rebuffed by its inhabitants and Queen

María Luisa could write to Madame de Maintenon in Paris:
'. . . *après Dieu c'est les peuples à qui nous devons la couronne* . . .
*Nous ne pouvons compter que sur eux, mais grâce à Dieu, ils font le
tout!*' It would indeed have been surprising if Castile, xenophobic at
the best of times, had taken kindly to British and German troops or
to a claimant to the throne chosen by the Catalans.

The first entry into Madrid took place in May 1705, but by the
spring of 1707 Philip was fighting back and, after his victories at
Almansa and Lérida, gained possession of the kingdoms of Valencia
and Aragon, subsequently abolishing their *fueros* as a punishment
for their support of the Archduke. During a counter-offensive in
the summer of 1710, the Allies won battles at Almenara and Saragossa and again occupied Madrid, only to beat a hasty retreat and
to suffer decisive defeats north of the capital at Brihuega and Villa
Viciosa on 9 and 10 December.

In the meantime Louis XIV had twice treated for peace with the
Allies, and if their demands had not been so stiff, the war might
well have been decided in favour of the Archduke and the Catalans.
On the first occasion, after the French defeat at Oudenarde and the
surrender of Lille in 1708, they stipulated not only that Louis
should recognize the Archduke as King of Spain, but that French
troops should co-operate in expelling his grandson. This was too
much for the old Sun King to swellow, and when negotiations were
resumed in 1709 after the Battle of Malplaquet, the conditions were
even more stringent: that the French forces alone should continue
the fight against Philip in Spain. With the Allies' grip on the
Peninsula confined to a few strong-points in Catalonia, Louis not
unnaturally decided to fight on.

The turning point came with the death of the Austrian Emperor,
Joseph, on 11 April 1711. The throne went to his brother, the Archduke, who was also elected Holy Roman Emperor. The English and
Dutch now lost interest in the further prosecution of the war. The
balance of power would be as much disturbed by reviving the empire
of Charles V as in countenancing a dynastic link between France
and Spain.

The belligerents thereupon embarked on new negotiations; and
unfortunately for Catalonia, the Tory government in England proved
less than scrupulous in implementing the solemn guarantees of
their Whig predecessors. It would be unfair to say that the Allies
summarily abandoned the Catalans—the 'Case of the Catalans' was
discussed *ad nauseam* during the long-drawn-out proceedings—but

the first consideration of the Allied powers was to obtain a hard-and-fast undertaking that the crown of France and Spain would in no circumstances be united and also to extract territorial concessions. Various solutions to the Catalan problem were put forward, including a proposal by the Emperor Charles VI that Catalonia should become a republic; this was vetoed by Bolingbroke on the grounds that it was not practical and would lead to perpetual warfare. In the end, all that was done was to incorporate a face-saving but entirely ineffectual clause in the Treaty of Utrecht, finally signed on 13 July 1713:

ARTICLE XIII. Seeing that Her Majesty the Queen of Great Britain does intercede on behalf of the inhabitants of Catalonia and does beseech that they be granted pardon and the restoration of their ancient rights and estates, His Catholic Majesty shall be pleased to grant not only that these rights be fully restored to them but that they shall henceforth enjoy all those privileges that do attach to the inhabitants of the two Castiles.

It was in vain that Catalan emissaries were sent to Utrecht, the Hague and London, or that Sir Robert Walpole protested that the Tories were little concerned with the honour of Queen Anne. The Catalans knew well enough what unconditional surrender would entail and had had a foretaste of what was in store for them when their allies hastily withdrew from Tarragona, abandoning it to the enemy.

An anxious debate now ensued. Was it better to surrender or to fight on in the hope that the Emperor Charles VI would find means of lending his support. The *Braços eclesiàstic* and *militar* were for submission so as to avoid further bloodshed, but there were other more headstrong voices, like that of Manuel Ferrer i Ciges, who exclaimed: 'Let the nation go down in glory!', and when the *Braç reial* declared in favour of continued resistance, the nobles of the *Braç militar* swung round, and the minority view prevailed.

Barcelona now closed ranks to prepare for a heroic defence which was to stir all Europe and to last for a year and two months. On 9 July 1713, a proclamation calling on the city to defend its liberties and privileges was read out in the streets to the sound of drums and trumpets; '*Priveligis o mort*' became the battle-cry of the inhabitants. Twelve thousand troops were enlisted under the command of Antonio de Villaroel and disposed to such good effect around the

ancient walls as to evoke the comment from the famous engineer,
Prosper Verboom: 'I could never have imagined that this city could
have been put in such a state of defence.'

Philip V's army of some 20,000 took up positions ten days later,
and the winter passed without progress. If at this stage Philip had
made any concessions over the cherished privileges, the siege might
well have ended, but the king is on record as saying: 'I would rather
surrender my crown than grant the Catalans their privileges, whatever the result,' while the Queen was equally obdurate: 'The king
will not concede them their privileges, because he would not be
king if he did.' Instead, Philip first called for reinforcements from
Sicily and Flanders, then found himself obliged to ask for help from
Louis XIV. As Voltaire was to write later in *Le siècle de Louis XIV*,
'Their stubborn resistance proved that Philip, even without his
[Austrian] competitor in the field, could not defeat them on his
own.'

With the arrival of the Duke of Berwick and French reinforcements on 7 July 1714, matters took a new turn. Under the direction of Verboom, parallels were dug towards the walls preparatory
to breaching them. The defenders, blockaded by sea, short of artillery-
men and with hundreds of houses in ruins, now found themselves
in desperate straits; but when Berwick called upon them to surrender
on pain of suffering all the rigours of war, the three *Braços* resolutely refused. At daybreak on 11 September, forty-five companies
of grenadiers formed up in the parallels, while forty-one battalions
launched a general attack. The breaches were stormed and the bat-
teries that guarded them overrun, and at eight at night a white
flag was at long last run up over the headquarters of the *Generalitat*.

In a stubborn attempt to maintain their regional laws and the
pluralistic concept of the Spanish monarchy, 'The Catalans were,' as
Jaime Vicens Vives has written, 'fighting against the current of
history and the price for this is usually very high.' So it was to
prove. Berwick, who had angrily replied to an eleventh-hour deputation from the city that 'Between a king and vassals there is no
capitulation on terms,' named a *Real Junta Superior de Justicia y
Gobierno* to take over the government of the Principality, and the
following day its president, Josep Patiño, presented himself first at
the Casa de la Ciutat, where he dissolved the Council of One Hundred and then at the Palau de la Diputació to read out a decree
abolishing the autonomous state of Catalonia:

The authority of the Diputación and Generalidad of Cataluña being terminated by the entry into this city and fortress of the armies of our sovereign king (may God preserve him), his Excellency the Marshal Duke of Berwick and Liria has commanded me that I order the deputies and *ohidores* of the *General* de Cataluña to put aside their insignia, to desist, together with their subordinates, from all exercise of duties, employment and office and to deliver up the keys, records and all else concerned with the said Diputación and its dependencies . . .

As might be expected, the immediate aftermath of defeat was the rounding-up of all military leaders and their exile to prisons in Castile, the disarming of Catalan troops and the hounding of civilians by a brutal soldiery. Verboom was instructed to construct a *ciutadella* (fort) in the middle of the city as a visible symbol of royal power, and this was completed with all speed. All symbols of the Council of One Hundred and *Generalitat* were obliterated—to the extent of removing the benches formerly occupied by the *Consellers*. Nor was the intellectual aspect forgotten. All books published in Catalonia between 1705 and 1714 were collected and destroyed; and in view of the students' part in the defence of Barcelona, the king decreed that its university be transferred to the small provincial town of Cervera.

Philip V and his counsellors thought long and hard before proclaiming the *Decreto de Nueva Planta* in January 1716, a 'new ground plan' for the centralized government of Catalonia and its integration with the rest of Spain. The views of his more extreme French and Castilian supporters emerge clearly enough in a memorandum presented by the Council of Castile:

It is necessary to abolish, efface and to suspend in their entirety the *fueros*, usages and customs of his Principality . . . and to impose the laws of Castile . . . to employ the Castilian language . . . so that books in Catalan must be forbidden, nor must it be spoken or written in schools and instruction in Christian doctrine must be in Castilian . . .

It is true that there were moderating voices. In his testimony to the king, one of the ministers, the Catalan-born Fransesc Ameller recommended that various institutions be allowed to function along traditional lines and wrote of the transfer of Barcelona University that 'it will be of much less use to the public, since Cervera is an inconvenient place and too small to accommodate so many students'. Josep Patiño, president of the interim Junta, questioned the practicality of introducing Castilian, since the people 'only speak their native language'; but the king was determined to garner the fruits of victory and to create a new Spain in the image of centralist France, as appears clearly enough from the preamble to the *Nueva Planta*: 'My arms, with divine assistance and because of the justice of my cause, having completely pacified the Principality of Catalonia, it is a matter of establishing government there . . . and ensuring that its inhabitants live in peace, quiet and plenty.'

The most important provision of the Decree was to establish a Captain General and a provincial high court or *Audiència* and to appoint *corregidores* (chief magistrates) and *regidores*, responsible for civil government, in the towns. All important posts were by royal nomination, while minor officials, such as *battles* (bailiffs), were to be appointed by the *Audiència*. The colonizing and centralizing purport of the Decree also emerges from Article 40: 'All prohibitions on persons from outside are to cease, since it is my Royal Intention that within my realms dignities and honours will be conferred reciprocally [*sic*] and not because of birth in one province or another.' Patiño's submission evidently carried some weight, since the only reference to language is that of Article 4, ruling that 'the proceedings of the *Real Audiència* shall be conducted in Castilian'. Only Catalan civil law remained untouched, the intention being that this would in time be supplanted by the Castilian.

It was to take Catalonia some fifteen years to adjust to these violent changes, which so abruptly swept away *fueros* and liberties established over centuries; and the *Nueva Planta* imposed an artificial political unity out of key with the deeply-held feelings and beliefs of its people and was to leave an abiding sense of grievance, which still survives and provides ammunition for the present-day separatists.

Nevertheless, if 19 January 1716 is the blackest day in history to later generations of nationalists, the *Nueva Planta*, by opening up domestic and foreign markets, channelled Catalan energies into industry and commerce. Economic revival began in agriculture, especially in the production of wine in the Penedès area and the export of brandy to an expanding market in England; and the profits were ploughed back into a new industry for the manufacture of cotton cloth. Corporations such as the Board of Commerce of Catalonia promoted an industrial revolution along the coasts of the

Peninsula; and during the period of 'enlightened despotism' under Charles III (1759–88) relations with the Court had so much improved that in 1772 the Catalan Company of Cotton Spinners entered into an agreement to process the fibre from the American plantations. It was in fact about 1780 that the image of the hard-working, pushful Catalan businessman first became current in Madrid.

Charles III and his ministers had meanwhile taken a decisive step forward in October 1765 by approving the *Autoritzacío als catalans per al comerç de Barlovent*, which ended Cadiz's American monopoly and allowed the ports of Santander, Gijón, La Coruña, Málaga, Cartagena, Alicante and Barcelona to trade direct with Cuba, Puerto Rico, Santo Domingo and the Island of Margarita. The more sweeping measures of 1778 opened up the whole of the Antilles, Central and Southern America; and, among others, the ports of Alfacs and Tarragona were beneficiaries. As a result, exports from Barcelona increased ten times in a single decade.

Such was the vitality of the region that within a century the population had doubled to reach almost a million—an increase all the more remarkable because it took place at a time when Catalans were emigrating *en masse* to other parts of the country, taking with them their traditional skills and crafts. Catalan colonies were established in almost every city of Spain, and many of the *émigrés* settled in Galicia, where they introduced improved methods of fishing and curing sardines and herrings. Traditionally, the greater part of the population had lived in the agricultural interior of Spain, but the demographic balance was now changing in favour of the regions of the periphery.

A disbalance was becoming apparent, of which A. Jutglar has written in his *L'era industrial a Espanya*:

Spanish geography, varied and distinct, exemplifies a Spain torn between two realities . . . of growing industrialization and commercial power along the coasts and of another country, fundamentally agricultural, at the heart of which is the phenomenon of Castile with its centralist tendencies and bureaucracy. This geographical phenomenon was to be aggravated during the whole of the nineteenth century and helps to explain a variety of events and tendencies, among them regionalism and, notably Catalan nationalism.

If Madrid regarded Catalonia's growing contribution to the national wealth with paternal approval—so a contemporary, José

de Cadalso, wrote that 'the industry of the Catalans is more profit-
able to the Crown than the poverty of millions of Indians'—the
Bourbons displayed no inclination to relax a rigid and negative
centralism, and indeed some of the provisions of the *Nueva Planta*,
which had lapsed by default, were re-applied with excessive zeal.
Miguel de Unamuno later summed up this short-sighted policy with
his usual perspicacity: 'A hollow unity, a unity without content,
unity for the sake of unity. There was no attempt to reconcile differences or to find harmony in discord; the aim was unity and
nothing else, unity stifling the least heterogeneity and differentiation . . . simplicity in a word . . . Naked unity, unity which is
nothing but unity. This unity is pure wilfulness . . . it is the dogma
of the infallibility of the man in command.'

By the last decade of the eighteenth century the intense economic
activity in the coastal region was bringing about profound changes
in Catalan society. In the mountainous hinterland life continued
along largely feudal lines, with the landed proprietors and clergy
securely entrenched. In Barcelona the great cotton boom gave birth
to a new middle-class bourgeoisie, whose industrial innovations were
to meet increasing opposition from the old guilds and the patrician
Ciutadàs honrats. At the same time the new textile factories created a demand for labour, met by an influx of workers from the
country districts and abroad. Unrest among the manual workers,
which found violent expression in the '*rebomboris de pa*' or bread
riots of 1789, set the pattern for the militant workers' movements
of the nineteenth century and did not go unnoticed in Paris, where
the French Revolution was in its first stages.

The first impact of the Revolution on Catalonia was that of the
dispossessed aristocrats, who flooded into the Principality from 1789
onwards and profoundly influenced the upper echelons of Barcelona
society with their ideas and culture. The Republic was not slow
in reacting and sent its agents across the border to disseminate revolutionary propaganda. From its inception in 1793 the Committee of
Public Safety entertained high hopes of fomenting a revolution in
Catalonia and forming a republic, hopes which emerge at their
most explicit in a memorandum prepared by General Dugommier
during his subsequent incursion:

Catalonia is a rich and superb province, both because of its agricultural resources and manufactures. It is renowned for its mines
and its ports on the Mediterranean. Above all, what must decide

us in attracting the Catalans is the certainty of establishing between France and Spain a bulwark more solid than the Pyrenees.
This is the tangible advantage of a Catalonia united with our
Republic. The Catalan is brave, active, hard-working and an enemy
of Spain; he has always had a high regard for liberty; and when
Equality is added, this queen of nations will soon unite with
those who fight for such principles. The flag of Fraternity will
herald our advance; and the Catalans, soon Francophile, will, I
predict, further our later designs on Spain.

Nothing was to prove farther from the truth. Catalonia was a
rootedly traditional country, and the French intervention in the
War of the Spanish Succession had been neither forgotten nor for-
given. If the Principality was deeply divided between the nobility and
clergy, the agricultural workers, the *Ciutadans Honrats*, the new
bourgeoisie, the factory workers and an emergent group of liberal
intellectuals, on two cardinal issues it was solidly united : disgust
for the decadent regime in Madrid and implacable hostility towards
France.

When the enlightened Charles III died in 1788, he was succeeded
by his near-imbecile son, Charles IV, who rapidly surrendered all
real authority to his masterful wife and her vain-glorious favourite,
Manuel Godoy, the so-called Prince of the Peace. It was not only
Catalonia which rejected Godoy's dictatorial and incompetent administration—which ultimately came to a summary end on the
verge of the Peninsular War as the result of a popular uprising at
Aranjuez.

Shortly after his appointment as Principal Secretary of State in
November 1792, Spain declared war on France as a protest against
the execution of Louis XVI. It is a measure of the extent to which
Catalonia now regarded herself as an integral part of the country
that neither now nor during the Peninsular War was there any
thought of breaking away. On the contrary, the Catalans embarked
on the *Guerra gran* in an access of patriotic fervour, at the same
time emphasizing their own role and continuing sense of oneness
in an outburst of ballads and poems in Catalan, foreshadowing
those of the *Renaixença* (see page 178) and speeding on their way
the spirited bands of young volunteers with dark blue capes and
streamered rosettes, rising in defence of their city :

> Al barret sense galó—l'escarapella hi ressalta,
> Lo gambeto blau turqui—i la bureta de grana.

Voluntaris Ciutadans,—tropa lleugera i galana:
A la guerra, fadrinets,—que la Ciutat nos demana.

Although Catalan had officially ceased to exist as a language, the commander of the Spanish army, General Ricardos, not only countenanced its use, but issued his orders in Catalan. In fact, he was absolutely dependent on Catalan support, since the army of 3,000 with which he invaded and soon occupied the Roussillon was entirely inadequate. Had the bombastic Godoy prepared the campaign with due care, there seems no reason why the lost counties of Roussillon and Cerdagne should not have been recovered; as it was, history repeated itself. The Spanish were soon in full retreat across the Pyrenees, and in November 1794 the fortress of Figueras surrendered to the French with the loss of 9,100 men and 171 cannon.

Catalan disgust with the effete government in Madrid and its fumbling conduct of the war knew no bounds:

> *Catalans, traició:*
> *Mòria tot traidor!*

Without reference to Madrid, a Catalan Assembly was formed; moneys were voted; a *sometent* called out the armed peasantry in their thousands; and by the time peace was signed in July 1795, the French were in full retreat across the frontier. Catalonia had saved herself by her own efforts and had demonstrated her contempt for the central authority by reconstituting what were in effect Corts and resorting to the forbidden *sometent*—indeed the war has been described as '*guerra essencialmente catalana i quasi civil*' ('a war essentially Catalan and quasi-civil').

The question remains, why did not Catalonia at this point prolong its Assembly and declare itself a republic? This is in fact what happened in the Basque province of Guipúzcoa under French tutelage—only to result in the loss of its *fueros* when it was returned to Spain after the Peace of Basle. The Catalans were more wary; they had suffered in the past at the time of the War of the *Segadors* and the Spanish Succession from reliance on foreign powers; and the Revolutionary regime in France was not such as to inspire confidence in its disinterestedness. Furthermore, it seems that feeling in the Principality cannot be described as more than regionalism; the quarrel was not with Spain, but with a corrupt and incompetent government. Nevertheless, Catalonia emerged with a revived, if diffuse, sense of nationhood, political, literary and dissentient, which was to be accentuated by the traumatic events of the Peninsular War.

XII

Two Campaigns

After the Peace of Basle the volatile Prince of the Peace returned
to the traditional policy of friendship with France and only a year
later issued a bombastic ultimatum to England. One of the immediate results was that Catalonia, in common with the rest of the
Mediterranean coast of Spain, was subjected to a stringent naval
blockade; and the destruction of the Spanish fleet at Trafalgar in
1805 still further reduced the possibilities of trading with America.
Worse was to follow, when Godoy was cowed into granting permission for the passage through Spain of Napoleon's army in its
attack on Portugal. Further French troops, at first welcomed as
friends and allies, began streaming across the Pyrenees and soon
threw off all pretence of being anything but foreign invaders.

In February 1808, General Duhesme crossed the southern end of
the Pyrenees with 14,000 men and began an unopposed advance on
Barcelona, which was treacherously occupied when General Lecchi
marched a column of troops past the fortress, apparently on his
way out of the city, then gave sudden orders to wheel and occupy it.
Since the authorities were creatures of Godoy, there was no immediate resistance; and the first bewildered reaction of Catalans who
opposed Godoy's despotic regime was one of relief. After the overthrow of Godoy and Charles IV at Aranjuez in March 1808, Napoleon's true intentions became brutally clear, when he compelled the
abdication of Ferdinand VII at Bayonne. Whatever his manifest
faults, Ferdinand now became the 'desired one' of all Spain, and Catalonia no less than the other parts of the country rose to the battle-
cry of 'Religio, Pàtria y Rey' ('Religion, Country and King').

The signal for country-wide revolt was the spontaneous uprising
of 2 May in Madrid against the occupying troops of Murat. A
Supreme Junta 'with all the attributes of authority' was formed in
the northern province of Asturias 'to sustain the liberty and independence of the nation against the infamous aggression of the
Emperor of the French', and shortly afterwards sent a deputation to
London, which was to set in motion British military intervention

in the Peninsula. Like all the other regions of Spain, Catalonia followed suit, though with its capital firmly in the hands of the French, it was not until 1809 that it proved possible to form a *Junta Superior del Principat*. In the meantime, revolutionary juntas took over on a local basis, notably at Gerona, Valls, Vilafranca and Lérida.

As elsewhere in Spain, the drive to form revolutionary juntas came from below and they came into being only at the expense of bloodshed and the murder of former supporters of Godoy and procrastinating officials, suspected of supporting the pretender, Joseph Bonaparte. At Terr, for example, a crowd of workmen and farmhands, led by a local shopkeeper, stormed the town hall, demanding weapons and the punishment of traitors who refused to give a clear lead, while at Tortosa an angry mob shot the military governor.

As at the time of the *Guerra gran*, the motives which inspired different sections of the community to take up arms were very mixed. For traditionalists, it was a straightforward matter of fighting for king and country and defending their religion against a Napoleon regarded as anti-god. The liberals saw the war as a struggle not only to free the country from the French invader, but to break loose from the authoritarian regime of the Bourbons. As for the peasants and workers, their fury was directed against anyone dubbed '*afrancesat*' and prepared to collaborate with, or even tolerate, the French. Since it was the well-to-do who were least anxious to stir up trouble with the occupying troops, they were automatically suspect. After the irregulars had routed a French force at Brucs, they at once turned on the landowners.

For his part, Napoleon issued a proclamation in his most florid style:

Conquerors of Athens and Neopatria, your ancient commerce with the orient will be restored. Catalonia will rise from the ashes. Your population, reduced after the conquest of America, will be more numerous than at the time of your splendour. Napoleon the Great will give you a new being. His paternal regard is fixed on you; your future is close to him and under his powerful protection. The French have always sustained you and helped you in your battles . . .

NAPOLEON THE GREAT extends his compassionate arms, seeing your country riven by a revolutionary fury excited by the vile English. Their policies are always directed towards your ruin. Your losses are the gain of those pirates. A hundred years ago they armed your ancestors against the Bourbons and abandoned them on the field of battle, as they will do with you . . .

Catalans, hark to my voice; open your eyes; consider your plight and the evils which surround you, and see that if you persist in delirium, your country will be plunged into the abyss. Virtuous Catalans, awake, unite, work for your salvation; take the initiative and destroy the monster which has devoured you and in its desperation plans to turn your country into a desert, strewn with corpses and ruins . . .

Napoleon received no answer to this impassioned plea, for reasons well-put by one of his own commanders in the Peninsular War, General Foy:

Catalonia is less a province of Spain than a small state under the sceptre of the Catholic Monarchs. Its customs, language and social organization are different from those of Castile . . . Nowhere in the Peninsula is there such a thirst for liberty and independence. Nowhere do parents transmit to their children more hatred for the French in their veins. They remember that, during the seventeenth century, we encouraged them in continual revolts against the kings of Spain and abandoned them to the mercies of an autocratic tyrant. They do not forgive us for having, at the beginning of the last century, imposed on them a king who humiliated their pride and destroyed their privileges. The Revolutionary war [*the Guerra gran*] in the Roussillon and Catalonia was conducted with slaughter and barbarity such as we never encountered in Navarre and Biscay. The peace brought no rapprochement. Catalonia, with its long coastline and populous commercial capital, has a community of interests with England. In fact, the war against France animates its ports and brings prosperity. The country demands a alliance which gives scope to its industry and nourishes its sources. In short, the Continental System is odious to it.

The struggle against the French in Catalonia was most effectively conducted by the armed peasantry, the so-called *miqueletes* and *sometents*. Their leaders, such as Milans del Bosch, Joan Clarós, Narcís Gay and the canon Rovira, became folk heroes; and every local junta maintained its own private army, which would overrun French outposts and harass supply lines, melting away at the threat of a set encounter with superior forces.

Duhesme early experienced the power of the *sometents*, when in June 1808 he was instructed to send columns to Valencia and also to Saragossa, in support of the French army in Aragon. The column destined for Valencia soon became bogged down at Tarragona and, with its communications cut, was compelled to return to Barcelona. A further 3,000 men, mainly Italian and Swiss under the command of Colonel Schwartz, set out for Lérida, but got no further than Brucs in the mountains west of Barcelona, when it was ambushed by a group of some 400 *sometents*. Unable to proceed, Schwartz formed his men into a hollow square with the artillery in the middle and began to retreat towards Barcelona. Reinforced by armed peasantry from the surrounding villages, the *sometents* poured such a devastating fire into the formation from the surrounding heights, that it broke up and the troops fled in utter confusion.

Although the Captain General of Catalonia and his regular officers complained of the unreliability and lack of discipline of the *sometents*, their own tactics of confronting well-trained and better-equipped French armies led to a series of disastrous defeats, as in the other parts of Spain. Nevertheless, during the first year of the campaign in Catalonia, the advantage was with the Spanish.

During this first phase General Duhesme, though securely in possession of Barcelona, found himself isolated, after the Spanish had cut his communications with France by the occupation of the strong-points of Figueras, Gerona, and Rosas on the coast. An attempt to capture Gerona was beaten off with heavy loss by an Irish garrison of only 350 men of the Ultonia Regiment under the gallant command of Colonel Peter O'Daly. Reinforced by the arrival of 8,000 troops from France under General Reille, Duhesme renewed the siege in August 1808, only to be thrown back and to lose his artillery and baggage train during their retreat to Barcelona, when his column was bombarded from the sea by a British naval detachment under Lord Cochrane and simultaneously attacked by the *miqueletes*.

Napoleon was now aroused to the danger of losing Barcelona and despatched a further force of 25,000 under General Gouvion St. Cyr to restore communications. St. Cyr first detached 12,000 men under General Reille to reduce the fortress of Rosas astride the coastal road. The ramshackle citadel was defended to such purpose by a force of 3,000 raw troops under O'Daly and a small naval detachment under Lord Cochrane, that it was not until 17 December 1808 that Duhesme's beleaguered garrison in Barcelona was finally relieved.

The siege of Gerona was resumed on 24 May 1809, and has gone down in Catalan military annals as the most heroic engagement of the whole campaign. It began badly for the French, as it was to continue, with St. Cyr under notice to relinquish his command to the aged Marshal Augereau. Since Augereau was ill in Perpignan, the operation began under the joint command of St. Cyr and General Verdier.

St. Cyr was notoriously selfish and morose at the best of times—not for nothing was he nicknamed '*le hibou*' ('the owl')—and promptly fell out with Verdier. On 4 September, General Blake and his army of Aragon succeeded in breaking through and reinforcing the hard-pressed garrison. An attempt by Verdier to restore the situation was met by a series of sorties on the part of the Spanish commander, Mariano Álvarez de Castro, to such good effect that the siege works were destroyed and the French lost 60 per cent of their effectives. At this point Verdier threw in his hand and retired to France.

Operations were continued by St. Cyr until he was at long last replaced by Marshal Augereau in October. After the failure of further attempts by Blake to relieve the fortress, the garrison was in desperate straits by November as a result of illness and starvation. Álvarez himself was feverish and prostrated by dysentery, but to one of his officers who suggested retiring, he snapped 'to the cemetery', and to another who complained of the shortage of supplies, 'When the last food is gone we will start eating the cowards, beginning with you.' But the outcome was now inevitable; and when Álvarez finally lapsed into delirium, his second-in-command surrendered to Augereau on 11 December 1809.

The heroic garrison was treated with the utmost brutality, and the stricken Álvarez was moved from one prison to another until he died in a dungeon at Figueras. It was widely rumoured in Spain that he had been poisoned. Augereau's retaliation, if unpardonable, may be explained on the score that the six months' defence of Gerona had cost the French army in Catalonia the best part of the campaigning season of 1809.

The occupation of Gerona opened the road to France, and with the capture of Lérida in April 1810 by Marshal Suchet—after one of the most brutal massacres of defenceless civilians in the whole history of the Peninsular War—the union of the French armies in Catalonia and Aragon left the whole of the eastern seaboard wide open to the invaders. The following year saw the progressive fall of all the remaining cities and strong-points in Catalonia: Tortosa was captured by Suchet in January 1811 and Tarragona in June, so enabling him to seize Valencia in January 1812.

The reasons for these Spanish reverses have been well summed up by Miguel Artola Gallego, writing in Vol. XXVI of the *Historia de España*:

> The crushing defeats of the Spanish regulars during the fourteen months preceding the loss of Tarragona were the result of a strategy devoted to the retention of cities and strongpoints and based on the deceptive security of walls and fortresses. The immobilization of large numbers of effectives in one place and in a posture of forced inactivity, without any guarantee of help from outside, left all the strategic initiative to the French. Popular support, one of the decisive factors of Spanish resistance, could hardly benefit from a garrison cooped up in a fortress, as long as the French, thanks to Spanish inactivity, enjoyed complete superiority in men and guns in each place where they decided to give battle.

After the fall of Tarragona the discouraged Marquess of Campo-verde decided to evacuate Catalonia, and further resistance to the French was left to a small force of 3,000 regulars under General Luis de Lacy. With the help of the *miqueletes* he resumed a guerrilla-style war and succeeded in liberating the smaller towns of Igualada, Cervera and Belpuig, so cutting the road to Lérida, but the forces at his disposal were too small to do more than harass French outposts and lines of communication. With Barcelona and the large towns securely in French hands, there was little significant change in the military situation in the Principality until Wellington's victory at Vitoria in June 1813 forced Suchet to abandon Valencia as part of a general French retreat and to fall back on Barcelona. By the early spring of 1814 Napoleon's needs were so desperate that the last French troops were withdrawn.

The last few years of the war had been a cruel period for the inhabitants of Catalonia. Agriculture was at a low ebb because of military operations, and imports of grain had been disrupted by the blockade; between the depredations of the French troops and the demands of the juntas, the *sometents* and the Spanish regulars, there was an acute shortage of food. Famine broke out in 1812 and was followed by epidemics, in which people died by thousands for lack of attention and medicines. Although the *Junta Superior del Principat* had refused to contribute to the war chest of the Central Junta in Cadiz, it had by its own efforts raised and supplied four armies— only to see them annihilated by the French. By 1812 it had reached the end of its resources and the soldiery were as starved and destitute as the peasants.

There was little or nothing to show for these homeric sacrifices; and indeed, with Barcelona continuously in French hands and the juntas on the run from one small town or village to another, no clear statement of aims emerged—except to continue the struggle indefinitely. So, after the abandonment of Catalonia by the generals in 1811, the embittered *Junta Superior* declared that 'The Catalan people is legion; its hate for tyranny is unshaken . . .' and 'The courage of a free people which fights to retain its liberty and independence will always triumph over armies that despise them. . . .'

Certainly the *sometents* and others who fought in Catalonia were poles apart in their ideas from the liberals of the Cadiz Cortes, brought up in the school of Montesquieu, Voltaire and Rousseau, who from their ivory tower in the Isla de León, declared the famous Constitution of 1812. Its central proposition was that sovereign power lay ultimately with the people and it provided for sweeping land reforms and curtailment of the privileges of the Crown, the Church and the aristocrats; but what has aroused the trenchant criticism of Catalan historians is that these reforms were to be accompanied by the centralization of government and, in particular, the division of the historic Principality of Catalonia into the provinces of Lérida, Barcelona, Gerona and Tarragona.

Ferran Soldevila sees in the Constitution 'the beginning of the disequilibrium which characterizes the history, not only of Catalonia, but also of Spain as a whole, during the nineteenth and part of the present century', and stigmatizes the Cadiz Cortes for taking 'yet another and most important step along the path of centralism and uniformity (the same legal codes, the same provincial organization, the same educational system etc.), to the point that the Cortes take their place as one of the series of great landmarks along that road: Casp, the marriage of Ferdinand and Isabel, and the victory of Philip V.'

If this is a point of view coloured by a deeply-held sense of Catalan nationalism and does less than justice to the other provisions of

the Constitution, the proposals of the Cadiz Cortes occasioned a
split between 'liberals' and 'absolutists', which was to be the great
divide of Spanish politics for the next half-century.

On his return from exile in France, Ferdinand VII was met at the
frontier by the Captain General of Catalonia, General Copóns, who
at once submitted to him a request from the ruling Regency that he
should proceed direct to Madrid so as to take an oath to abide by
the Constitution. He contented himself with the declaration that
'Thanks to God, I am in Spain: it is a miracle from heaven', and
made his way to Saragossa and Valencia, meanwhile sounding popular opinion on the subject of his restoration.

In Valencia he received a triumphant welcome from sixty-nine
'serviles' or dissident right-wing deputies of the 'apostolic' party,
who petitioned him to reject the Constitution and to return to traditional forms of government. At this point General Elio, a confirmed
conservative, who, like most of the generals, considered that they
alone had won the war and were entitled to impose their authority,
offered the king the support of his second Army. Ferdinand forthwith repudiated the Constitution, and a week later General Eguía,
with a division of Elio's army, entered Madrid, dissolved the Cortes
and proceeded to the arrest and imprisonment of as many of the
ministers and liberal deputies as he could hunt down. This was the
curtain-raiser to the persecution of liberals up and down the country;
and the simultaneous refusal to make concessions to the Spanish
colonists led to final rupture with most of the possessions in Latin
America and dealt a crushing blow to the economy.

In Catalonia, opinion was divided. The populous coastal area and
large towns, particularly Barcelona, were liberal, while the mountainous northern district was a stronghold of the absolutists. Many
liberals fled abroad and found exile in London and Paris; others, like
General Luis de Lacy and Milans del Bosch, a hero of the resistance
movement during the Peninsular War, took to the field again with
their guerrillas. The rebellion was unsuccessful: Milans del Bosch
escaped into France, but de Lacy was caught, transferred to Majorca
for fear of a popular uprising, and summarily shot. Elsewhere in
Spain the royalists were unable to contain the renewed upsurge of
liberal ideas, and in 1820 an army destined for South America re-
belled, and its revolutionary leader, Rafael de Riego, marched in
triumph to Madrid. Ferdinand was thereupon compelled to swear
allegiance to the Constitution, which he had so long withheld.

The new situation—the so-called 'liberal triennium'—which saw new links established between liberals in Barcelona and their counterparts abroad, especially in Italy, lasted for only three years. In October 1822, the plenipotentiaries of Russia, Prussia, Austria and France decided that liberalism had gone too far in Spain; and in spite of British disapproval, a French army once again crossed the Pyrenees. Catalonia was the only part of Spain to put up a stiff resistance. Although the absolutists, based on Seu de Urgell, collaborated with the invaders, an army under general Espoz y Mina, the famous guerrilla leader of the Napoleonic war, contested every town and village, but was eventually compelled to surrender in November 1823, when Barcelona fell after a four-month siege.

While the French remained in occupation of the city repressive measures were kept within bounds, but with their withdrawal and the appointment in 1827 of a French adventurer, Charles d'Espagnac, as Captain General of Catalonia, Barcelona was subjected to a reign of terror. Its citizens were imprisoned, transported or shot, senselessly and without trial. Rather than undergo torture or asphyxiation in sealed chambers, many committed suicide; and matters reached such a pitch that influential Catalans in Madrid began petitioning the king for d'Espagnac's removal. Two circumstances led to his final downfall: Ferdinand's marriage in 1829 to his fourth wife, María Cristina of Naples, and the *coup d'état* of 1830 in France, resulting in the replacement of the authoritarian Charles X by the more liberal Louis Philippe. Profiting by the severe illness of her husband, from which it seemed unlikely that he would recover, the Queen arranged for d'Espagnac's dismissal in November 1832. Only the intervention of the troops saved him from the fury of the Catalans and he later paid for his crimes when he was murdered in 1839 during the first Carlist War.

Before his death in September 1833, Ferdinand had remarked that 'Spain is a bottle of beer and I am the cork. Without me it would all go off in froth.' He was speedily proved right; civil war broke out only a few days after his funeral.

Liberals and absolutists had been wrangling over the succession since Ferdinand's rejection of the Salic law, introduced in 1713 by Philip V, which provided that a woman might never succeed to the throne of Spain. In 1789 the law was repealed by the Cortes at the instigation of Charles IV, but the decision was not made public until forty years later, shortly after Ferdinand married María Cristina. If she had borne a son there could have been no argument about the succession; but both of her children were girls. In the circumstances Ferdinand's brother, Don Carlos, maintained that the so-called Pragmatic Sanction of 1789, agreed a year after his own birth in 1788, was invalid and had long since lapsed for want of its being promulgated at the time. He therefore refused to recognize the Infanta Isabella as the heir to the throne and was banished to Portugal.

It was perhaps the Duke of Wellington who framed the most trenchant epitaph to Ferdinand VII: 'To bequeath a civil war to one's country! One may love a woman very well, but one should not quite incur a civil war for her sake . . . The fact is that when an old man falls in love with a young woman there is no saying what may be the consequences.' They were indeed drastic, since the Carlist Wars, which broke out again in 1847 and 1872, were much more than a dynastic struggle. Don Carlos was a devout and convinced Catholic, who fiercely resented the erosion of the Church's political influence and the waning powers of the Inquisition. The Carlists gained their main support from the Basques and from the absolutists in Catalonia, whose primary object was to maintain their own institutions against encroachment from Madrid. At the hour of his greatest triumph in 1837, when his army threatened Madrid, Don Carlos was nevertheless careful to promise no more to the Catalans than a revival of industry in the region and refrained from any reference to the re-establishment of their *fueros*.

Both sides were deeply divided. The liberals, from whom María Cristina drew her support, were split between the 'moderates', a mildly conservative centre party comprising most of the professional classes, the landowners and bureaucrats, and the more extreme '*exaltados*' or 'progressives', headed by General Baldamero Espartero.

At the time of Ferdinand VII, Barcelona and the coastal area were overwhelmingly liberal, and a *Junta auxiliar consultativa* formed in Barcelona addressed a memorial to the Queen, pledging its support and proclaiming the city 'the most stalwart bulwark of Spanish liberties', but at the same time demanding a programme of reforms, subsequently approved by the prime minister, Alvarez Mendizábal.

The war was fought with the utmost ferocity, especially after the death of Don Carlos's supremo, General Zumalcárregui, in 1835, when, after the brief reappearance of the notorious Charles d'Espagnac, the Catalan-born General Cabrera took over command of the Carlist forces in Catalonia and Aragon. These brutalities came to a head when Cabrera's own mother, Maria Grinyó, was shot by

9. General Ramón Cabrera y Griño, commander of the Carlist forces in Catalonia.

a firing squad in reprisal for the shootings by the Carlists of the mayors of Valdegorfa and Torrecillas. Cabrera promptly retorted with the execution of three woman hostages. One of his greatest successes was the capture of the government-held fortress of Morella at the centre of the mountainous Maestrazgo, lying back from the Mediterranean to the north-east of Valencia and Castellón de la Plana.

On the night of 25 January 1838, a small party of Carlist volunteers scaled the precipitous rock rearing up from the centre of the

F*

town and, by removing the seat of an overhanging privy, penetrated the castle precinct. Their shouts of 'Viva Cabrera ! Viva Carlos V !' panicked the garrison and governor into surrender. Thereafter, Cabrera's black flag, with its white skull and crossbones, floated above the fortress, which became the Carlist headquarters in Spain, until its recapture by General Espartero in May 1840 brought the war to an end.

The war between absolutism and liberalism had ended in victory for the liberals; but Queen María Cristina herself did not long survive the success of her troops. The liberals were deeply divided between progressives, headed by the triumphant Espartero, and the moderates under General Narváez. The Queen, who favoured the moderates, came to Barcelona for discussions with Espartero, but was unable to reach agreement and shortly afterwards relinquished the Regency to him.

In Barcelona, now the economic hub of Spain, the bourgeoisie were soon in arms against Espartero and his progressive government over his support of the workers; and in 1842 the city was bombarded by government troops. Although the war between absolutists and liberals was to break out on two further occasions during the nineteenth century, in the Principality politics were henceforth to be dominated by two main issues: the struggle of the manual workers for better conditions and the right of association, and the campaign for regional autonomy mounted by the bourgeoisie and the middle classes.

XIII

War in the Streets

At the beginning of the eighteenth century some 40 per cent of Spaniards lived in the coastal areas of the country as against 60 per cent in the interior. By 1760 the balance had radically changed: the large central area, including the two Castiles, now accounted for only 49 per cent of the population and the periphery for 51 per cent. The most populous of the coastal regions was Catalonia; and although the birth-rate in the Principality fell off during the nineteenth century, this was more than offset by a mass immigration of agricultural workers from Andalusia to work in its textile mills. It is therefore hardly surprising that Catalans should have increasingly demanded more 'say' in the ordering of the country's affairs and those of Catalonia in particular.

From the outset, a distinction must be made between the aims of the bourgeoisie and factory owners and those of the manual workers. At times, when the prosperity of the region was affected, they coincided. Thus, when the American empire was lost during the early decades of the nineteenth century and markets were largely made good by the sale of manufactured products to the rest of Spain, both sides were united in a demand for protective tariffs. And, although it was the bourgeoisie which was most pressing in its demands for regional autonomy, it was prepared to lay aside its principles when the economy was at stake. When Cuba, long regarded as a preserve for Catalan mercantile enterprise, demanded a similar autonomy and the Spanish Cortes was disposed to grant it, the Catalan bourgeoisie bitterly contested the measure; yet on the entry of the United States into the subsequent war for independence, the Catalanist Union demanded peace:

> Upon feeling the first cold shivers of a general collapse, the instinct of self-preservation prompts every soul to utter the same cry: 'Let us save Catalonia!'; for the Catalans have not put forth a century of heroic efforts to create an advanced civilization in this part of Spain in order to be flung, in a moment of intoxication,

on to the altar of an unrealistic phantasy, which is that national honour must be satisfied with bloodshed in battle.

The attitude of the bourgeoisie towards the factory workers was no less ambivalent. While claiming more freedom for itself in the shape of an autonomous Catalonia, it was resolutely opposed to the social betterment of its workers in the form of higher wages or the recognition of trade unions. An extreme statement of this attitude was that of the *Comissió de Fàbriques* in 1835, which in denying the right of workers to associate for their mutual benefit, argued cynically that: 'Since the operative is free to leave the factory as and when it suits him, so the owner may dispense with his services when convenient.'

If there had been a willingness for concessions on the part of the bourgeoisie it would no doubt have led to a healthier home market and a sense of community, which could only have promoted the cause of autonomy. As it was, a lack of capital for the development of industry during the period of moderate government from 1844–68 and its control by a small number of family firms led to stubborn opposition to any attempts to improve wages and working conditions—on the grounds that Catalonia could face foreign competition only if prices were kept low. For all the sound and fury on the subject of autonomy, it therefore took second place to more immediate commercial issues; and at times of crisis the bourgeoisie habitually fell back on the forces of law and order wielded by the central government in Madrid.

The labour movement took definite shape in 1830 with the organization of trade unions (*sociedades de resistencia al capital*) by the textile workers in Barcelona. There had been strikes as early as 1823 and 1827, but in 1835 a conflict between the unskilled workers (or *miserables*), and better-trained artisans who sided with the militia and employers, led to the burning of churches and of some modern factories. In 1838 a Liberal government reluctantly recognized the right of assembly for purposes of mutual aid, which was to lead to the formation of the co-operatives, workers' athenaeums, choruses and cultural centres, so typical of the labour tradition in Catalonia, in an attempt to combat drinking and gambling (many workers were previously paid off in company-owned taverns).

The situation was given a new twist by the installation of automatic machinery (*selfactines*) during the mid-1850s. Fearing the loss of their jobs, the workers, like the Luddites in England before them,

resorted to rioting and the burning of factories. The authorities reacted with savage reprisals: the police arrested the leaders of the
Central Junta of the Working Class, formed to oppose the installation of the *selfactines*, and its chairman was summarily shot. A
decree of 1855, ordering the dissolution of the labour unions and
giving control of the mutual aid societies to the military, occasioned
a general strike in Barcelona from 2 to 11 July, the first of its kind
in Spain and a curtain-raiser to the perennial labour troubles and
terrorism for which Barcelona was to become a byword. From its
inception the Catalan labour movement was Anarchist-inspired—
the natural result of a political system in which the right to vote
was linked with the payment of property tax. Since the workers were
denied political expression, their object was to force the government
and their employers to grant better wages and working conditions by
direct action. In this, Catalonia was typical of countries with a semi-
feudal land system, in which the labour force for new industries was
largely recruited from peasants who had immigrated to the cities,
and it inevitably became a hotbed for the ideas of Proudhon and his
Russian disciple, Bakunin.

On the break-up of the First International in 1874 after the split
between Bakunin and Marx (who believed that the remedy lay in
more and better socialist government, rather than in individual
action), the Catalan Unions remained predominantly Anarchist. This
was later to result in a polarization between the Socialist UGT
(*Unión general de trabajadores*) in Madrid and the industrial areas
of the Basque country, and the Anarchist CNT (*Confederación
nacional de trabajo*) in Catalonia. It is ironical that the term Syndical-
ism, denoting the action of workers to obtain immediate satisfaction
of their demands (without necessarily resorting to violence), should
have been taken over by the Franquist regime to describe its gov-
ernment-controlled unions. This was, of course, because of the
apolitical connotation of the word and the consistent refusal of
Anarchists and Syndicalists to become involved in government (and
so to dissociate themselves from bourgeois demands for regional
autonomy).

In June 1870 a branch of the First International, FORE (*Federación de obreros de la región de España*) was set up in Barcelona and
affirmed the Anarchist views of Bakunin. Although it was promptly
outlawed, it proved impossible to check the march of unionism. An
extension of the franchise in 1890, which removed the limitation
on voting to taxpayers, did little to placate the workers, disillusioned

by political manoeuvring. Their prime concern was the positive betterment of working conditions; and during the latter decades of the nineteenth century, social struggles grew increasingly violent.

There were attacks, many of them perpetrated by Catalan Anarchists in revenge for repressive measures or the execution of their comrades, on King Alfonso XII and his successor, Alfonso XIII; on property owners and employers; and on leaders of the Church and government. Two prime ministers, Antonio Cánovas and Eduardo Dato, were assassinated, as was Cardinal Soldevila of Saragossa. On 7 December 1893, a bomb was thrown into that rallying ground of the socially *arrivés* in Barcelona, the Teatre de Liceu, causing several deaths. In the aftermath, there were hundreds of arrests and five Anarchists were tortured and executed. Another bomb, tossed into the Corpus Christi procession in June 1896, caused a further six deaths and was followed by widespread arrests, further torturings and executions at Montjuic Castle, and a law against terrorism. This was used as a pretext for arresting union leaders in no way concerned with the attacks; but instead of breaking the unions, as employers had hoped, it simply swelled the ranks of the Anarchists, while the workers, for whom conditions had not materially changed over the past century, were still further estranged from their employers.

1909 saw an unprecedented outbreak of violence, which has gone down in the annals of Barcelona as the 'Tragic Week'. In July of that year, in the wake of a defeat in the unpopular colonial war in Morocco, the Government attempted to mobilize the reservists. It was well known that the better-to-do were able to dodge the draft by payments to the state; a strike committee was formed; and on 25 July the workers took to the streets and left churches and convents smoking from one end of the city to the other. The uprising was put down by government troops at the cost of eighty-three lives; and Fransesc Ferrer, director of an Anarchist school, was executed, together with four other workers, in the face of international protest. The prime minister, Antonio Maura, who had ordered the repressive measures at the behest of the autonomist Lliga Regionalist (see page 180 was thereafter forced to resign.

What was to become the central organization of Spanish Anarchosyndicalism, the CNT, was first formed in 1911. Dissolved by the government shortly afterwards, it won formal recognition in 1914, and by 1917 was by far the largest union in the country, with 714,000 members. Although it numbered a minority favouring the establishment of workers' co-operatives by terrorist methods, its

10. Workers during the Barcelona strike of 1903, from *Cu-Cut*!

leadership was dedicated to the improvement of living conditions, but without direct participation in politics or the recovery of separate nationality for Catalonia. So, Salvador Seguí, Secretary General of the Catalan CNT (whose murder led to the subsequent assassinations of Eduardo Dato and Cardinal Soldevila), defined its position in 1919:

> We are, and we shall be, opposed to those gentlemen who claim a monopoly of Catalan politics, not so as to achieve the freedom of Catalonia, but to defend better their class interests. And I assure you that these reactionaries, who call themselves Catalanists, fear nothing so much as the rising up of a Catalonia that is not subject to them.

The methods used in dealing with the militants only encouraged the spread of Anarchosyndicalist ideas. The law permitted their detention for a fortnight without trial; they frequently spent their term in jail in making converts; and the system of *conducción ordinaria*, whereby a suspect was marched on foot between mounted members of the *Guardia Civil* from one place to another aroused sympathy for the movement up and down the country.

During the economic boom of the First World War, when Barcelona was supplying both belligerents, social struggle intensified. Groups of employers organized bands of gunmen under a German freebooter, the Baron von Koenig, and revived the *sometén*, so as to break strikes, of which the most important against the foreign-owned *La Canadiense*, (the Barcelona Traction, Power and Light Company), lasted for two months and led to a thirteen-day general strike throughout Catalonia. There was an unsuccessful attempt to reactivate the moribund 'free' or 'yellow' unions organized by the Catholic Church (which had shown itself singularly uninterested in the plight of the workers). Naturally the unions retaliated; and from January 1919 to October 1920 there were some 300 assaults, either by armed unionists on the owners or authorities, or by *vigilantes* on workers and union leaders.

This war in the streets flared up sporadically during the turbulent years leading up to the outbreak of civil war in 1936. The period also saw the increasing involvement of the CNT in the political issues of republicanism and federalism (see pages 182 to 183) and the formation of rival Socialist and Communist unions, as the result of developments in Russia and abroad. However, the CNT was still overwhelmingly the most powerful union in Catalonia when the war began. According to official figures for the country as a whole, the CNT numbered 1,577,000 members in 1936; the Socialists, strongest in Madrid and the Basque country, 1,447,000; the Communists, 133,000; and right-wing organizations, 549,000.

Like the manual workers, the Catalan manufacturers formed bodies to further their own interests, principally to obtain protective tariffs and to combat the demands of their employees. The first was the Industrial Institute of Catalonia founded in 1848, followed by the *Fomento del trabajo nacional* in 1879. The nineteenth century saw steady expansion, especially in the textile industry, which received a great boost in supplying uniforms during the Crimean War. It nevertheless remained in the hands of family concerns, the so-called 'thirty families' of industry and suffered from lack of capitalization. Attempts to establish heavy industry in the form of steel-making failed for lack of accessible mineral deposits, and the initiative passed to Bilbao and the Basque provinces; again, many of the most significant developments, such as the railroads, the telephone system and *La Canadiense*, were financed by foreign investment.

Nevertheless, Catalonia was the most powerful economic force in Spain at the beginning of the twentieth century, and 42 per cent of all foreign imports reached Spain by way of Catalan ports. There was a sense of euphoria among the bourgeoisie and middle classes, who sent their children to study in Paris and London, changed the face of Barcelona during 1870–1900 by pulling down the mediaeval walls and opening up tree-lined *boulevardes* in Parisian style, and for whom the patent of urban aristocracy was the ownership of a box at the opera house, the Teatre Principal (hence a natural target for Anarchist violence). Catalan prosperity was symbolized by the great international exhibition of 1888, attended by some 400,000 visitors, some of whom were accommodated in a ship fitted out as a floating hotel.

The First World War brought huge profits to the textile industry (about 600 million pesetas over and above its normal income), but its organization was still on a small scale, and contracts were met only by pressing into use antique hand-looms; it is of relevance that in 1925 the average firm operated only 5,000 spindles as against 40,000 in the rest of Western Europe. Unlike the Basques, who also reaped large profits from the War and seized the opportunity to develop banks, now among the strongest in Spain, the Catalan business community failed to invest at home. From this period dates a relative decline in the paramount importance of Barcelona as a centre of commerce—a tendency which was accentuated during the Franquist era by the siting of new industries elsewhere in Spain, partly, one suspects, so as to counter pressure for Catalan autonomy, based on considerations of population and industrial preponderance.

This demand for autonomy, first in the form of regionalism and later in demands for a federal state, became a major preoccupation of an ebullient bourgeoisie and middle class from the last decades of the nineteenth century onwards. In their darkest days Catalans had never lost sight of their identity as a people apart; but since the coming of the Bourbons, the Catalan language, although spoken colloquially, had not been taught in schools or used officially, nor was it considered a suitable medium for literature. The significance of the so-called *Renaixença* was that by reviving pride in Catalan achievement during the Middle Ages and more particularly in the language itself, it stimulated attempts to obtain a political structure appropriate to an individual national entity.

An important preliminary stage was the publication in 1815 of *La Gramàtica i apologia de la llengua catalana* by Josep Pau Ballot, an elderly priest and professor of rhetoric, which was at once a dictionary and eulogy of the language. The importance of his book, incomplete as it was philologically, is often overlooked; and the *Renaixença* is generally held to date from the publication in 1833 of the poem *La pàtria* by Bonaventura Carles Aribau. Curiously enough, it was composed simply as one of various birthday tributes, in several languages, to the Madrid banker, Gaspar de Remisa; but it was the first poem of any importance to have been written in Catalan for almost three centuries, and its nostalgic feeling for country and language caused other poets, including Joaquim Rubió i Ors, to follow Aribau's example. The reinstatement of the *Jocs florals* (see page 99) in 1859 stimulated other major writers, among them the poet Jacint Verdaguer (1845–1902), the novelist Narcís Oller (1845–1930) and the dramatist Àngel Guimerà (1845–1924) to use their native language, which henceforth became recognized outside Spain as a legitimate and expressive literary vehicle.

The importance of language as an assertion of national individuality cannot be overstressed—witness the similar revival of Welsh or Basque; and it was only logical that Catalans should later use it on historical and political levels. Catalanism, as the movement towards political identity became known, found early and conservative expression in a book, *La tradició catalana*, by the Bishop of Vich, Josep Torras i Bages, published in 1892. However, his dictum that 'Catalonia will be Christian or it will not be at all' found no echo in anti-clerical circles; and a more influential spokesman for the middle classes was Valentí Almirall, a disciple of Fransesc Pi i Margall, who had been a president of the First Republic during its brief existence from February 1873 to January 1874. Between 1879 and 1881 Almirall published the first modern newspaper in Catalan, *Diari Català*, and in 1882 founded the *Centre Català*, the first of various Catalanist associations, which banded together as the *Unió Catalanista* and in 1892 put forward a programme for Catalan autonomy, at the

11. Insignia of the Unió catalanista, one of the first organizations to promote Catalan autonomy.

same time proposing that the central government should be left in control of matters such as foreign policy, defence, postal services and relations with the Church.

It was in the face of the economic, social and political disruption following on the loss of Cuba and the war with the United States in 1898 that the *Lliga regionalista* (Regionalist League) was founded in April 1901. Its position and the opposition which it raised in Madrid have been well put by Jaime Vicens Vives in his *Approaches to the History of Spain* (University of California Press, 1967):

> Fundamentally the dispute involved not only the possibility of accepting the indigenous and authentic culture of Catalonia as one mode of the Hispanic essence, but also the possibility of providing the state with an efficient and modern structure whose leaders, instead of playing politics, would seek solutions for the country's most urgent and dramatic problems. In order to present both tendencies in the best possible light, Catalan nationalists asked for an autonomous regime. Their proposal was encumbered by its own antiquated concepts and by the fear that it would lead either to the break-up of the Spanish state that had emerged at the Renaissance, or else to the decline of Castile's historic mission as the national entity that had founded that state.

In seeking regional autonomy the Lliga was not separatist in its aims, as emerges very clearly from the statement of Prat de la Riba (1870–1917), who both became leader of the Lliga and edited its daily newspaper, *La veu de Catalunya* (*The Voice of Catalonia*), that 'Catalan nationalism has never been separatist, it has always favoured the fraternal unity of the Iberian nationalities within a federative organization'.

Although Prat was the theoretician of the movement and his book, *La nacionalitat catalana*, had great posthumous influence, he was not a good speaker and his views on social matters were retrograde; and the political activities of the Lliga were directed by the more daring and reformist Fransesc Cambó. It was nevertheless scathingly described by Almirall as wanting to 'make Catalonia an instrument of reaction against every modern expansive idea, on the political as well as on the moral and religious level'—a criticism which was to become increasingly true as, over the years, the Lliga grew to be the embodiment of bourgeois conservatism.

The Lliga nevertheless succeeded in bringing the issue of Catalanism to the forefront of Spanish politics, when in 1906 it formed an alliance with the Republicans, Socialists, the Catalan left and the Carlists—the so-called *Solidaritat Catalana*. By gaining forty-one out of the forty-four Catalan seats in the 1907 elections for the Spanish Cortes, the *Solidaritat* won a resounding victory for the cause of autonomy. Although the coalition achieved none of its immediate aims and lasted no more than a year, it brought home to politicians in Madrid the possibility of Republicans and Catalanists making common front. A formula was therefore found, which, without introducing radical social reform—feared as much by the Catalan bourgeoisie as the royalist ministers in Madrid—went some way to meeting the demands of the Catalanists.

It was proposed that the *diputaciones*, responsible for local administration, should combine on a regional basis as *mancomunidades* to take over the functions of the separate *diputaciones*. Even this very limited measure was vetoed by the Senate; but in December 1913 the conservative prime minister, Eduardo Dato, implemented it by the back door, authorizing the *mancomunidades* by administrative decree rather than by obtaining parliamentary approval.

The *Mancomunitat* of Catalonia was inaugurated in 1914 in the former palace of the *Generalitat* in Barcelona under the presidency of Prat de la Riba. He had hoped that other regions with aspirations to autonomy, such as the Basque provinces and Galicia, would form their own *mancomunidades* as a stepping stone to a federal Spain; but this was not to be.

Although its functions were purely administrative and it had access only to local taxes, the *Mancomunitat* was able to borrow substantial funds and at once set to work to improve roads, railways, telephones and other services neglected by the central government. Its most impressive achievement was in the field of education: new schools were built with facilities for teaching in Catalan as well as Castilian and support was given to the universities and the Institute for Catalan Studies as also to a wide range of specialized institutions concerned with industry, science and medicine. The *Mancomunitat* was unable to make progress in the broader political sphere or to advance the cause of regionalism, since it was essentially bourgeois in character and lacked support from the workers and middle class.

By 1917 the monarchy was passing through a crisis as a result of social discontent and the debilitating colonial war in Morocco. There was unrest in the army, a general strike throughout Spain in August, and agitation for a new Cortes with powers to alter the constitution and to move towards regional autonomy. Matters were papered over, and a number of radical and republican groups were formed in Catalonia, among them *Estat catalá, Acció catalá*, the Republican Catalan Party, the Socialist Union of Catalonia and the Union of Rabassaires—a militant peasant organization formed to combat the ancient institution of the *Rabassa Morta*, which limited the cultivators' tenure of the vineyards to the life of the vines. At the same time, there was a tendency for the unions—even the CNT— to become more directly involved in the political struggle.

Street fighting, strikes and assassinations had brought the country to a state of near-anarchy; and matters reached a head when King Alfonso XIII was arraigned by a committee of the Cortes for responsibility for the military disaster at Anual in Morocco. Without waiting to stand trial, Alfonso decided to resort to a military dictatorship: that this 'solution' should have succeeded was because the Catalan bourgeoisie, little as it respected the king, was equally apprehensive in the face of mass demonstrations.

There had been street fighting in Barcelona on 11 September 1923; and on the following day the Captain General of Catalonia, Miguel Primo de Rivera, made contact with the Lliga, promising a greater measure of autonomy and an end to labour disturbances. The general's troops then proceeded to occupy key positions in Barcelona, and despite protests from the government, which shortly resigned, the king ordered Primo de Rivera to form a Military Directory.

Although the new dictator had proclaimed that 'Catalonia has nothing to fear from our coming to power', repressive measures followed thick and fast: the use of the national flag and of Catalan in official documents were forbidden; newspapers were banned; cultural societies were disbanded; and a year and a half later the *Mancomunitat* was suppressed. To placate the bourgeoisie harsh measures were taken against the labour unions, and the CNT was dissolved. Some of the left-wing leaders, notably Francesc Maciá, who was to organize a small military expedition into Catalonia from France, went into exile.

Among the moderates, protest was cultural rather than political: many more books were printed in Catalan, a win by the Barcelona Football Club or success in a foreign musical festival were hailed as national triumphs, and even the dancing of the *sardana* became a gesture of defiance. At the same time, the militants of the CNT who still remained in the country formed the activist FAI (*Federación anarquista ibérica*), which on occasion resorted to terrorism, as did the more extreme Catalanists. In 1924 the Bandera Negra ('Black Flag'), a cell of *Estat catalá*, attempted to blow up a train on which King Alfonso was travelling to Barcelona.

The dictatorship was not without its successes—at least it ended the war in Morocco and restored relative calm to the streets; and anything was preferable to the corruption of the old order, presided over by the *caciques*, or party bosses. Nevertheless, by January 1930, during the general depression in Europe, there was a general feeling of disillusionment, even among the bourgeoisie, who had seen a steep fall in the value of the peseta. Deserted by the army, Primo de Rivera was dismissed by the king and two months later died in a Paris hotel.

The fifteen months following the fall of the dictatorship saw an effervescence of republicanism throughout Spain and the appearance in Catalonia of a small, but active Communist group. Meanwhile, a Revolutionary Committee was formed in San Sebastián by a group of senior Republican politicians and declared itself in favour of recognizing Catalan autonomy. Although the CNT did not take part in the proceedings, it departed so far from its apolitical position as to instruct its members to vote for the Republicans in the event of elections. Jumping the gun, two captains of the garrison at Jaca incited their troops to mutiny in December 1930; they were captured and shot, but the tide was flowing fast, and the eminent intellectual, Don José Ortega y Gasset, wrote a famous article, proclaiming: 'Spaniards! Your state is no more! Reconstitute it! *¡Delenda est monarquía!*'

At this juncture the king found it impossible to refuse a demand for municipal elections, which were announced for 12 April 1931. In Catalonia, the political hero of the hour was Fransesc Maciá, who had gained stature as the result of his expulsion from Barcelona on his attempted return from exile in September 1930. With his white hair, luminous eyes and aristocratic bearing (he was a landowner and devout Catholic) he became known as l'Aví (the grandfather). Maciá returned again, this time unhindered, and at once began to organize the Catalanists of the left as the *Esquerra republicana de Catalunya* (Catalan Republican Left) in preparation for the elections.

The result was a body blow for the more staid and conservative Lliga and *Acció catalá*, the Esquerra receiving an unprecedented 47 per cent of the votes in Barcelona and the Republicans, with solid working-class support, winning throughout Catalonia. In the country as a whole, the Republicans secured a huge majority in the larger cities and provincial capitals—in some places, such as Eibar in the Basque provinces, a Republic was proclaimed forthwith; and the king, having issued a dignified statement, in which he said that he was aware of losing the love of his people and was unwilling to be the cause of a civil war, left Madrid for exile.

XIV

The Republic

Two days after the elections, on 14 April 1931, Fransesc Maciá made his appearance on the balcony of the historic building of the *Generalitat* and read out a proclamation to the crowd which had jammed the Plaça de Sant Jaume, declaring a Catalan Republic. It was to be 'an integral part of the Iberian Federation' and he further announced that he was to act as its first president.

Republican flags appeared in the streets as if by magic; and even the soldiery, released from their barracks, joined a jubilant crowd in singing the 'Marseillaise'. Five weeks later an assembly was elected to draft a statute giving shape to Catalan autonomy, which was the subject of a referendum held in August 1931. 562,691 votes were cast in favour and 3,276 against. There were 1,105 spoiled papers and 195,501 abstentions, no doubt including many of the supporters of the Lliga, which had refused to take part in the Assembly.

Maciá now embarked on a triumphal progress to Madrid to present the draft to the newly elected Cortes. Madrid had in fact declared for a republic only hours after Barcelona, but with the significant difference that it was not to be federal, but, as stated in the preamble of the draft Constitution, 'a democratic republic of workers of all classes, organized in a regime of liberty and justice'. The Constitution also incorporated some highly controversial anti-clerical clauses, providing for the suspension of payments by the state to priests after a period of two years and the dissolution of religious orders judged to be dangerous (this was clearly framed against the Jesuits). These and the Catalan Statute provoked heated opposition, and all the old arguments for and against once again broke surface—for example, that it would destroy national unity and, on the other side, that Spain was taking too much in taxes from Catalonia and giving little in return. After five months of recrimination the Constitution was approved and promulgated in December 1931.

In deference to feelings in Madrid, Maciá had already agreed that the new entity should be called the Government of the *Generalitat* rather than the Catalan Republic, as originally proposed, and as it finally emerged the Statute was much watered down.

Instead of reserving to the Catalan State all matters except defence, foreign affairs, customs and relations with the Church, the measure approved by the Cortes listed the functions to be exercised by the revived *Generalitat*. Most of these, apart from responsibility for public order, were secondary; and Catalonia was to be entitled only to a proportion of the taxes sufficient to pay for the services administered by the *Generalitat*. What particularly angered the Catalans was the Socialists' veto on Catalonia's right to legislate on social matters—clearly enough dictated by a desire to extend their own influence at the expense of the CNT. Article 13 further forbade the federating of different autonomous regions, so as to forestall a possible union of Catalonia, Valencia and Majorca and the emergence of an entity resembling the former Crown of Aragon.

For all its limitations, the Statute left the *Generalitat* with widespread powers. One of the results was to counter the Castilianization of the bureaucracy in services now run by the *Generalitat*, although most of the existing officials, given the choice of transferring, remained at their posts. Control of the police as also of the administration of civil justice passed to the *Generalitat*; and although education remained in the hands of the Spanish state, it was agreed that the University of Barcelona should become autonomous and that teaching might be either in Castilian or Catalan. In fact, 80 per cent of the students and staff opted for classes in Catalan. It was in the spheres of culture and local government that there were the most marked signs of revival: all over the province there was a new spirit of co-operation abroad, and this was reflected in a marked absence of the riots and anti-clerical demonstrations so prevalent in the rest of Spain at the time.

The Esquerra received a massive vote of confidence when elections for a Catalan parliament were held in November 1932, receiving almost twice as many votes as the rival Lliga. Under the presidency of Lluis Companys the Corts met in December after a lapse of more than two centuries; its first task was to draft a constitution making the *Generalitat* a limited presidential regime and delegating executive powers to its First Councillor—at that time, Fransesc Maciá, leader of the victorious Esquerra.

Maciá, who had in the first place demanded outright nationalism for Catalonia, wisely moderated and broadened his programme to include social measures and won support across the board. Only the large landowners and industrialists, at one extreme, and the CNT at the other held aloof. The wealthy, most of whom had a stake in the land, were apprehensive about agrarian reform, while the CNT, which had at first supported the Esquerra, found itself progressively excluded from governmental decisions.

This conflict arose because the *Generalitat* found itself obliged to enforce legislation promulgated by the Spanish Ministry of Labour, controlled by the CNT's main rival, the Socialist UGT. As a result, measures inappropriate to the labour situation in Catalonia were passed, and the moderate leaders of the CNT were supplanted by extremists of the FAI (see page 182). A splinter group was formed by thirty of the moderates (the so-called *treintistas*) who favoured Syndicalist ideas and indirect participation in government as a pressure group; but in the upshot a great mass of the working population was alienated from Catalanism, even as represented by the radical Esquerra. A further unfortunate repercussion was the formation by the more narrowly nationalistic elements of the Esquerra of the *escamots*, urban shock groups, devoted to a rigid maintenance of 'public order' amounting to systematic persecution of the blue-collar workers of the CNT.

Fransesc Maciá died on Christmas Day, 1933, and was succeeded as President of the *Generalitat* by Lluis Companys, to the left of Maciá politically, a former lawyer for the CNT and founder of the Union of Rabassaires. At this same juncture it happened that the Catalan parliament was debating a bill on farm leases, framed to liberalize the contracts of the *Rabassa Morta* (see page 182). The Lliga withdrew from the Corts in protest and, when the bill was passed in April 1934, induced the Madrid government to lodge an appeal with the Tribunal of Constitutional Guarantees. Companys refused to accept the Tribunal's decision that the law was unconstitutional, and the Corts forthwith voted in favour of an exact duplicate.

In the face of popular demonstrations in the Principality and the walk-out of all the Catalan deputies (except those of the Lliga) from the Spanish Cortes, the prime minister, Ricardo Samper, began urgent negotiations with the *Generalitat*, but far from finding a way out of the impasse, he only succeeded in antagonizing the right wing deputies of the CEDA (*Confederación española de derechas autónomas*), who withdrew their support from his government. A new administration was formed by Alejandro Lerroux, a political opportunist, who in his radical days in Barcelona had admonished his following to 'Enter and sack the decadent civilization of this unhappy country! Destroy its temples, finish off its gods, raise the skirts of its novices and teach them to be mothers! Fight, kill, and die!', but now invited members of the Catholic CEDA to join his cabinet. For the left, the entry of the CEDA into the government represented a first step towards Fascism, while the Republicans denounced it as a monstrous betrayal of the Republic to its enemies.

Reaction was immediate. In Madrid the UGT declared a general strike and Socialist militants attempted to storm the Ministry of the Interior. In the Asturias, the miners had been preparing for the contingency and were in possession of arms and dynamite. A Socialist republic was proclaimed there on 5 October; within a few days the military and civil guards had been overpowered, and for a brief period the province became a revolutionary Soviet. The rebellion was quelled only after Lerroux called General Francisco Franco to the War Office and the Foreign Legion was sent against the miners.

In Catalonia the CNT stood aloof, but a Workers' Alliance called a general strike, and on the night of 6 October, Companys addressed a mass meeting from the Palace of the *Generalitat*:

> Liberal, democratic and republican, Catalonia cannot absent itself from the protest that has swept the country, nor fail in proclaiming its solidarity with our brothers in the Spanish lands engaged in a fight to the death for freedom . . . In this solemn hour, in the name of the people and Parliament, the government over which I preside assumes all the functions of power in Catalonia, proclaims the Catalan State of the Spanish Federal Republic, and when relations with the leaders of this general protest against Facism are established and strengthened, invites them to establish in Catalonia the provisional government of the Republic.

Companys had sought an assurance from Domenec Batet, Captain General of Catalonia, himself a Catalan, that the military would remain neutral; but at dawn next day the artillery began bombarding the Palace of the *Generalitat* and the City Hall. The *escamots* laid down their weapons; they had previously opposed the arming of the members of the Workers' Alliance. By this and their earlier alienation of the CNT, they had incapacitated the only elements capable of serious resistance; and Companys found himself obliged to surrender. The dubious role of the *escamots*, sometimes described as Fascist, has been defended by certain Catalan nationalists, but the facts speak for themselves.

All the members of the *Generalitat* and the Barcelona City Council, apart from the representatives of the Lliga, together with numbers of rabassaires and union militants, were now arrested and dispersed in prisons over Spain. Companys and his colleagues were later sentenced to thirty years' imprisonment. Three of the military in charge of law and order were sentenced to death by court martial, but subsequently reprieved under pressure from Alcalá Zamora, the President of the Republic. Companys had perhaps acted precipitately, but his action is understandable enough in view of the wave of fascism then spreading over Europe.

If the first two and a half years of the Republic were called the 'red biennium' by the rightists, the second were known by the left as the 'black biennium'. The new government now set to work to undo the partial reforms of its predecessor; peasants were driven from the land, union leaders were dismissed, and the jails became crowded with political prisoners. Right-wing deputies pressed for the repeal of the Catalan Statute; and in November 1934 the Cortes compromised by suspending the Catalan Corts and appointing a Captain General to take the place of the president of the *Generalitat*, now dominated by the Lliga.

As the government's five-year term of office drew to an end, the parties of the left in Catalonia began preparing to fight the elections. In May 1935 the extremist FAI started negotiations for the return of the more moderate Syndicalist *treintistas* to the CNT, while the Marxists of the left (but not the Socialists or Stalinists) united as the POUM (*Partido obrero de unificación marxista*). A popular front was now formed by the Esquerra, *Acció catalá*, the Union of Rabassaires, the Socialist Union, POUM, the Catalan Proletarian Party and the Communist Party of Catalonia. Huge portraits of Maciá with the single word 'Catalans!' appeared on the walls, and thanks to the last-minute action of the CNT in advising its members to vote, the front won a resounding victory over its opponents of the Lliga, as did leftists all over the country in the elections of February 1936.

The immediate outcome was the formation of a left-wing Republican government by Manuel Azaña, which forthwith emptied the jails of prisoners, political and otherwise. The immensely popular Lluis Companys returned to Catalonia, where he was welcomed by delirious crowds and at once resumed the presidency of the *Generalitat*. The Catalan parliament now sought and obtained a declaration from the Tribunal of Constitutional Guarantees that its suspension had been illegal and put into effect the farm lease law of 1934 (see page 187) without objection from the Madrid government.

Thanks to the prestige and popularity of Companys, there was little disturbance of law and order in Catalonia, but during the next few months the rest of the country was overwhelmed by a mounting crescendo of violence. Churches were burnt, lands were seized, while strikes, riots, demonstrations and assassinations were legion. It is on record that between 16 February and 15 June 1936, there were 160 burnings of churches; 339 strikes, local or general; 146 bombings and 269 political assassinations.

The fact is that, although the elections had been a triumph for the left in terms of elected deputies, the Popular Front with 4,176,156 votes had won fewer than the combined parties of the right and centre (which included the Carlists and Basque Nationalists) with 4,464,648, and the country was split down the middle. Among the factory workers and under-privileged peasantry there was bitter antagonism to the bourgeoisie and landowners, which exploded in the attacks on churches—the Church had not taken part in the elections one way or the other, but was regarded as the symbol and stronghold of the better-to-do. Not unnaturally the middle classes regarded the indiscipline of the Anarchists and their open demands for the collectivization of industry and appropriation of agricultural land with heart-felt dismay, heightened by the increasing incidence of violence—hence the emergence of paramilitary groups, such as the Falange, founded by José Antonio Primo de Rivera, a son of the former dictator, and dedicated to an authoritarian regime of 'order'.

The problems with which the Republic was faced and not surprisingly failed to solve have been well put by N. Tuñón de Lara in *La España del siglo XX*:

An archaic economy and weighing upon it the agrarian problem and the predominating role of the big banks; a powerful Church whose spiritual power had so often over the centuries mingled with the temporal power; an army which had, during the first thirty years of the twentieth century, drifted towards militarism; regions with marked national characteristics (Catalonia, Euzkadi, Galicia) in need of freedom to develop; intellectual minorities whose knowledge was in sharp contrast to the cultural backwardness of the majority of the population; and an old, rickety State, as anachronistic as the social classes it served, which had to be reconstructed anew to render it effective and, what was more important, to create institutions that would make uninterrupted development towards a democratic life possible.

There is no better example of the gulf between the two sides and the impossibility of bridging it than the revolt of the Asturian miners (page 188). During the initial stages, there was a certain amount of unprovoked violence; some churches and convents were burnt and several priests were killed; a number of middle-class women were raped; and a detachment of civil guards was shot in cold blood. During the reign of terror which followed the miners' surrender, and in violation of the terms agreed with General López Ochoa, the legionaries butchered more than a thousand civilians.

It was clear that sooner or later the army would play its part in the deepening crisis. As early as 1932, General Sanjurjo, who had been witness to an atrocity perpetrated at the village of Castilblanco in the Extremadura, when four civil guards were mutilated and murdered by members of the CNT, had staged a *pronunciamento* in Seville. It was unsuccessful; but the words of his manifesto, 'A passionate demand for justice surges upwards from the bowels of the people, and we are moved to satisfy it . . . Revolution will always be a crime or an act of insanity when Law and Justice exist' echoed the views of many of his colleagues.

One of Azaña's first acts on taking power had been to dismiss Generals Franco and Goded from their positions in the War Ministry because of their involvement in the suppression of the Asturian uprising. It seems that Franco was not involved in a military plot at the time, enemy though he was of the left, but that he called upon the prime minister before his 'banishment' to the Canaries in March 1936 and bluntly warned him of the seriousness of the situation. Thereafter, the conspiracy rapidly took shape under the direction of General Mola, recently transferred from Morocco to become military governor of the Carlist stronghold of Pamplona. In the aftermath of the abduction and murder of the right-wing leader Calvo Sotelo by Republican police officers, the army revolted in Morocco on 17 July, and on the morning of Sunday, 19 July 1936, the insurgents were crossing the Strait of Gibraltar.

It would be inappropriate to describe the ensuing events of the Civil War in any detail, but some account of its course in Catalonia seems in place.

Companys had prior warning, when his police discovered an arms cache and insurgent leaflets in the house of a prominent rightist, and indeed warned the prime minister in Madrid, Casares Quiroga—but to no effect. He therefore called in the leaders of the CNT, the only organization strong enough to offer effective resistance; and its members took matters into their own hands on the evening of 18 July by raiding arms depots and seizing weapons. The army, too, had been making plans, and General Fernandez Burriel of the cavalry, who was to direct the uprising until the arrival of General Goded from Majorca, ordered out his troops at dawn on 19 July with instructions to join up in the Plaça de Cataluña in the centre of Barcelona.

By now the streets were packed with armed workers, spearheaded by the Anarchists and supported by the civil guard and the police. Improvised armoured cars were hurled against the artillery, and so fierce was the resistance that the rebel columns were unable to make junction. General Goded, who had secured Majorca without difficulty, arrived by plane at midday, but failed to rally his troops and was himself captured when his headquarters in the old building of the Captaincy General was stormed and taken towards evening. By now the Plaça de Cataluña was heaped with bodies, and Goded later broadcast a dignified appeal, relayed by all the radio stations in Republican hands, for his followers to surrender.

By the evening of 20 July all remaining resistance had been overcome; 500 people had been killed and 3,000 wounded in the two-day battle. The heroes of the hour were the CNT; and their leaders, Joan García Oliver, Buenaventura Durruti and Marianet Vásquez went straight from the firing line, rifles in hand, to see Companys at the Palace of the *Generalitat*. As reported by García Oliver, he then made the following diplomatic statement:

The CNT and the FAI have never had the treatment they deserved. You have always been harshly persecuted and I, who was formerly with you [as a lawyer] found myself compelled to oppose you for reasons of politics. Today you are masters of the city and of Catalonia . . .

You have conquered and the power is yours. If you do not need me or do not want me to remain as President of Catalonia, tell me now, and I shall become one more soldier in the fight against Fascism. If, on the other hand, you feel that I, my party, my name and my prestige can be of use in this struggle—for though it has ended in this city, we do not know how or when it will finish in the rest of Spain—then you may count on me and my loyalty as a man who is convinced that a whole shameful past is dead and who fervently wishes that Catalonia should in future be numbered amongst the most progressive countries in the world.

The Anarchists were torn between their traditional policies of libertarian revolution and non-participation in government and the obvious need to co-operate with the other parties of the left who had fought beside them. In the upshot they decided to accept Companys's offer, and an Anti-Fascist Militias Committee was set up, comprising five members from the CNT, three from the UGT, four from the Esquerra and other Republican parties, one from the Union of Rabassaires, one from the POUM and one from the newly formed and Communist-dominated PSUC (*Partit socialista unificat de Catalunya*).

During the first confused days of the revolution there was a wave of atrocities and assassinations all over Spain; and in this respect it seems that there was little to choose between the Nationalists and Republicans, although executions by Franco's army were carried out as a cold-blooded matter of policy, whereas on the Republican side it was a matter of the wholesale and undisciplined settling of old scores.

In Barcelona, the bourgeoisie attempted to pass themselves off as workers by going about the streets without ties; scores were nevertheless 'taken for a ride' by being driven down the Rabassada road to the suburbs and there shot and dumped. These outrages were condemned by the union leaders, and, to their credit, Companys and his Councillor for Culture, Ventura Gassol, intervened personally by smuggling out the rightist leaders of the Lliga and numbers of clerics, including the Archbishop of Tarragona, the Bishops of Vich and Gerona and the Abbot of Montserrat, on to ships for France and Italy. Every church in the city was burned down, except for the cathedral and the Monastery of Pedralbes, while the different unions looted and occupied the large houses of the upper classes and other outposts such as the building of the *Fomento del trabajo nacional*, the Hotel Colón, the Teatre Principal and the Jockey Club.

Control of all the utilities, such as the tramways, and of large industrial concerns, such as the Ford Iberia Motor Company and the

G

CAMPSA oil company passed to the CNT, which fixed wages and employed former managers as 'technicians'. Smaller shops and businesses were taken over by their workers and clerks, and even cinemas were 'collectivized', the profits going to the building of a school and a clinic. On the whole these arrangements worked effectively enough—although there was an increasing shortage of raw materials for manufacturing industry—and the reorganized metallurgical and chemical factories were to become one of the Republic's main sources of ammunition, arms and fighting vehicles. Collectivization also took place in the country districts, but not without opposition from the Rabassaires, who were unwilling to relinquish control of the land, even to bodies of their own choosing.

Neither the Socialist authorities in Madrid nor the Communist-orientated PSUC in Barcelona, which was small in numbers and relied on infiltration into the government to extend its influence, favoured collectivization under the auspices of the rival CNT. For its part, the CNT found itself increasingly obliged to collaborate with the government and other parties, since the banks, on which it relied for the financing of its new enterprises, were controlled by the PSUC, which lost no opportunity of blaming the CNT for inevitable shortages. As Victor Alba, who was in Barcelona at the time, writes in *Catalonia, a Profile*, London, 1975:

> PSUC propaganda was sometimes amusing. The CNT had issued a poster that showed a sleeping worker with the caption: 'A loafer: a fascist.' The PSUC popularized a burlesque of this poster, with three drawings: one, with a sleeping worker, had the well-known caption; another, with two men sleeping, was captioned 'Two loafers, two fascists'; and the third, which showed three men asleep, bore the caption 'Three loafers: a committee.'

Similar differences between the CNT and the PSUC were evident in the organization of the columns which the Committee of Militias sent to Aragon to check a Nationalist advance into Catalonia and if possible to take Saragossa and occupy the Basque country. While the PSUC was always for a centrally controlled army with a regular chain of command, the motto of the Anarchists was 'Let us organize the indiscipline.' The CNT militia did not wear uniform and commanders were chosen from ex-soldiers or experienced militants as the occasion demanded—much in the manner of their forbears, who had so fiercely resisted the attempts of a central government to conscript them into a regular army at the time of the War of the *Segadors*.

Although Saragossa was never captured, its lights, as George Orwell put it, twinkling at night ahead of the Republican lines 'like the portholes of a great long liner', the amateur soldiers acquitted themselves well and stabilized the front for some eighteen months in the face of a numerically superior Nationalist army. The aims of Durruti, in command of the CNT contingent, remained frankly revolutionary:

> I will be the first to enter Saragossa: I will proclaim there a free Commune. We shall subordinate ourselves neither at Madrid nor Barcelona, neither to Azaña nor Companys. If they wish they can live in peace with us; if not we shall go to Madrid . . . We shall show *you*, Bolsheviks, how to make a revolution.

The PSUC improved the occasion by blaming the CNT for the stalemate on the Aragon front; but it seems that in reality supplies were held up by the Communists, that the Ministry of Defence in Madrid was loath to support the offensive for fear of a link-up between the autonomous regions of Catalonia and the Basque provinces, and also that troops were progressively transferred to fronts where the threat from the Nationalists was more serious.

As time went on, the revolutionary aims of the CNT caused an open rift with the PSUC. In the eyes of the CNT it was now or never: a proletarian revolution could only be achieved in the heat of battle. The slogan of the PSUC, the party of law and order in the Republican camp, was 'Win the war first.' Given the refusal of the Western democracies to supply military aid, it was the only party to be backed up by munitions from abroad and followed the Soviet line. At the outset, this was to present a common front against Hitler with the other European countries and to avoid charges of fomenting a revolution in Spain; later, when secret negotiations began for the Hitler–Stalin pact, there was a turn-about, and Russian policy was to withdraw aid from Republican Spain, leaving the field clear to the Nationalists and their Fascist allies.

Conflict between the PSUC and the CNT came to a head in Barcelona on 3 May 1937, when the police, commanded by a member of the PSUC, occupied the CNT-controlled telephone building. During the next week, barricades went up in the streets and more people were killed and wounded in hand-to-hand fighting between elements of the two organizations than in the days of the preceding July. An uneasy truce followed; and in June the central government under Juan Negrín, who was increasingly to come under the thumb of the Russian Ambassador and the Communists, clipped the wings of the *Generalitat* by taking over public order in Catalonia. As an immediate result, the Communist-controlled police shut down all radio stations except that of the PSUC and confiscated weapons in the possession of the CNT.

The PSUC, although daily growing in numbers and prestige thanks to its backing by the Russians, was not yet strong enough to precipitate an outright show-down with the CNT. Instead, it lashed out at the POUM, many of whose members were Trotskyites and *émigré* intellectuals. Its political secretary, Andreu Nin, was arrested and reputedly tortured to death by agents of the Soviet NKVD, while its executive committee underwent trial in Barcelona. The vendetta continued until the end of the war, with its militant members going to ground in non-Communist units of the Republican army.

The *Generalitat* and CNT now found themselves isolated and divided, neither of them being in a position to advance their respective aims of autonomy or revolution. In the hey-day of Soviet influence, with the NKVD acting at will, the Communists, aided and abetted by Negrín, virtually took over the direction of the war. On the pretext that Catalonia was not pulling its weight in the war effort, the units of the Esquerra, POUM and the Anarchists were withdrawn from Aragon and scattered about the other fronts.

The *Generalitat* found itself still further circumscribed when the government moved from Valencia to Barcelona in October 1937. In April 1938, when the Nationalists succeeded in driving a wedge between Catalonia in the north and the Republican-held territory in the south—Madrid and part of New Castile, Valencia and portions of Andalusia—Companys was moved to write to Negrín that, at a time when Catalonia was being invaded, there was no Catalan war sub-committee, that the *Generalitat* was unrepresented on the Superior War Council and that its President was kept in ignorance of confidential information on the military situation.

During the spring of 1938 the Italian airforce stepped up its indiscriminate bombing of Barcelona, culminating in the raid of 18 March in which 1,300 people were killed and 2,000 injured, almost all civilians. Little damage was done to military objectives, and according to the German Ambassador in Salamanca, Franco knew nothing about them and was furious because of mounting protest from abroad. Mussolini, on the other hand, declared himself delighted that the Italians 'should be horrifying the world by their aggressiveness for a change, instead of charming it by the guitar.'

In face of the mounting Nationalist offensive from Aragon, food shortages, and the disruption of industry after the occupation of the hydro-electric stations at Tremp to the north-east, conditions in Barcelona deteriorated. The Communist-controlled secret police, SIM (*Servicio de investigación militar*), attempted to counter sagging morale by rounding up suspected members of the Fifth Column and Falange and at the same time conducted a vicious private campaign against 'defeatists' of the CNT and POUM, many of whom were summarily tried, tortured and murdered.

As a last fling, and under Communist pressure, the government launched an attack across the Ebro on 24 July 1938, with the object of restoring communications between Catalonia and the Republican enclave around Valencia in the Levante. Despite sweeping initial gains, the battle was lost by the beginning of November, and it was now only a matter of time before Catalonia was overwhelmed, and Nationalist troops under General Yagüe entered Barcelona on 26 January 1939.

A mass exodus from Barcelona had begun on 24 January, and the roads to France were jammed with columns of refugees, with bombs and driving rain to add to their misery. By 10 February some 10,000 wounded, 170,000 women and children, 60,000 male civilians and 250,000 men of the Republican army had crossed the frontier, among them Companys and some of his ministers and the President of the Republic.

After the Nazi occupation of France, Companys was arrested and handed over to the Spanish authorities. He was secretly court-martialled at Montjuic Castle on the grounds of 'military rebellion' and executed on 15 October 1940, but not before he had made one last request—that he be allowed to remove his shoes, so that he might die with his feet touching Catalan soil. Whatever his mistakes, he has so passed into history as a patriot and a martyr.

XV

The 'Catalan Problem'

In the wake of defeat Catalonia suffered all the repression and curtailment of civil liberties which have been the pattern of its more recent history. The Falangists, who surfaced like magic on the entry of the Nationalist army, had previously put it about that Catalonia would not lose its autonomy under a new regime; but General Franco, confident of victory, had as early as 5 April 1938, revoked the Catalan Statute:

> The Nationalist Rising meant, in political terms, a break with all institutions opposed to its programme of restoration. And it is clear that whatever the shape of life in the future, the Statute of Catalonia, unwisely granted by the Republic, was no longer legally valid after the 17th day of July 1936. It is therefore unnecessary to make any declaration to this effect.

A decree of February 1939, dissolving the unions, the Republican and left wing parties, and banning the Freemasons, was followed by a law annulling all the legislation of the Catalan parliament. And yet again the use of any language except Castilian was proscribed. This applied not only to schools and universities, but even to telephone conversations—and telephone boxes bore notices to this effect. The publication and sale of books and newspapers in Catalan were forbidden, and cultural institutions were suppressed. Internationally known painters, such as Joan Miró or Picasso (who was not born in, but had worked in, Barcelona) came under the cloud of official disapproval; and, as so regularly happens in Spain and South America, streets were re-christened, the names of Catalan personalities being replaced by those of the heroes of the new regime.

The *Generalitat* again disappeared and local government was put into the hands of officials appointed from Madrid. Even the conservative Lliga, whose leader, Fransesc Cambó, had made approaches to Franco in 1936, became a dead letter.

After the war was over the new regime passed a retrospective and arbitrary law of 'political responsibility', decreeing that all persons

ES-SERVEIX-BEURE-Y-MENJAR-A-TOTES-HORES

PERE ROMEU - 4 GATS

CARRER Ð MONTESION·

12. A Picasso sketch (c. 1900) of Els Quatre Gats café, a gathering place for artists and writers. Picasso is seen in the foreground.

who had resisted the army from the outbreak of war on 18 July 1936, were guilty either of rebellion or of aiding and abetting it. The maximum penalty was that of death, for rebellion—and many of the mayors of villages in which murders had taken place were automatically executed. Most of the Republican and left-wing leaders had escaped across the border, but it has been estimated that there were some 15,000 executions in Catalonia during the peak period of 1939–40, while another 150,000 persons were imprisoned with sentences of up to thirty years (few of them in fact served more than a fraction of this term). Whereas in Spain generally the accused were dubbed 'reds', in Catalonia they were termed 'red separatists': Spanish rightists have rarely drawn a distinction between separatism and autonomy.

The first reaction of the larger part of the bourgeoisie and moneyed classes was to accept the fact of assimilation and to extract the maximum benefit from it. Some, indeed, like the historian Ferran Valls i Taberner actively recanted and stated publicly that the mistake had been to assume that a love for Catalonia implied political Catalanism and that the right road for the future was to co-operate in rebuilding Spain under the umbrella of the Nationalist Movement. Others, more venal, such as the so-called *estraperlistas*, devoted their energies to exploiting shortages of raw materials and the black market of the post-war years.

During this early period there was a general expectation that, with the end of World War II, the Allies, if victorious, would put an end to the Franquist regime and that the position would revert to that of 1936, so that in spite of stirrings among the Communists and Anarchosyndicalists and a smallscale but foredoomed attempt at invasion across the Pyrenees by Communist exiles in 1944, the tendency was to sit back and await events outside Spain.

Almost thirty years of Nationalist government saw a gradual, but profound change in social and economic conditions. General Franco proved a great deal more astute than his enemies had anticipated. Irrigation, hydro-electric schemes and industrialization financed by foreign loans and money from the lease of American bases have transformed the economy. A new middle class of the right centre has emerged in the cities, while housing standards have improved and it is a commonplace for working class families to own a small car, a television set and a refrigerator—though these are more expensive than in other countries of the West.

A few hard figures demonstrate that, in the economic area at any rate, the claim of Franco's minister in charge of Economic Development, López Rodó, that 'Never was so much achieved in such a length of time', was near the truth. Between 1960 and 1970 imports went up from 721 to 3,018 million dollars, and exports from 725 to 966 million (the deficit being made up by revenue from tourism and the inflow of money from abroad); average income increased from 290 to 818 dollars per annum (with a projected 2,000 in 1980); the number of cars per 1,000 of the population from 9 to 70; while the number of workers engaged in both industry and services had outstripped those employed in agriculture, although agricultural exports had doubled.

The relative economic preponderance of Catalonia has declined, although Catalonia still accounts for upwards of 30 per cent of Spanish industrial production. The reasons for this have been the opportunist attitude of the Catalan bourgeoisie, which tended to produce consumer goods in small workshops for a captive market during the period of self-sufficiency following the Civil War; the failure to build up the banks, now largely in Basque and Castilian hands; and the policy of the government to establish new industries in less-developed parts of the country. The growth rate of the population has been rather less than in the rest of Spain, but this has to some extent been compensated for by immigration from the agricultural districts of the south. Between 1950 and 1960, of the 979,000 persons who emigrated to the cities, 423,000 went to Catalonia; before the recent recession the tide was later to Western Europe.

In the cultural, if not the political sphere, matters began to change in 1955-6, when Spain was admitted to the United Nations and the increasing dependence of the economy on the massive influx of tourists resulted in a new awareness of liberties and amenities outside Spain, over which the censorship of the press and radio had previously drawn a veil. In 1945 only two books were printed in Catalan; by 1968 the number had risen to 500, but more thorough-going liberalization did not take place until the Caudillo was on his deathbed.

In a decree of 23 October 1975, Prince Juan Carlos, while re-affirming that Castilian 'be used by all state organizations, public administration, in the administration of Justice, local authorities and all other official institutions', conceded that 'All regional languages are part of Spain's cultural heritage and must be accorded national status . . .' (Article 1); that 'Regional languages may be used by all means of diffusion whether oral or written, and particularly at meetings and events of a cultural nature' (Article 2); but that 'No Spaniard shall be the object of discrimination for not knowing, or not making use of, a regional language.' (Article 4).

As regards the recognition of political parties, other than the official *Movimiento Nacional*, Franco remained inflexible until the last. In deference to foreign opinion the regime took some limited and tentative steps towards a more democratic society, but remained overwhelmingly authoritarian. Any open discussion of politics was conducted on the theoretical plane, and for all practical purposes the country remained in a political vacuum. Similarly, trade union activity was funnelled into the official *Sindicatos*, vertically organized according to trade and including representatives both of labour and management. In the latter stages, discussion of wages and working conditions was permitted, but since differences were settled from above by the Minister of Labour, the *Sindicatos* had none of the bargaining power of free trade unions.

Especially as the standard of living improved, the workers began reorganizing their own underground unions. Influenced by exiles from abroad, increasingly out of touch with the situation inside Spain, the UGT and CNT discounted the possibility of working within the official *Sindicatos*, and attempts to reconstitute mass organizations in secret led only to repeated arrests and the imprisonment of their leaders within the country. After 1950, the Communist party, which suffered a massive set-back after its dubious role in the Civil War, stole a march on its rivals by instructing its members to infiltrate the official unions; and a potent force was the so-called Workers' Commissions (*Comisiones obreras*). Working on a factory to factory basis, sometimes within the *Sindicatos*, they backed up their demands by strikes, increasingly frequent and numerous since 1962, which the authorities found themselves unable to prevent.

The students, too, grew dissatisfied with the party-controlled SEU (*Sindicato democrático de estudiantes*), which was dissolved in 1965 in the face of mounting protests, 'sit-in's' and strikes. Various illegal unions, some of them Maoist and Trotskyite, appeared, only to be suppressed. In Barcelona, the University was temporarily closed in 1966 after two years of agitation and clashes with the police, centring on the questions of better educational facilities and free representation untrammelled by interference from the State.

The overriding desire of the mass of Spaniards who had lived through the Civil War was for a period of peace, during which they could resume their normal life and activities. The paternal and (within strict limits) progressively more tolerant Franquist regime met this requirement, especially as all sections of the community benefited from the country's economic revival. With the emergence of a new generation for which the War is past history, there is a new spirit abroad and Spaniards are reaching out for new freedoms. Among the first straws in this wind of change were the appearance of near-pornographic magazines on the bookstands, followed after Franco's death by a spate of free-ranging publications on politics. Since then outspoken criticism of the Franquist regime in the newspapers has become a commonplace.

Amidst the melting pot of ideas, none are more hotly contested than the arguments for regional autonomy or separatism—as demanded by the extremists of the ETA in the Basque country, whose violence has been the mirror image of the Franquists' ruthless ban on language, local culture or folklore, to the extent of a veto on flying the national flag. Of all the regions with aspirations to autonomy—Catalonia, Euzkadi, Galicia, Valencia, and to a lesser extent the Balearics and Canaries—Catalonia, with its long historical tradition and highly developed language and literature, perhaps has the strongest claim.

The post-War history of Catalanism has step by step followed the earlier pattern. As at the time of Primo de Rivera, it first re-emerged in purely cultural manifestations: *sardana* dancing, attendance at Mass in Catalan, competition in the Floral Games or support of a local football team. When the prohibition on publishing books in Catalan was relaxed, a growing number of writers and intellectuals used their native tongue, but, as at the time of the *Renaixença*, their books were bought and read only by the well-to-do and middle classes. Paradoxically, neo-Marxist writers, who defend the Cuban revolution and attack American imperialism, have had little to say about social conditions in Catalonia itself; and a lack of contact with the younger working class generation is aggravated by the fact that, by and large, only middle and upper class families can afford to send their children to university.

Forthright support for Catalanism came from some of the young priests, who, after 1960 and following the initiative of Pope John XXIII and the Vatican Council, began conducting litany and Mass in Catalan and taking an active interest in social matters and the plight of the deprived *xarnegos*, the underprivileged immigrants from the south. In this they were hampered by traditional Catalan distrust of the Church and lack of support from the episcopal hierarchy—an honourable exception was the former Abbot of Montserrat, Aureli María Escarré, who in 1963 wrote in *Le Monde*:

> The real subversion existing in Spain is that of the government. Spain—and this is the great problem—is still divided into two parties. What we have behind us is not twenty-five years of peace, but only twenty-five years of victories. The conquerors, including the Church, which was obliged to fight on their side, have done nothing to close the gap between victors and vanquished . . .

and again,

> The great majority of Catalans are not separatists. We have a right, like any other minority, to our customs, which have their own proper place within Spain. We are Spaniards, but not Castilians.

Escarré subsequently resigned as Abbot-Bishop in 1967 at the prompting of the Vatican and went into exile.

On the basis of history, culture, demography, the economic preponderance of the periphery and the disproportion between taxes levied in Catalonia and what is spent by the government in the region, middle class intellectuals have put forward a variety of schemes for solving the 'Catalan Problem', ranging from outright independence to federalism along Swiss lines and broadly approximating to the original proposals of Maciá in 1931 (see page 185). Some writers have even suggested that Portugal should be included in a broad Iberian federation, to include Catalonia, Euzkadi, Galicia and the rest. Reaction from centralists has predictably been that such arrangements would lead to the break-up of the Spanish State and that Catalanists wish to exploit Spanish markets on their own terms. In the words of the Spanish wit Wenceslao Fernandez Florez, 'Catalonia is the only metropolis that is trying to secede from her colonies.'

There has for long been a strong current of Catalanist opinion among the upper and middle classes, but in the recent past one question has been the extent to which it was shared by the working population, traditionally more concerned with social and agrarian reform and the betterment of working conditions. The attitude of landowners and urban entrepreneurs hardly held out the prospect of improvement in a future autonomous Catalonia under their control. The *xarnegos*, an important element of the population, often ill-housed and relegated to the least rewarding jobs, are a special case, whose plight received belated attention with the publication of Fransesc Candil's best-selling *Els altres catalans*. Their children are brought up to speak Catalan, and intermarriage with native-born Catalans is frequent—but to what extent are they Catalanists?

While political parties and free unions were suppressed it was difficult to do more than guess, but the answers to such questions are now emerging. The legalization of the unions and opposition parties, including the Communists, in April 1977 and the success of the parties of the centre and left in the elections of the following June are shaping a new pattern. In Catalonia—in contrast to the rest of Spain—the left won a clear majority, and mass demonstrations in favour of autonomy and the release of political prisoners have left no doubt as to its attitude. In spite of anxious glances towards the army, pledged to maintaining the unity of Spain, the Government was prompt to enter into negotiations with Josep Tarradellas, President of the *Generalitat* in exile. The first result was the royal decree of 29 September 1977, re-establishing the *Generalitat*, to include representatives of the main political parties, seven advisers and delegates from the four provinces of Catalonia.

The fifteen ministers of the new *Generalitat*, with Tarradellas at their head, have been authorized to decide on all questions of administration and local government, while matters of defence, Foreign Affairs and the budget of the state as a whole have been left in the hands of the Madrid government. The *Generalitat* has, however, been recreated without prejudice to the future status of Catalonia, to be decided—no doubt with much hard bargaining—when a new Spanish Constitution is drafted and approved by the Cortes.

As to the future, the good sense of the Spanish people has proved all the *émigré* commentators on present-day Spain to be wrong in their pessimistic predictions: for example, the Communists under Santiago Carrillo have taken a very moderate line of Eurocommunism; and the fiery Pasionaria returned from Moscow with great éclat, only to be relegated to relative obscurity. This account of the Catalans ends at an exciting moment in their history. It is no longer reasonable to suppose that the clock can be put back to 1932 by a simple re-enactment of the Catalan Statute. All that can be said with any certainty is that the Catalans (and also the Basques) have a deep and justifiable sense of historical identity; and until a satisfactory framework is evolved, in which cultural expression and a natural pride in achievement past and present are duly recognized, and the region is given effective control of its domestic affairs, the Catalan Problem will remain an open wound.

Glossary of Catalan Terms

AGUTZIL (Castilian: ALGUACIL.) An official charged with maintaining law and order.

ALMOGÀVERS Catalan mercenaries of the Middle Ages, renowned both for their courage and savagery.

AUDIÈNCIA The supreme judiciary, consisting of seventeen judges and sitting in Barcelona.

BANDOLERS Bandits of the sixteenth and seventeenth centuries.

BRAÇ (pl. BRAÇOS) One of the three Estates constituting the CORTS of Catalonia (q.v.). The BRAÇ ECLESIÀSTIC representend the clergy; the BRAÇ MILITAR, the nobility; and the BRAÇ REIAL, the towns.

CANCELLER The Chancellor of Catalonia, a cleric who presided over the first chamber of the AUDIÈNCIA (q.v.).

CASA DE LA CUITAT The town hall of Barcelona.

CAVALLER A knight, member of the lesser aristocracy.

CEDA (Castilian.) *Confederación española de derechas autonomas* (Confederation of Autonomous Rightist Parties).

CIUTADÀ HONRAT A hereditary rank enjoyed by the most distinguished citizens of Barcelona and other towns.

CNT (Castilian.) *Confederación nacional de trabajo* (The Anarchosynicalist Confederation of Labour).

COMTAT—A county.

CONSEJO DE ARAGÓN (Castilian.) The Council of Aragon, formed by Ferdinand the Catholic to supervise the affairs of the Crown of Aragon and sitting in Madrid.

CONSELL DE CENT The Council of One Hundred, or City Council of Barcelona.

CONSELLOR-EN-CAP The president of the CONSELLORS (q.v.).

CONSELLORS The five councillors forming the executive of the CONSELL DE CENT (q.v.).

CONSTITUCIÓ A statue or law authorized by the CORTS (q.v.).

CORONA DE ARAGÓN (Castilian.) The Crown of Aragon, formed

by the amalgamation of the kingdoms of Aragon and Valencia and the principality of Catalonia.

CORTES (Castilian.) The parliament of Castile, and later of Spain.

CORTS The parliament of Catalonia, summoned by the king for passing laws or granting subsidies.

DIPUTACIÓ The standing commission of the CORTS (q.v.), consisting of three DIPUTATS (q.v.) and three OIDORS (q.v.), elected triennially.

DIPUTAT One of the commissioners of the DIPUTACIÓ (q.v.), who severally represented the three BRAÇOS (q.v.).

DONZELL See CAVALLER.

DRESSANES The royal Dockyards in Barcelona.

DRET A tax.

ESQUERRA *Esquerra republicana de Catalunya* (Catalan Republican Left).

ESTAMENT An Estate (see BRAÇ).

ETA *Euzkadi Ta Azkatasuna* (Land and Freedom of the Basques, the militant separatist movement).

FADRISTERN The younger brother of a Catalan family.

FAI (Castilian.) *Federació anarquista ibérica* (Iberian Anarchist Federation).

FORÁN A Majorcan peasant.

FORE (Castilian). *Federación de obreros de la región de España* (Workers' Federation of the Spanish Region, the former Spanish branch of the First International).

FUR (Castilian: FUERO.) A royal charter of rights, first granted to a town or city, but later used of the laws and liberties of an entire state, such as Navarra.

GENERALITAT Originally used of the Estates of the Catalan people as a whole, the name became synonymous with the DIPUTACIÓ (DEL GENERAL DE CATALUNYA) q.v.

GOVERNADOR The Governor of Catalonia and deputy to the viceroy or LLOCTINENT (q.v.).

GREMI A guild.

HEREU The heir to the bulk of a family property.

INSACULACIÓ The system of balloting for public office introduced by Ferdinand the Catholic.

JURAT A town councillor in the Gerona region.

LLIGA REGIONALISTA The Regionalist League, the autonomist movement formed by Prat de la Riba in 1901.

LLIURA Monetary unit. A *lliura* or pound equalled 20 *sous* or 240 *diners.* During the seventeenth century the *lliura* was worth 10 Castilian *reales* or just under a *ducado* or ducat.

LLOCTINENT GENERAL The viceroy of Catalonia, an office created by Ferdinand the Catholic.

LLOTJA The bourse or gathering place of the merchants of Barcelona.

MALS USOS The 'Evil Practices' tying a peasant to his lord.

MANCOMUNITAT A regional directorate of local authorities.

MAS, MASIA A farmstead.

MASOS RONÈCS Peasant farmsteads.

MASOVER A peasant holding, a MAS (q.v.) under lease.

MENESTRAL An artisan or rural labourer.

MERCED (Castilian.) A reward or favour granted by the king to his vassals.

MILITAR See CAVALLER and BRAÇ.

MIQUELETES Irregular troops, guerrillas.

OBSERVANÇA One of the most important of the CONSTITU-CIONES (q.v.), decreed in 1481 and precluding arbitary action by the king.

OIDOR One of the three officials responsible for auditing expenditure and, with the three DIPUTATS (q.v.), making up the DIPUTACIÓ (q.v.); also used of a judge of the AUDIÈNCIA (q.v.).

PAGESOS DE REMENÇA Serfs who could obtain personal liberty by a monetary payment to their SENYOR (q.v.).

POUM (Castilian.) *Partido obrero de unificación marxista* (The Trotskyite Marxist Workers Party of Unification).

PRAGMÀTICA A royal ordinance made outside the CORTS (q.v.).

PSUC *Partit socialista unificat de Catalunya* (United Socialist Party of Catalonia, the Catalan branch of the Spanish Communist Party.

QUINT A fifth part of the revenues of certain towns, claimed by the Crown.

RABASSA MORTA A form of land holding entitling a farmer to cultivate a vineyard until the death of the vines.

RABASSAIRES Farmers cultivating vineyards under the terms of the RABASSA MORTA (q.v.).

RENAIXENÇA The patriotic literary revival of the nineteenth century.

SALA One of the three chambers of the AUDIÈNCIA (q.v.).

SEGADOR A harvester.

SENYOR (Castilian: SEÑOR.) A Catalan baron and lord of his villagers and retainers.

SEU *Sindicato democrático de estudiantes* (Democratic Syndicate of Students, the official union dissolved in 1965).

SIM (Castilian.) *Servicio de investigación militar* (Military Investigation Service, the Communist-dominated secret police at the time of the Civil War).

SÍNDIC An agent of the cities and royal towns in the CORTS (q.v.).

SOMETENT A call to arms. The armed contingents called out by the towns in emergency.

TAULA A bank.

TAULA DE CANVI The Exchange or City Bank of Deposit in Barcelona.

TERCIO (Castilian.) An infantry regiment, nominally of 3,000 men.

UGT (Castilion.) *Unión general de trabajadores* (the Socialist General Workers' Union).

USATGES Literally 'usages'. A written code defining the reciprocal rights of the sovereign and his subjects, first promulgated in 1068 and the basis of Catalan rights and liberties.

VELLÓN (Castilian.) Coinage made of silver-copper alloy or of pure copper.

VISITA (Castilian.) An enquiry into the conduct of royal officials in the king's dominions.

XARNEGOS Immigrant workers from the south of Spain.

Further Reading

GENERAL

(See also the very full bibliography in Vilar, Pierre, *La Catalogne dans L'Espagne moderne*, listed below.)

Balaguer, V., *Historia de Cataluña y de la Corona de Aragón*, 5 vols., Barcelona, 1860–3.

Bleiberg, Germán (ed.), *Diccionario de historia de España*, 2nd ed., Madrid, 1968.

Bofarull y Brocá, *Historia crítica de Cataluña*, 9 vols., Barcelona, 1876.

Brenan, Gerald, *The Spanish Labyrinth*, Cambridge, 1969.

Castro, Américo. *The Spaniards, An Introduction to their History*, Berkeley and Los Angeles, 1971.

Collier, Basil, *Catalan France*, London, 1939.

D'Abadal, Ramon et. al., *Moments crucials de la història de Catalunya*, Barcelona, 1962.

Ford, Richard, *A Handbook for Travellers in Spain*, London, 1845.

Peers, E. Allison, *Catalonia Infelix*, London, 1937.

Russell, P. E. (ed.), *Spain, A Companion to Spanish Studies*, London, 1973.

Soldevila, Carlos, *Cataluña, sus hombres y sus obras*, Barcelona, 1955.

Soldevila, Ferran, *Història de Catalunya*, 2nd ed., Barcelona, 1963 (the best modern history of Catalonia).

Història dels Catalans, Barcelona, 1961.

Trueta, J., *The Spirit of Catalonia*, Oxford, 1946.

Vicens Vives, Jaime, *Approaches to the History of Spain*, Berkeley, 1967.

Vilar, Pierre, *La Catalogne dans l'Espagne moderne*, 3 vols., Paris, 1962 (an indispensable economic history).

PREHISTORY AND MEDIAEVAL

Balari Jovany, José, *Origenes historicos de Cataluña*, 2 vols., Abadía de San Cugat del Valles (Instituto Internacional de Cultura Romanica), 1964.

Bosch Gimpera, Pere, *Prehistoria catalana*, Barcelona, 1919.

Chaytor, H. J., *A History of Aragon and Catalonia*, London, 1933.

Forey, A. J., *The Templars in the Corona de Aragón*, Oxford, 1973.

Froissart's *Chronicles*, Everyman ed., London.

Hillgarth, J. N., *The Spanish Kingdoms 1250–1410*, Vol. I, Oxford, 1976, continuing.

Lévi Provençale, Évariste, *Histoire de l'Espagne musulmane*: Vol. I, *La Conquête et l'émirat oméiyade (710–912)*, Paris, 1950.

Vol. II, *Le Califat oméiyade de Cordoue (912–1031)*, Paris, 1953.

Lewis, A. R., *The Development of Southern French and Catalan Society 718–1050*, Austin, Texas, 1965.

Lot, Ferdinand, *L'Espagne chrétienne de 711 à 1037*, Paris, 1928.

Lowe, Alfonso, *The Catalan Vengeance*, London, 1972.

Menéndez Pidal, Ramón, *La España del Cid*, 2 vols, Madrid, 1956.

Moncada, Francisco de, *Expedición de las catalanes y aragoneses contra turcos y griegos*, reprinted Paris, N.D.

Oman, Sir Charles, *The Art of War in the Middle Ages*, London, 1933.

Poema del Cid, (Menédez Pidal, R., *Cantar de mío Cid*, 3 vols., Madrid, 1954; Merwin, W.S. (trans.), *The Poem of the Cid*, London, 1959).

Read, Jan, *The Moors in Spain and Portugal*, London, 1974.

Russell, P.E., *The English Intervention in Spain and Portugal in the time of Edward III and Richard II*, Oxford, 1955.

Schneidman, J. L., *The Rise of the Aragonese-Catalan Empire 1200–1350*, 2 vols., New York and London, 1970.

Vicens Vives, Jaime, *Fernando el Católico, principe de Aragón, rey de Sicilia (1458–1479)*, Madrid, 1952.

Historia de las remensas en el siglo XV, Barcelona, 1945.

Juan II de Aragón (1398–1479): monarquía y revolución en la España del siglo XV, Barcelona, 1953.

'Los Trastámaras y Cataluña' in *Historia de España*, Vol. XV., ed. R. Ménendez Pidal, Madrid, 1970.

SIXTEENTH TO EIGHTEENTH CENTURIES
(See also 'General')

Braudel, Fernand, *The Mediterranean and the Mediterranean World in the Age of Philip II*, 2 vols., London, 1972.

Elliott, J. H., *The Revolt of the Catalans*, Cambridge, 1963.

Kamen, H., *The Spanish Inquisition*, London, 1965.

War of the Succession in Spain, 1700–15, London, 1969.

Lynch, J., *Spain under the Hapsburgs*, 2 vols., Oxford, 1964 and 1969.

Marañon, G., *El Conde-Duque de Olivares*, 3rd ed., Madrid, 1952.

Merriman, R. B., *The Rise of the Spanish Empire in the Old World and the New*, 4 vols., New York, reprinted 1962.

Nada, John, *Carlos the Bewitched*, London, 1962.

Vicens Vives, Jaime, *An Economic History of Spain*, Princeton, 1969.

NINETEENTH CENTURY AND MODERN
(The literature on Catalonia since the Civil War is so extensive that the reader is referred to the bibliographies in the books by Victor Alba and José Amodia, listed below.)

Alba, Victor, *Catalonia, a Profile*, London, 1975.

Amodia, José, *Franco's Political Legacy*, London, 1977.

Candel, Fransesc, *Els altres catalans*, Barcelona, 1964.

Carr, Raymond, *Spain: 1808–1939*, Oxford, 1966.

Centro Español de Documentación, *Terrorismo y justicia en España*, Madrid, 1975.

González Casanova, J. A., *Federalisme i autonomia a Catalunya, 1868–1938: Documents*, Barcelona, 1974.

Hermet, Guy, *The Communists in Spain*, London, 1974.

Holt, Edgar, *The Carlist Wars in Spain*, London, 1967.

Orwell, George, *Homage to Catalonia*, London, 1952.

Read, Jan, *War in the Peninsula*, London, 1977.

Riba, J. Mercador, *Barcelona durante la occupación francesa*, Madrid, 1949.

Rossinyol, Jaume, *Le problème de la Catalogne*, Paris, 1974.

Thomas, Hugh, *The Spanish Civil War*, London, 1965.

Ullman, Joan C., *The Tragic Week: A Study of Anti-clericism in Spain, 1875–1912*, Cambridge, Mass., 1966.

Vallès, Edmon, *Història grafica de la Catalunya contemporània*, Barcelona: Vol. I, 1974; Vol. II, 1975.

White Book, Catalonia, Buenos Aires, 1956.

LANGUAGE, LITERATURE AND ART

Casanelles, Antonio Gaudì, A Reappraisal, London, 1967.
Castellet, J. M. and Molas, J. (eds.), Ocho siglos de poesía catalana, Madrid, 1969 (bilingual text).
Desclot, Bernat, Crònica, ed. M. Coll i Alentorn, Barcelona, 1948.
Durliat, M., L'Art catalan, Paris, 1964.
Elcock, W. D., The Romance Languages, London, 1960.
Espiñas, Josep María, Vuit segles de carrers de Barcelona, Barcelona, 1974.
Fuster, Joan, Nosaltres els valencians, Barcelona (Ediciones 62), 1962.
Gili, Joan, Introductory Catalan Grammar, London, 1943.
James (Jaume) I, Chronicle (Llibre dels Feits), tr. John Forster, London, 1883.
Llull, Ramon, Blanquera, A Thirteenth Century Romance, tr. E. Allison Peers, London, 1926.
  The Book of the Beasts, tr. E. Allison Peers, London, 1927.
  The Book of the Lover and the Beloved, tr. E. Allison Peers, London, 1923.
  The Tree of Love, tr. E. Allison Peers, London, 1926.
Muntaner, Ramon, Chronicle, tr. Lady Goodenough, London (The Hakluyt Society), 1920.
Nola, Maese Ruperto de, Libro de guisados, manjares y potages, reprinted from the Logroño ed. of 1529, Madrid-Palma de Mallorca, 1969.
Peers, E. Allison, Fool of Love, A Life of Ramon Llull, London, 1949.
Penrose, R., Miró, London, 1970.
Peter (Pere) IV the Ceremonious, Crònica del rey d'Aragó, ed. Joseph Corubeu, Barcelona, 1885.
Pladavall, Antoni, Els Monestirs catalans, Barcelona, 1970.
Ruiz i Calonja, Joan, Història de la literatura catalana, Barcelona, 1954.
Soldevila, Carlos, Cataluña, arte, vida, paisaje, Barcelona, 1951.
Terry, A., Catalan Literature, Vol. 7 of A Literary History of Spain, ed. R. O. Jones, London and New York, 1972.
Triadú, Joan (ed.), An Anthology of Catalan Lyric Poetry, Oxford, 1953.
Various authors, Un segle de vida catalana, 2 vols., Barcelona, 1961.

Index